Affine Analysis of Image Sequences

T0254483

Distinguished Dissertations in Computer Science

Edited by C.J. van Rijsbergen, University of Glasgow

The Conference of Professors of Computer Science (CPCS), in conjunction with the British Computer Society (BCS), selects annually for publication up to four of the best British PhD dissertations in computer science. The scheme began in 1990. Its aim is to make more visible the significant contribution made by Britain in particular by students to computer science, and to provide a model for future students. Dissertations are selected on behalf of CPCS by a panel whose members are:

C.B. Jones, Manchester University (Chairman)

S. Abramsky, Imperial College, London

H.G. Barrow, University of Sussex

D.A. Duce, Rutherford Appleton Laboratory

M.E. Dyer, University of Leeds

D. May, Inmos Ltd, Bristol

V.J. Rayward-Smith, University of East Anglia

M.H. Williams, Heriot-Watt University

AFFINE ANALYSIS OF IMAGE SEQUENCES

Larry S. Shapiro

Sharp Laboratories of Europe, Oxford

CAMBRIDGE
UNIVERSITY PRESS

CAMBRIDGE UNIVERSITY PRESS
Cambridge, New York, Melbourne, Madrid, Cape Town, Singapore, São Paulo

Cambridge University Press
The Edinburgh Building, Cambridge CB2 2RU, UK

Published in the United States of America by Cambridge University Press, New York

www.cambridge.org
Information on this title: www.cambridge.org/9780521550635

© Cambridge University Press 1995

First published 1995
This digitally printed first paperback version 2005

A catalogue record for this publication is available from the British Library

ISBN-13 978-0-521-55063-5 hardback
ISBN-10 0-521-55063-7 hardback

ISBN-13 978-0-521-01978-1 paperback
ISBN-10 0-521-01978-8 paperback

To the memory of my late father Cedric,
and to my mother Tessa for her untold sacrifices.

If asked what aspect of vision means most to them, a watchmaker may answer "acuity", a night flier, "sensitivity", and an artist, "color". But to the animals which invented the vertebrate eye, and hold the patents on most of the features of the human model, the visual registration of *movement* was of the greatest importance.

G.L. Walls, *The Vertebrate Eye and its Adaptive Radiation.*
Hafner Publishing Company, New York, 1967 (page 342).

Contents

1 **Introduction**   1
  1.1 Motivation   1
  1.2 Approach   1
  1.3 Application: Model–based image coding   4
  1.4 Thesis outline   5

2 **Corner extraction and tracking**   9
  2.1 Introduction   9
  2.2 Feature–based correspondence   9
  2.3 Corner detection   13
  2.4 The matcher   16
  2.5 The tracker   24
  2.6 Conclusions   33

3 **The affine camera and affine structure**   35
  3.1 Introduction   35
  3.2 Camera models   36
  3.3 Affine stereo/motion equations   43
  3.4 Affine structure using local coordinate frames   44
  3.5 Affine structure without local coordinate frames   52
  3.6 Conclusions   59

4 **Clustering using maximum affinity spanning trees**   61
  4.1 Introduction   61
  4.2 Maximum affinity spanning trees   62
  4.3 Clustering concepts   71
  4.4 The affinity measures   81
  4.5 Termination criteria   86
  4.6 Implementation   87
  4.7 Results   91
  4.8 Conclusions   99

5 **Affine epipolar geometry**   100
  5.1 Introduction 100

5.2   The affine epipolar line 101

5.3   The affine fundamental matrix 103

5.4   Solving the affine epipolar equation 103

5.5   Experimental results 111

5.6   Epipolar geometry and CI space 112

5.7   Conclusions 114

6   Outlier rejection in an orthogonal regression framework   115

6.1   Introduction 115

6.2   Linear regression 116

6.3   Previous work on outlier rejection 120

6.4   Outlier rejection techniques 122

6.5   Error analysis 134

6.6   Affine epipolar geometry revisited 138

6.7   Conclusions 140

7   Rigid motion from affine epipolar geometry   144

7.1   Introduction 144

7.2   Motion ambiguities 145

7.3   Rigid motion: two views 146

7.4   Rigid motion: three views 158

7.5   Conclusions 161

8   Affine transfer   162

8.1   Introduction 162

8.2   Transfer using local coordinate frames 162

8.3   Transfer without local coordinate frames 163

8.4   Affine transfer using CI space 166

8.5   Results 168

8.6   Conclusions 168

9   Conclusions   175

9.1   Summary 175

9.2   Future work 175

A   Clustering proofs   177

A.1   MAST generation 177

A.2   Cluster Formation 178

B   Proofs for epipolar geometry minimisation   182

B.1   Cost function E_1 182

B.2   Cost function E_2 183

B.3   Cost function E_3 184

B.4   Line–to–point and point–to–point cost functions 184

C Proofs for outlier rejection   **186**
    C.1 Matrix perturbation theory 186
    C.2 Variance proofs 188

D Rotation matrices   **190**
    D.1 Angle–axis form 190
    D.2 Euler–angle form 191
    D.3 KvD form 191

E KvD motion equations   **192**
    E.1 KvD image motion equations 192
    E.2 Epipolar–based image coordinates 194

Bibliography   **195**

Index   **207**

Acknowledgements

As always, there are many people to thank. Foremost among them is Professor Mike Brady, whom I thank not only for his wise supervision, tremendous enthusiasm and ready accessibility, but also for affording me the freedom to develop my own research project and pursue the directions that intrigued me most. Andrew Zisserman was an enthusiastic collaborator on the affine structure and motion theory, and I am indebted to him for his fount of good ideas and his general interest in my work.

My gratitude extends to my colleagues in the Robotics Research Group, particularly the Brady Bunch. I sincerely thank Paul Beardsley, Andrew Blake, Roger Fawcett, Nicola Ferrier, Phil McLauchlan, David Murray, Ian Reid, Phil Torr, Bill Triggs, Han Wang and Charles Wiles for valuable discussions and for commenting on my work at various stages.

The ORS awards scheme (UK) and Foundation for Research Development (RSA) funded this research, and Bill Welsh (BT Research Labs) and Chris Harris (Roke Manor) kindly supplied certain of the image sequences.

My close friends Paul Lyne, Mike and Tracy Nicolle, Adrian Polliack, Laurence Pujo, Isabel Purcell, Anthony Weaver and Parveen Yaqoob contributed greatly to the "Oxford experience", sharing doctoral trials and tribulations and substantially augmenting my practical joke library! I also offer heartfelt thanks to Joy, Norman, Michelle, Anthea, Mark and Mia Goldberg, my "surrogate family" who have made England feel so much like home.

I am grateful to my thesis examiners, Dr. Andrew Blake and Professor Don Pearson, for putting forward my thesis for the Distinguished Dissertations Award; to Professor C.J. van Rijsbergen of the BCS, for his assistance with bringing this book to press; and to David Tranah of Cambridge University Press, for his professionalism and flexibility.

Finally, none of this would have been possible without the unfailing love and continuous encouragement I received from my mother Tessa, grandmother Ethel, and from Tammy and Jonathan – albeit all the way from South Africa.

Chapter 1

Introduction

1.1 Motivation

Sight is the sense that provides the highest information content – in engineering terms, the highest bandwidth – to the human brain. A computer vision system, essentially a "TV camera connected to a computer", aims to perform on a machine the tasks which our own visual system seems to perform so effortlessly. Since the world is constantly in motion, it comes as no surprise that time–varying imagery reveals valuable information about the environment. Indeed, some information is *easier* to obtain from a image sequence than from a single image [62]. Thus, as noted by Murray and Buxton, "understanding motion is a principal requirement for a machine or organism to interact meaningfully with its environment" [100] (page 1). For this reason, the analysis of image sequences to extract 3D motion and structure has been at the heart of computer vision research for the past decade [172].

The problem involves two key difficulties. First, the useful content of an image sequence is intricately coded and implicit in an enormous volume of sensory data. Making this information *explicit* entails significant data reduction, to decode the spatio–temporal correlations of the intensity values and eliminate redundancy. Second, information is lost in projecting the three spatial dimensions of the world onto the two dimensions of the image. Assumptions about the camera model and imaging geometry are therefore required.

This thesis develops new algorithms to interpret visual motion using a single camera, and demonstrates the practical feasibility of recovering scene structure and motion in a data–driven (or "bottom–up") fashion. Section 1.2 outlines the basic themes and describes the system architecture. Section 1.3 then discusses potential applications of this research, with special focus on low bit–rate image communication. Finally, Section 1.4 explains the organisation of the thesis and displays a subset of the results.

1.2 Approach

The first problem mentioned above, namely high data throughput, is overcome by noting that not all image pixels carry the same amount of information [23]. In particular, distinctive feature points (or *corners*) provide a large amount of local information, imposing even more constraint on the motion parameters than edge points. These corners are curvature extrema on the image intensity surface, and are being increasingly used in vision applications [10, 33, 36, 39, 54, 77, 96, 105, 107, 134, 157].

The projection operation is modelled as an *affine camera* [98], a generalisation of the familiar orthographic and scaled orthographic camera models. This provides a good approximation to the perspective projection model when the field of view is small and when the variation in depth of the scene along the line of sight is small compared to its average distance from the camera (of which more later). The affine camera requires no camera calibration, so enables the identification of quantities that can be computed under parallel projection without calibration, such as affine epipolar geometry (Chapter 5) and new views of an object (Chapter 8). When calibration *is* needed, the precise stage at which it must be introduced into the computation can be determined, e.g. aspect ratio is required to compute rigid motion parameters (Chapter 7).

Finally, a displacement–based formulation is used (in preference to a velocity–based (or *optic flow*) method) in order to exploit long–range temporal information and avoid the ill–conditioning that arises in the case of small motions.

1.2.1   System architecture

The architecture is shown in Figure 1.1. Images are processed as they enter sequentially in time, with three distinct layers of computation:

1. *Low–level vision*: A set of corners is extracted from each incoming image and matched to the corners from previous images, generating an "image trajectory" for each feature. The feature extraction, tracking and prediction modules operate wholly within the image plane, and each feature is treated independently.

2. *Medium–level vision*: The image trajectories are then grouped into putative objects, representing the projections of rigid bodies in the world moving independently of one another and of the viewer. Two different segmentation modules are developed for this purpose, namely clustering and outlier rejection. Each object's structure and motion parameters are then computed, and this knowledge is passed back to the low–level routines to assist the correspondence process. All modules in this layer use three–dimensional information, without needing object–specific data (e.g. prior object models).

3. *High–level vision*: The final stage of processing depends on the goal of the computation, e.g. the objects can be matched to a prior database for recognition, coded efficiently for bandwidth compression, and so on. The modules in this layer operate at the symbolic level, using high–level object knowledge.

This architecture is a motion analogue of the framework Ullman proposed for human perception of abstract shape properties and spatial relations [152]: the image trajectories form the *base representation* for use by subsequent visual processes (or "visual routines"); the layer 2 modules are *universal routines*, which can be usefully applied to any scene; and the layer 3 modules are *situation–dependent routines*, which are more specialised and depend on the goal of the computation.

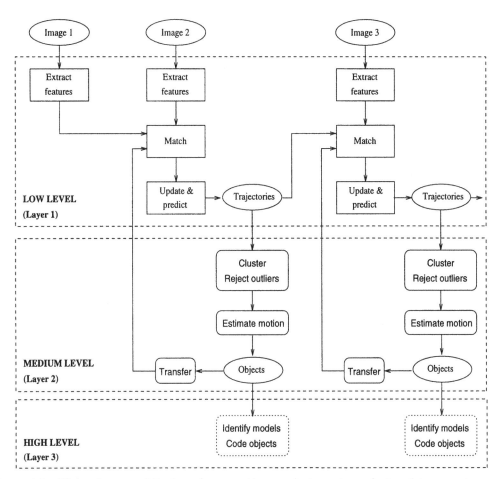

Figure 1.1: *Three–layer architecture for a motion analysis system, designed to operate over long, monocular image sequences.*

The flow of information through the framework is straightforward: grey–level images form the inputs to layer 1 and image trajectories are its outputs. These trajectories feed into layer 2 where they are grouped into objects and passed onto layer 3, which finally generates the appropriate symbolic representations. The first two layers are entirely data–driven; they depend only on the input, and are guided by general organisational principles rather than object–specific knowledge. It is these first two layers that form the subject of this thesis.

1.2.2   Themes

Several philosophies underpin the research in this thesis. First, the proposed algorithms use *all* available features. This overcomes a key limitation of many existing point–based structure and motion algorithms (e.g. [79]), which operate on the minimum amount of data required; such approaches are extremely sensitive to errors and noise, and often rely crucially on the selection of an appropriate "local coordinate frame". The advantages of our approach include improved noise immunity, the ability to identify outliers ("rogue observations") and avoidance of the computational burden of selecting a suitable frame.

Second, consideration is given to the statistical performance of the algorithms, with noise models constructed to assess confidence in the computed parameters. Least–squares minimisation is performed in the *image plane,* where the noise enters the system, rather than in the scene.

Third, three–dimensional information is introduced without computing explicit depth (or even Euclidean structure). This accords with recent trends to move away from the "vision as photogrammetry" approach; indeed, the timely "shape and motion without depth" paradigm of Tomasi and Kanade [145] is shown to be even more general than they themselves realised!

Finally, emphasis has been placed on developing reliable algorithms, and the system has been widely tested on both simulated and real data.

1.3   Application: Model–based image coding

An important reason why motion analysis is such an active research field is that it has a large number of practical applications. These include automatic vehicle driving ("road following"), aerial surveillance, medical inspection, mobile robot navigation and global model construction; good reviews of these and other applications can be found in [4, 65, 106, 134, 172]. The application of interest here is *low–bandwidth image coding,* a vital component in emerging videoconferencing and videophone systems [76, 161].

The goal of image coding is to reduce, as far as possible, the amount of data needed to reconstruct a faithful duplicate of the original picture. Current video coding research envisages systems operating over 64 kbit/s Integrated Services Digital Network (ISDN) channels, and therein lies the problem, for full–motion video has extremely demanding bandwidth requirements. For instance, a 512×512 image, 8 bits deep, contains roughly 2×10^6 bits; contrary to Descartes' beliefs, a picture is clearly worth much more than a thousand words! At 25 frames/second, the limited transmission capacity dictates the need for substantial compression. These demands stretch classical coding algorithms [44, 102] (e.g. transform coding) to the limit, and they exhibit poor performance when there is significant motion in the scene, dropping several frames per second or reducing spatial resolution.

The obvious difficulty with conventional waveform coding is that is doesn't explicitly consider image *content*; knowing the statistical properties of an image doesn't explain what it depicts. A new class of techniques has therefore emerged, termed *intelligent image coding* or *model–based image coding* (MBIC) [5, 110, 162]. Their objective is to *understand* the scene by modelling the objects, yielding a higher–level (and hence more compact) representation. The transmission data are thus not the images themselves but instead *parameters to represent them,* making this application a natural candidate for cross–fertilisation between image communication and computer vision ideas.

Figure 1.2 shows a block diagram of such a system. At the transmitting side, images are analysed to extract properties of the objects in the scene, such as shape, motion, colour and texture. The transmitter and receiver then both possess a model of the scene, and when motion occurs, the relevant parameters are measured and transmitted. The receiver then applies these movements to its model and generates a new synthetic image. The models can also be updated to refine earlier calculations and add previously obscured portions. Research activity in this field has intensified over the last five years, and impressive compression ratios (of the order $10^4 - 10^5$) have been reported in preliminary tests [44]. Although accurate and reliable motion estimation is obviously of the utmost importance in such systems, almost all efforts to date have concentrated on the role of the *model* [5, 6, 34, 103, 162] (Figure 1.3(a)). This approach doesn't generalise easily, since models are then needed for every object in the world, and the models have to be *located* in the image before processing can begin.

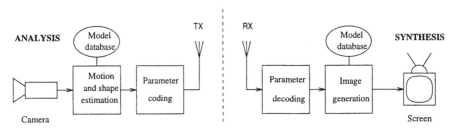

Figure 1.2: *Model–based image coding (MBIC) system.*

The quest for a generalised model–based image coding system would thus be greatly aided by an ability to code scenes *without* object recognition, even if only partial coding was achieved. Three important advantages accrue from the use of low–level primitives (Figure 1.3(b)), namely *generality, opportunism* and *graceful degradation*. A system that doesn't need to know what it is looking at will obviously work on a wider variety of scenes. It can also take *advantage* of any "out of the ordinary" properties (e.g. earrings). Furthermore, it will fail more gracefully than a scheme that has been unsuccessful in locating its model.

The argument here is not that valuable model knowledge should be discarded; rather, that both top–down *and* bottom–up approaches are needed, and that both could be accommodated in a single framework (perhaps along the lines of Figure 1.1). The system presented in this thesis indicates the utility of corner features in scene segmentation and motion and shape estimation; with complementary edge information, a generalised MBIC system can be envisaged that will build its own models out of low–level primitives that appear in almost every natural scene.

1.4   Thesis outline

The thesis layout follows the order of processing in Figure 1.1. The broad sweep of topics covered (correspondence, tracking, clustering, outlier rejection, structure from motion, epipolar geometry and transfer) makes a single literature survey impractical; instead, relevant previous work is discussed in the appropriate chapters.

Chapter 2 describes the first layer of the architecture, showing how corner features are extracted and tracked through the image sequence (Figure 1.4(a)). The remaining chapters

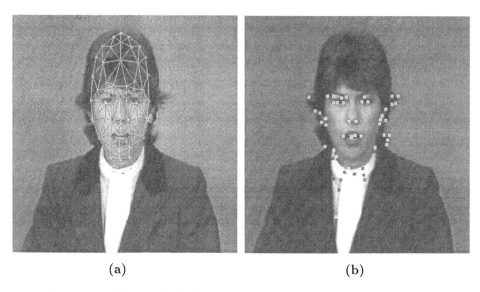

(a)   (b)

Figure 1.3: *Comparison between high–level and low–level approaches: (a) Traditional MBIC, where a wire frame model is fitted to the face; (b) Towards generalised MBIC using low–level primitives (corner features).*

then develop various modules in the second layer. **Chapter 3** first introduces the affine camera model, providing the theory and notation needed by subsequent chapters. The literature on "affine structure" (scene structure up to an arbitrary 3D affine transformation) is reviewed and placed in a common framework, and new algorithms are proposed. **Chapter 4** builds on these affine structure concepts, presenting a novel local, parallel, clustering algorithm (based on graph theory) to group the trajectories into putative objects (Figure 1.4(b)).

Chapter 5 derives the equations of epipolar geometry and defines the special form of its fundamental matrix. Various least–squares formulations are examined to ensure a noise–resistant solution for these parameters. Figure 1.4(c) and (d) shows a typical set of computed epipolar lines. Affine epipolar geometry is then used in two ways. **Chapter 6** defines a new outlier rejection scheme operating in an orthogonal regression framework, and rejects unreliable corners from the main body of data on the basis of inconsistent affine epipolar geometry (Figures 1.5(a) and (b)). **Chapter 7** then shows how the rigid motion parameters may be computed *directly* from the affine epipolar geometry: specifically, the scale factor between views, the projection of the axis of rotation and the cyclotorsion angle about the optic axis are determined, along with their confidence estimates. Figure 1.5(c) shows a typical axis of rotation. Kalman filtering is employed to give optimal estimates over time.

Finally, **Chapter 8** employs affine structure concepts to perform transfer, i.e. to generate new views of an object or fill in points that have disappeared (Figure 1.5(d)). This forms the feedback link to the low–level correspondence process, thus completing the processing chain.

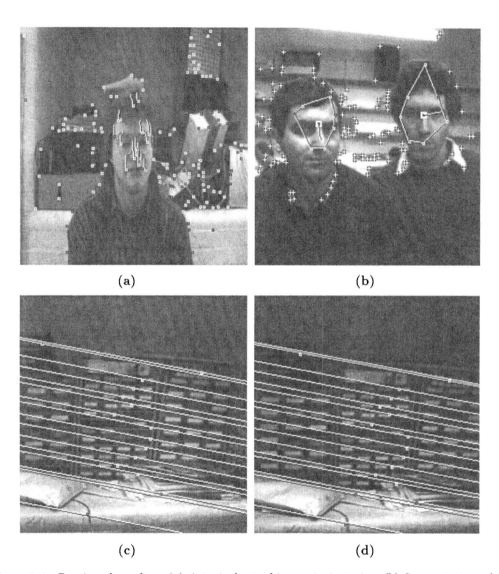

(a)

(b)

(c)

(d)

Figure 1.4: *Previewed results : (a) A typical set of image trajectories; (b) Segmentation of a dynamic scene (by clustering); (c)(d) Left and right epipolar lines.*

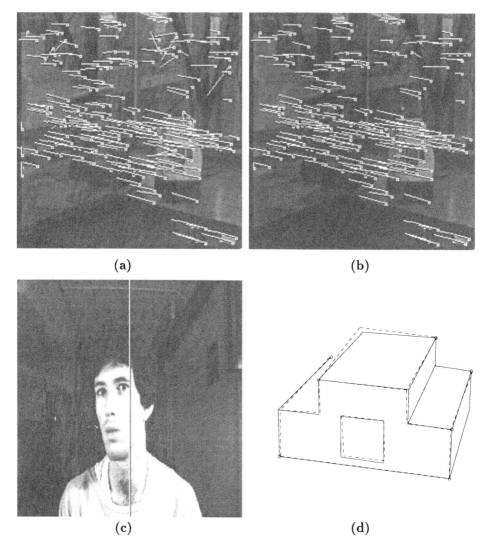

(a)   (b)

(c)   (d)

Figure 1.5: *Previewed results: (a)(b) The benefits of outlier rejection (before and after); (c) Projected axis of rotation (for a shaking head); (d) Transfer to a new view (dashed lines) superimposed on the correct view (solid lines), using a core point–set (circles).*

Chapter 2

Corner extraction and tracking

2.1 Introduction

The first competence required of a motion analysis system is the accurate and robust measurement of image motion. This chapter addresses the problem of tracking independently-moving (and possibly non–rigid) objects in a long, monocular image sequence. "Corner features" are automatically identified in the images and tracked through successive frames, generating *image trajectories*. This system forms the low–level front–end of our architecture (cf. Figure 1.1), making reliable trajectory computation of the utmost importance, for these trajectories underpin all subsequent segmentation and motion estimation processes.

We build largely on the work of Wang and Brady [156, 157], and extend their successful corner–based stereo algorithm to the motion domain. Their key idea was to base correspondence on both similarity of local image structure *and* geometric proximity. There are, however, several ways in which motion correspondence is more complex than stereo correspondence [90]. For one thing, objects can change between temporal viewpoints in ways that they cannot between spatial viewpoints, e.g. their shape and reflectance can alter. For another, the epipolar constraint is no longer hard–wired by once–off calibration of a stereo-rig; motion induces *variable* epipolar geometry which has to be continuously updated (if the constraint is to be used). Furthermore, motion leads to arbitrarily long image sequences (instead of frame–pairs), which requires additional tracking machinery. The benefits are that temporal integration facilitates noise resistance, resolves ambiguities over time, and speeds up matching (via prediction).

Our framework has two parts: the *matcher* performs two–frame correspondence while the *tracker* maintains the multi–frame trajectories. Each corner is treated as an *independent* feature at this level (i.e. assigned an individual tracker as in [26]), and is tracked purely within the image plane. Section 2.2 justifies this feature–based approach and establishes the utility of corners as correspondence tokens. Section 2.3 explains how to extract corners and Sections 2.4 and 2.5 describe the matcher and tracker subsystems.

2.2 Feature–based correspondence

Image sequence analysis begins with an attempt to find a vector field describing image changes over time. There are three main techniques [62, 100, 134]: *feature–based* methods extract image features and track their movement from frame to frame; *gradient–based* methods use spatial and temporal partial derivatives to estimate image flow at each location in the image; and *correlation–based* methods use similarity in brightness patterns to determine motion vectors.

The feature–based approach has several advantages. First, feature extraction reduces the vast amount of data present in an image, without necessarily eliminating salient information [134]; indeed, Brady noted that "not all information is created equal" (page 259) [23], and that different locations in an image impose differing degrees of constraint on the motion parameters. For instance, a smooth image region often provides so little constraint that the computation has to be supported by regularisation, allowing smoothing conditions to dominate the information actually available in the raw image data.

Second, Verri and Poggio [154] showed that in general, the observed image velocity field (or *optic flow*) differs from the true image motion field (the theoretical projection of the 3D velocity field), except where image gradients are strong, e.g. at edge or corner locations. Computing dense flow fields can thus be counter–productive, which militates against the naive use of gradient or correlation methods.

The central question which then remains is: at what level above grey–scale intensities should matching take place? Should the basic matching elements be low–level descriptors (e.g. corners, edges, blobs) or high–level objects? With low–level features, images are matched feature–by–feature without being interpreted, thus complicating the correspondence problem (e.g. there are many candidates in I_2 for each feature in I_1). With high–level features, images are first analysed separately and described in terms of familiar objects (e.g. a beige fax–machine sitting on a brown desk); this greatly simplifies the correspondence problem by eliminating ambiguity in the matching stage, but the burden of work is transferred to the recognition modules. The low–level approach is preferred for the three important reasons discussed in Section 1.3, namely *generality, opportunism* and *graceful degradation.*

Although our framework is not specifically modelled on the human visual system (HVS), it seems reasonable to take account of relevant psychophysical evidence, which supports our approach. Ullman [151] illustrated that during motion analysis, the HVS neither performs "grey–level" matching nor relies on elaborate form perception; instead, it explicitly extracts "correspondence tokens" prior to motion correspondence, these tokens being elementary constituents at the level of Marr's raw primal sketch [90].

2.2.1   The case for corners

Low–level descriptors may be classified into three main types: region–based, edge–based and point–based. This section explains why point features ("corners") are suitable matching tokens.

Regions (or "blobs") [41, 149] correspond to smooth surface patches, or loci of zero–dimensional change [23]. Tracking such regions is difficult, since minor differences between frames (due to image noise or image motion, say) can lead to very different segmentations in consecutive frames [164]. Despite recent progress by Meyer and Bouthemy [95] (who tracked convex–hull approximations to region boundaries) and by Etoh and Shirai [40] (who used advanced statistical region descriptors), further theoretical and empirical work is needed before region tracking becomes feasible.

Edges are loci of one–dimensional change [23], located where the change in intensity is significant in one direction. They are generally detected by finding either maxima in the first image derivative [25] or zero–crossings in the Laplacian of the Gaussian of the image [52, 90]. Their usefulness in motion algorithms is limited by the "aperture problem", which arises from a locally linear expansion[1] of the spatio–temporal image intensity function $I(x, y, t)$: without assumptions about the nature of the flow $\boldsymbol{\mu}$, only the component of flow *perpendicular* to the edge element ($\mu^{\perp}$) can be found [39, 62, 100]. Unfortunately, the assumptions invariably lead to inaccuracies in the estimated flow, particularly at motion boundaries [134]. The use of higher order derivatives is unsatisfactory since differentiation accentuates noise [62]. Moreover, until the recent advent of snakes [75], arbitrarily curving edges were difficult to describe and track, and simultaneous tracking of multiple open edge contours with automatic snake initialisation still remains an open problem.

Point features are distinctive image points corresponding to objective 3D scene elements, that are accurately locatable and recur in successive images. They have the advantage of being discrete and distinguishable, so they can be explicitly tracked over time. Popular point features include local maxima of directional variance [96], knots in elastic strings [22], distinguished points along edge curves (e.g. maximum curvature points [94], inflection points [10], zeros and discontinuities of curvature [22]), junctions and line terminations [90], and centres–of–gravity of iso–density contours [135].

We employ the term "corners" to refer to point features that are loci of two–dimensional intensity change, i.e. *second–order features*. This includes points of occlusion (e.g. T, Y and X junctions), structural discontinuities (e.g. L junctions) and various curvature maxima (e.g. texture flecks or surface markings). Corners impose more constraint on the motion parameters than edges, for the *full* optic flow field $\boldsymbol{\mu}$ is recoverable at corner locations. Until recently, corners were neglected in favour of edges; reliable detection of edges was difficult enough, and corners were even harder to extract accurately because of their susceptibility to noise. Advances in the last five years, however, have shown that corners can be computed both reliably and efficiently, and they are increasingly being used in vision applications (e.g. [15, 24, 26, 29, 31, 35, 55, 80, 121, 134, 139, 141, 145, 147, 158]).

Although corner features have mainly been used in factory– or laboratory–type environments, where physical corners arise from man–made objects (Figure 2.1(a)), they are equally useful in more "natural" scenes. For instance, Figures 2.1(b)–(d) show corners detected on images of a human face, which has no right–angles or sharp discontinuities; the facial features are rounded and the skin surface is smooth. Although (impressively) the detected corners do often correspond to salient facial features (e.g. nostrils, corners of eyes, tips of eyebrows, endpoints of mouth), what is more important is that the corners are *stable, robust* beacons which are extracted automatically from the given image sequence. For example, the eyes, mouth and nostrils are robustly localised even when the head moves, and the mouth and eyes open and close.

---

[1]The first order Taylor series expansion of $I(x + \delta x, y + \delta y, t + \delta t)$.

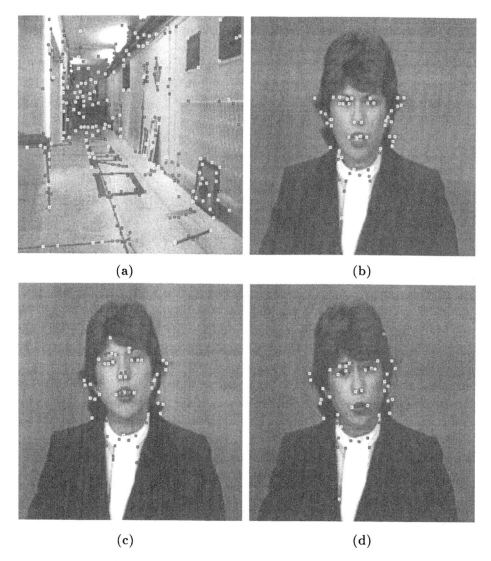

(a)   (b)

(c)   (d)

Figure 2.1: *Corners (marker colour set for maximum contrast): (a) A typical laboratory scene; (b)(c)(d) Three frames in the standard CCITT sequence "Clair". Her eyes close in (c), and her mouth closes in (d).*

2.3 Corner detection

Numerous strategies have been proposed for extracting corner features, with landmark contributions (in chronological order) by Moravec [96], Kitchen and Rosenfeld [77], Nagel and Dreschler [39, 105], Asada and Brady [10], Harris and Stephens [54], Noble [107], Wang and Brady [157], and Smith [134]. Good reviews and critical analyses of these systems can be found in [33, 36, 107, 134]. We employ the curvature–based corner detector of Wang and Brady. Section 2.3.1 describes this corner finder and Section 2.3.2 discusses the problem of false corners.

2.3.1 The Wang–Brady corner finder

If a grey–level image is considered as a height surface, the total image surface curvature is approximately [157]

$$\kappa \approx D_t^2 I / |\nabla I|, \qquad |\nabla I| \gg 1, \tag{2.1}$$

where D_t^2 is the second order directional derivative along the edge tangential direction t. That is, κ is proportional to the second derivative along the edge tangent, and inversely proportional to the edge strength (image gradient)^2. Corners are defined at points where κ is high and attains a local maximum. Several refinements are then introduced [157] to improve robustness to noise, such as false corner response suppression (to prevent corners being wrongly reported on strong edges). The final corner operator generates a response Γ which attains a local maximum at a corner location (Figure 2.2):

$$\begin{cases} \Gamma = \left(\frac{\partial^2 I}{\partial t^2}\right)^2 - S\,|\nabla I|^2 \longrightarrow \max \\ \Gamma > R \\ |\nabla I|^2 > E \end{cases} \tag{2.2}$$

For an image location to be labelled a corner, then, both the image curvature and the gradient perpendicular to the edgel at that location must be maxima and must exceed specified thresholds. This particular corner detector was chosen since it ran faster (at 14 Hz on T800 transputers), and produced better localised corners [134, 157], than the best competing corner detector at the time (that of Harris and Stephens [54]). Note that Γ doesn't only find corners lying along edges (as in the Medioni–Yasumoto scheme [94]); points with sharp autocorrelations (e.g. texture flecks) also give strong corner responses. This is important since such points are potentially robust features, and because visually striking features (e.g. moles) may be isolated, i.e. not lie on continuous edges.

The four parameters to specify are: S, a measure of image surface curvature; R, a threshold for the corner response; E, an edge strength measure; and M, the side of the square area over which Γ must be maximal. This remainder of this section summarises experiments with these four parameter settings and with Gaussian smoothing. Understanding this parameter variation is important if the system is to work reliably in practice (e.g. for coding).

---

[2]Equation (2.1) is exact for 3D vectors; the approximation arises from the use of 2D normal and tangential vectors.

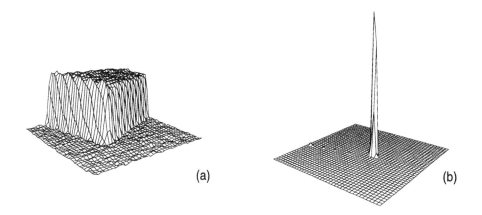

Figure 2.2: *Corner detection: (a) Image intensity surface; (b) Corner response function* Γ.

The mask size M controls the extent over which the corner position must be a local peak, and indirectly defines the minimum separability between corners. Typical values are 3, 5, 7 and 9 pixels, and Figure 2.3 shows corners extracted from an image using two different mask sizes. The larger mask rejects the high frequency intensity variations (noise) and reduces clutter, at the expense of a longer search time and a reduced "local effect"; however, the strongest corners appear for all mask sizes. A mask size of 7 proves satisfactory for our application.

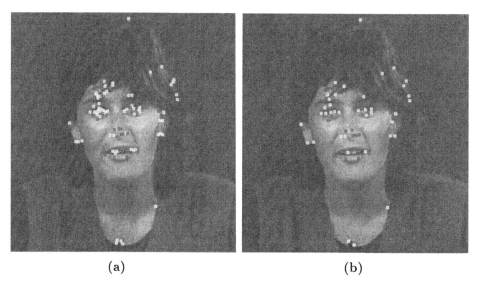

Figure 2.3: *Mask sizes* M. *A frame in the CCITT sequence "Miss America", with all other parameters held constant* $(E = 10\ 000,\ R = 0,\ S = 0.4)$: *(a)* $M = 3$; *(b)* $M = 7$.

Parameters R, S and E are closely related. S suppresses the corner response along edges by subtracting a fraction of the edge strength $|\nabla I|^2$ from Γ. Figure 2.4 shows the response for two different values of S. Notice that most of the corners along the outer shirt boundary with $S = 0$ disappear when a larger scale value is used. Increasing S beyond 0.3–0.4 (depending on the edge jaggedness and the second order differentiation mask) has little effect on edge response suppression, since any corners remaining along the edge must then arise from significant curvature changes. However, as $S \to \infty$, $\Gamma \to -\infty$ and useful corners begin to disappear. A balance must thus be struck between S and R; S must be sufficiently large to cancel out spurious edge responses, but beyond that, it simply introduces an "offset" which R can compensate for. We limit S to the range $[0; 1]$, with a default value of 0.4, and set $R = 0$. The edge strength threshold E is needed to maintain the validity of Equation (2.1), with $\sqrt{E} \gg 1$; a value of $E = 10\,000$ works well. The results are not unduly sensitive to changes in these parameter values.

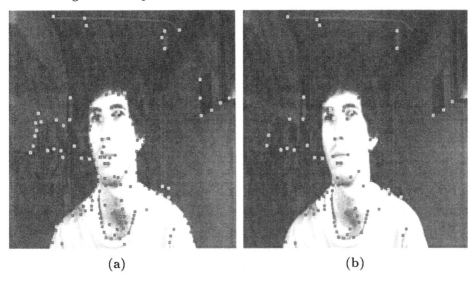

(a)   (b)

Figure 2.4: *Scale sizes S. A frame in the "Curl" sequence, with all other parameters held constant ($E = 10\,000$, $R = 0$, $M = 7$): (a) $S = 0$; (b) $S = 0.6$.*

Finally, Gaussian smoothing (with standard deviation σ) displaces the corner position by an amount linear in σ [157]. This displacement is negligible (less than half a pixel) for $\sigma = 0.5$. The number of corners shrinks with increasing σ, because the "blurring effect" suppresses the high frequency intensity variations (Figure 2.5); the benefits are noise reduction and suppression of some false edge responses too strong for S to sift out. Most salient corner features are preserved with $\sigma = 0.5$; $\sigma = 1$ blurs excessively, destroying useful information. The $\sigma = 0.5$ Gaussian is therefore applied to the images prior to corner extraction.

2.3.2   False corners

Image corners are assumed to be projections of physical 3D corners, termed *objective* structure (due to their viewpoint invariance) [26]. This is a key assumption, since correspondence tokens must be well–founded in the scene [151]. Unfortunately, other scene phenomena can also generate second–order intensity variations in the image and hence be marked (incorrectly) as corners. If these "false" corners are not identified, they will obviously introduce

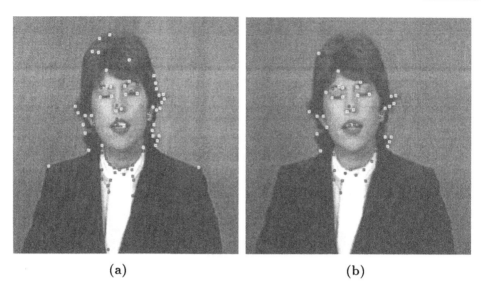

(a)   (b)

Figure 2.5: *Gaussian smoothing. A frame in the "Clair" sequence, with all other parameters held constant ($E = 10\,000$, $R = 0$, $S = 0.4$): (a) $\sigma = 0$ (75 corners); (b) $\sigma = 0.5$ (47 corners).*

error into the subsequent stages, since their motion is in general inconsistent with that of the true object. (Outlier rejection is discussed in Chapters 4 and 6.)

Examples of this *subjective* structure (which varies with viewing position) include profile edges and conjunctions of edges lying at different depths. Figure 2.6(a) shows edges from different objects meeting along an occluding boundary. The problem of profile edges (bounding contours) is shown in Figure 2.6(b): the tip of the nose is labelled a corner in the profile view, but not in the frontal view. This problem is less serious than that of false junctions since with small inter–frame motion, curvature maxima tend to remain local maxima until they disappear (rather than sliding along the edge). Hence, they give useful information for a limited period, and are then retired. (A rigorous analysis of projected space curves, particularly extremal boundaries, can be found in Cipolla [30].) Other sources of error include shadow lines and specularities.

2.4   The matcher

The matcher receives as input two grey–scale images, I_1 and I_2, along with their respective corners, $\mathbf{x}_i$ and $\mathbf{x}'_j$ (where $i = 0 \ldots n{-}1$ and $j = 0 \ldots n'{-}1$). Its task is then to match $\mathbf{x}_i$ to $\mathbf{x}'_j$. This is the well–known *correspondence problem*, whose worst case enumeration is nn' possible matches. Constraints from the physical world are usually imposed to reduce this computational effort [90]. For instance, Thacker et al. [141, 142] noted four popular heuristics in stereo matching: *uniqueness, restricted search strategies, local image properties* and *disparity gradients*. The first three apply equally to the motion correspondence problem, albeit in a slightly modified form, and are used in our matcher as follows:

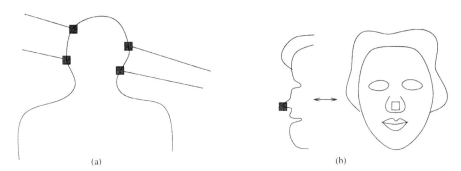

Figure 2.6: *False corners: (a) Junctions between edges belonging to different objects; (b) 3D edge curvature maxima are viewpoint dependent.*

- Each corner may only pair with one other corner.

- Small search neighbourhoods are utilised since corners do not move far between consecutive frames (the high frame–rate ensures small inter–frame motion). This leads to efficient, local matching operations.

- Local image patch correlation is employed to verify matches, resolve ambiguities and measure the confidence in each match. This is effective because the small inter–frame motion leaves the intensity pattern around a corner largely unchanged between successive frames.

Sections 2.4.1 and Section 2.4.2 describe the matching algorithm, Sections 2.4.3 gives results, and Section 2.4.4 relates the matcher to previous work. The two–frame matcher is described here in *bootstrap* mode; Section 2.5 will discuss the modifications when predictions are available.

2.4.1 Strong matches

Consider two sets of corners superimposed on a single system of image axes, with a search window centred on a corner in I_1. All corners from I_2 lying in this window are candidates for the match (Figure 2.7(a)). *Normalised cross–correlation* is then performed between the image region surrounding the I_1 corner (the "template") and the image region surrounding each candidate corner in I_2 (the "patch"). The winning candidate is the one with the highest correlation value c_{max}, provided c_{max} exceeds a specified threshold. (This threshold is necessary since the "best" corner in the window need not be a valid match, e.g. the true feature may have disappeared.) The size of the correlation patch is the mask size M, which defines the critical set of pixels used to select the corner in the first place.

The procedure is then repeated, working back from I_2 to I_1, and matches are only accepted if they concur in both directions. This technique ("mutual consent pruning") is widely used [26, 134, 141, 155] to resolve conflicting attractions, where the preference of one feature for another is not reciprocated (Figure 2.7(b)). A match that survives this pruning is termed a *strong* match.

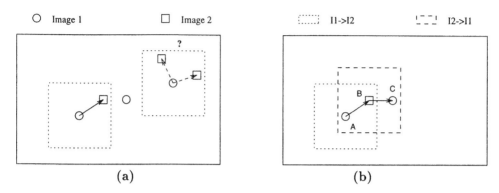

(a)   (b)

Figure 2.7: *A search window (dotted rectangle) centred on the reference feature in I_1 (circle). All features from I_2 (squares) falling within it are candidates for the match: (a) A small intensity patch around each candidate is correlated with the patch around the reference feature; (b) Feature A in I_1 chooses B in I_2, but B prefers C to A. Mutual consent pruning flushes out these "love triangles".*

Various correlation measures are possible [16, 123, 134, 141]. We choose the one used in [155], an adaptation of the standard *product moment coefficient* [97], which assumes a linear dependence between two N–point data sets $\{x_i\}$ and $\{y_i\}$,

$$c = \frac{S_{xy}}{S_x S_y} = \frac{\sum_{i=1}^{N}(x_i - \bar{x})(y_i - \bar{y})}{\sqrt{\sum_{i=1}^{N}(x_i - \bar{x})^2}\sqrt{\sum_{i=1}^{N}(y_i - \bar{y})^2}}, \quad -1 \leq c \leq 1,$$

where $\bar{x}$ and $\bar{y}$ are the sample means, S_x^2 and S_y^2 are the standard deviations, and S_{xy} is the covariance. Perfect positive (negative) correlation is indicated by $c = 1$ ($c = -1$). This 1D analysis is extended to 2D by raster–scanning the pixels in the blocks of interest. Hence, to correlate template T with image patch P, both of them square with side $W = 2w + 1$ pixels, the correlation measure (after simplification) is

$$c = \frac{W^2 \sum_k \sum_l T_{i+k,j+l}\, P_{i+k,j+l} - \sum_k \sum_l T_{i+k,j+l} \sum_k \sum_l P_{i+k,j+l}}{\sqrt{W^2 \sum_k \sum_l T_{i+k,j+l}^2 - \left(\sum_k \sum_l T_{i+k,j+l}\right)^2}\sqrt{W^2 \sum_k \sum_l P_{i+k,j+l}^2 - \left(\sum_k \sum_l P_{i+k,j+l}\right)^2}},$$

where (i, j) indexes the centre pixel of the block, $\{T_{i,j}\}$ and $\{P_{i,j}\}$ are the respective intensity values, and k and l range from $-w$ to $+w$ inclusive. Only positive correlation values are considered ($0 \leq c \leq 1$), since negative c simply indicates template inversion. Perfect correlation obtains when $c = 1$, so c serves as a measure of match confidence.

An advantage of this particular correlation measure is that it compares the *relative structures* of the image patches, rather than their absolute intensities. In fact, c is invariant to a 1D affine transformation between the data–sets, i.e. $c = \pm 1$ when $y_i = ax_i + b$, where a and b are scalars. Assuming that the albedo ρ of the surface patch doesn't change over time, a will account for automatic gain control of the camera, uniform changes in scene lighting, and changes of object pose relative to a constant light source, while b will account for a change in the intensity offset (see Appendix A in [128]).

2.4.2   Forced matches

There are several reasons why there may still be unmatched corners in I_1 and I_2:

1. A feature may disappear permanently due to occlusion, i.e. it appears in I_1 but not I_2 (a *ghost*).

2. A previously obscured feature may become visible as new structure sweeps into view (or previously–seen structure reappears), i.e. it appears in I_2 but not I_1 (an *intruder*).

3. A feature may appear intermittently ("flash" on and off) due to instability in the corner detector (e.g. Γ oscillating about R). This causes both ghosts and intruders.

4. A feature may only appear once, due to shot noise. This leads first to an intruder and then to a ghost.

It is impossible to distinguish between these scenarios on the basis of only two frames; in fact, it is precisely scenarios 3 and 4 that have made corner detection unattractive in the past, especially for stereo matching. However, sustained observation of the features greatly simplifies this task (Figure 2.8).

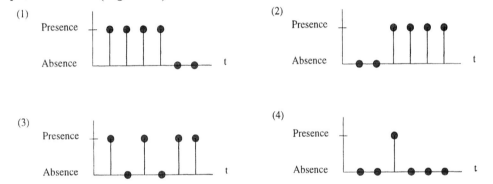

Figure 2.8: *Observing a corner over time allows discrimination between the four scenarios.*

With this in mind, we require the matcher to generate a best position estimate (BPE) for *every unmatched corner* in I_1, i.e. to "feed the corner forward" into the next frame. It is not possible at this level to hypothesise the motion of a point based on the motion of its neighbours, since corners are sparse and the scene contains non–rigid, independently moving objects (which haven't yet been segmented). Thus, the corners *needn't* move in a locally consistent manner (Figure 2.9(a)).

In leaving no corner in I_1 unpaired, the matcher differs from [26, 141, 157] where a large proportion of the corners may be unused at any one time. The assumption here is that the third scenario has happened, i.e. the corner has flashed off and will flash on again soon. If this *is* true, the BPE will be a good estimate, since the feature is still visible and does have some second–order structure (even if it isn't particularly strong). If the corner has in fact disappeared permanently, the tracker will soon realise this, since the corner will not reappear and the correlation values of the forced matches will be low.

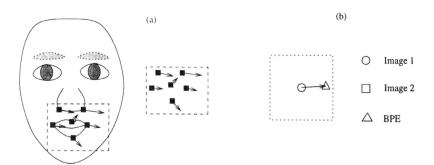

Figure 2.9: *(a) A valid (but locally inconsistent) image motion field arising from nonrigidity and independent motion (mouth opens while head moves); (b) An unmatched corner in I_1 (circle) is given a* forced *match (triangle) with confidence c_{bpe}. The BPE is computed by correlation search in the window.*

The BPE is computed by a correlation test over the whole search window, using every location as a candidate. The position with highest correlation (c_{bpe}) is accepted (Figure 2.9(b)). This is called a *forced* match. (A fuller discussion of the implementation details and optimisations is given in [128].) On the next cycle ($I_2 \rightarrow I_3$), the ghost point is treated as a true corner in I_2, in the hope that it will find a strong match in I_3 (signalling reappearance).

This search procedure is expensive, since an $n \times n$ window has n^2 possible positions. However, it is a local operation (so could be done in parallel), and is only performed for unmatched points. Also, n^2 is the worst–case scenario; when predictions are available, the search space is substantially reduced (see Section 2.5.2). Most important, however, is that forced matching need only be performed as a bootup or recovery process; it will be shown later that once the image has been segmented, higher level information (in the form of affine epipolar geometry and affine structure) is available to assist the matcher with unmatched points (see Chapter 8). This feedback approach was explored recently for the projective case in [16]. Moreover, certain algorithms do not require the points to be tracked through every frame (see Chapters 5 and 7), in which case the strong matches suffice.

2.4.3   Results

The algorithm has been implemented in C on SUN SPARC workstations, and tested on a wide range of sequences. All search windows are square, centred on the pixel of interest. Elliptical [26] or circular [114] search regions have also been used in other correspondence algorithms; square regions were chosen for simplicity and computational efficiency. An 11×11 window is used for initial candidates[3].

Figure 2.10 shows a head rotating about an axis parallel to the optic axis (a "curl" flow field characteristic), with the matches decomposed into strong and forced matches. Together, these vectors accurately convey the direction of motion, testifying to the temporal

---

[3]The size of the candidate search window relates to the expected motion in pixels, which in turn depends on the objects being tracked (e.g. a snail vs a missile), the frame–rate and the camera focal length.

consistency of the corners. The forced matches also clearly contribute valuable information, verifying that it is beneficial to propagate these corners; there are also clearly incorrect matches, highlighting the need for outlier rejection (see Chapter 6). Experiments have shown the number of forced matches and incorrect motion vectors to decrease with Gaussian smoothing, confirming that the best corners are retained.

Figures 2.11 and 2.12 show the composite two–frame matches (i.e. with strong and forced matches combined) on head and car sequences. In all cases, the motion direction emerges clearly, giving a clear indication of where (and in what direction) image motion occurs. The accuracy of the displacement vectors despite the small motion indicates that the corners are well localised, and this proves a solid foundation for multi–frame trajectories. It is also apparent that corners are a sparse shape representation; additional information (e.g. edge motion) would obviously be a useful complement (especially when finding motion boundaries, as in [50, 134]).

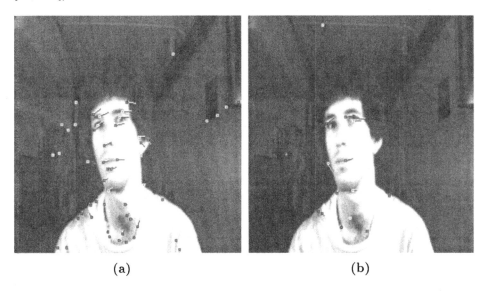

(a)   (b)

Figure 2.10: *Two–frame matches for the "Curl" sequence ($\sigma = 0.5$, double–length vectors): (a) Strong matches (54 corners); (b) Forced matches (15 corners).*

2.4.4   Previous work

Seminal work on the motion correspondence problem was done by Ullman [151], and numerous algorithms have since been proposed. This review is necessarily brief; additional reviews can be found in [126, 134].

Solutions to the "two–frame matching problem" are broadly based on classic calibrated stereo algorithms [9, 13, 112, 113, 141]; however, the familiar stereo epipolar constraint cannot be used to define search regions when the relative camera/scene motion is unknown. Algorithms may be classified according to the matching criteria they employ. Measures of *corner similarity* are typical, the idea being that each feature has a set of attributes

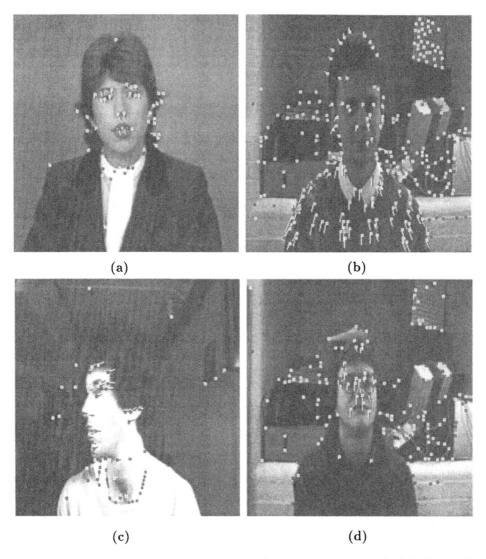

(a)   (b)

(c)   (d)

Figure 2.11: *Combined strong and forced matches (double–length vectors): (a) Clair nods her head downwards and opens her mouth slightly (CCITT); (b) Ian looms towards the camera (diverging flow pattern) amidst a cluttered background; (c) Larry shakes his head; (d) Richard nods his head.*

(a)   (b)

Figure 2.12: *Combined strong and forced matches (double–length vectors): (a) Salesman moves his arms and hands, turns the object and ripples his shirt; (b) Jeep drives forwards.*

which is invariant under the appropriate transformation. Barnard and Thompson [13] used "matching probabilities", which were inversely proportional to the sum of squares of the brightness difference between small patches centred on the corners in I_1 and I_2; the DROID system [26] used feature attributes of smoothed image intensity and intensity gradients at the corner position; Lawton [84] used correlation of small patches (assuming a static environment and purely translational motion); and Smith [134] used a feature vector comprising the unsmoothed image brightness and the centroid of his corner nucleus.

Another approach to matching low–level primitives is to form a *minimal mapping*. Scott and Longuet–Higgins [125] required the overall sum of the squared inter–image distances travelled by features to be a minimum; unfortunately, this failed for large rotary motions [126]. Ullman [151] minimised the "entropy" ($-\sum_i \log P(v_i)$) between matches in an attempt to obtain the most probable distribution of velocities (in accordance with a given probability distribution function $P(v)$); however, he didn't provide the grouping mechanisms to form the higher level primitives required for his theory to work (e.g. to form points into lines). Barnard and Thompson [13] used iterative relaxation of a matching surface to find the optimal solution; this is computationally expensive.

Geometric constraints are also popular, using either local support for a match (e.g. disparity gradient validation checks [112, 113]) or more global notions of shape (e.g. Shapiro and Brady [127] used a modal approach to shape description and matching). The former are not really useful here due to the sparseness of corners [141], and the latter are fundamentally limited by their global nature.

2.5 The tracker

The tracker oversees the matcher: it supervises the initial startup (*boot mode*), secures the transition to normal operation (*run mode*), performs prediction and maintains an image trajectory for each feature. Each corner is tracked individually at this early stage of processing since the segmentation is unknown. The matcher in Section 2.4 runs until the predictor kicks in, whereafter the tracker in Section 2.5.1 is used.

Two important issues to consider when designing the tracker are how to cope with uncertainty in corner motions and how to perform (and utilise) predictions. Figure 2.13(a) shows a typical solution, with a corner location predicted on the basis of its known history. If no corner is found at (or near) the prediction, further predictions are made for subsequent frames, accompanied by a decrease in prediction confidence (hence a larger search window). Our experiments with this approach (using a Kalman filter [158]) have shown it to be unsuitable in two respects. First, after several frames elapse without sighting the corner, the uncertainty in its position leads to a prohibitively large number of potential match candidates. Matching the corner is then almost impossible, since the correlation measure doesn't have the required discrimination power. Second, if the corner "manoeuvres" (i.e. violates the assumed motion model) while it has flashed off, it is never found again.

Our solution is to contain the uncertainty as quickly as possible (Figure 2.13(b)). Thus, when a corner doesn't appear at the predicted position, a full search is mobilised. If the corner has manoeuvred, it is found immediately; if it has genuinely disappeared (as opposed to simply flashed off), the correlation values indicate this. The increased computational cost of this strategy is partly offset by the reduced number of candidates for each match, and is justified by the improvement in the trajectories.

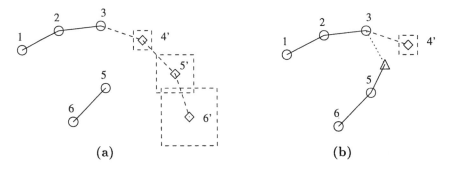

(a)   (b)

Figure 2.13: *Two tracking approaches, with a manoeuvring corner: (a) Predict and allow uncertainty to grow unchecked; (b) Contain the uncertainty immediately.*

Section 2.5.1 discusses matching with prediction, Section 2.5.2 defines the predictors and Section 2.5.3 describes trajectory maintenance. Points in the previous frame (I_{t-1}) are denoted by $\mathbf{x}_i$, points in the current frame (I_t) by $\mathbf{x}'_j$, and predicted positions (in I_t) by $\hat{\mathbf{x}}'_i$.

2.5.1   Tracking with prediction

Finding a suitable role for prediction in corner tracking is a tricky problem. On the one hand, past behaviour can be a valuable indicator of future behaviour, since physical objects possess inertia; ignoring "motion trends" therefore discards useful information. On the other hand, prediction requires a motion model, and while the predictor works well when this model is valid, it fails badly when the model is incorrect. There are thus two possible approaches to matching:

- match the actual data $\mathbf{x}_i$ to $\mathbf{x}'_j$

- match the predictions $\hat{\mathbf{x}}'_i$ to $\mathbf{x}'_j$

The second approach is more typical, but only has merit when $\hat{\mathbf{x}}'_i$ is *closer* than $\mathbf{x}_i$ to the corresponding point $\mathbf{x}'_i$; when it is further away, the prediction actually *complicates* the problem by misleading the matcher. Since occasional predictor failure is inevitable, the key is knowing when to trust the predictions. We use local patch correlation to indicate predictor success, and revert to the original image data when the predictor appears to fail.

Strong matches are first obtained from the raw data (as in Section 2.4.1), and prediction is then used to confirm the reliability of these matches. For every matched corner $\mathbf{x}_i$, the correlation value of its predicted position $\hat{\mathbf{x}}'_i$ is computed and compared against the correlation value of the strong match $\mathbf{x}'_i$, to decide whether the match is reliable and to identify weak corners[4] (Figure 2.14). Note that prediction is used here solely to verify matches and reject unsuitable features; the basic matches are formed from the *original images.*

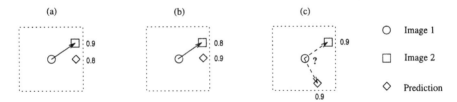

Figure 2.14: *Strong matches and their predictions. The strong match is accepted if (a) its correlation value beats the prediction correlation value, or (b) it is close to the predicted position with a similar correlation value. The corner is destroyed if the strong match is far away from the prediction with a similar correlation value (a weak corner).*

Now the unmatched corners remain. If a prediction is available, a small region around the predicted position is searched for a BPE, and this is accepted if the correlation value is high enough. If it isn't (or no prediction is available), a full correlation search is performed, centred on the original corner. Thus, when the predictor works, we save greatly on time, but when it fails, we fall back on the full search method. If the prediction gives a good correlation

---

[4]Weak corners arise in areas of uniform texture, caused either by a poor corner (low Γ) in a region without much structure, or a good corner (high Γ) in a highly (but similarly) textured area. Either way, such corners are unsuitable for tracking and are destroyed.

value but is actually incorrect, this become apparent in several frames' time when the corner hasn't reappeared, and the feature is then retired.

2.5.2   Predictors

The general form of predictor used is

$$\mathbf{x}(k+1) = \sum_{i \geq 0} w_i \, \mathbf{x}(k-i), \tag{2.3}$$

where $\mathbf{x}(k)$ is the image position in frame k and w_i are fixed weighting factors. The number of frames needed for startup is $i+1$. At best, these predictions are approximate since the predictors operate purely in the *image plane,* without attempting to model three–dimensional motion or camera projection. However, the aim here is *not* to deduce world motion parameters, but rather to take advantage of trends in image motion to improve efficiency and reject unsuitable features.

Two predictors are examined: a constant velocity model and a constant acceleration model. For the constant velocity case ($\frac{\partial^2 \mathbf{x}}{\partial t^2} = 0$), the finite difference forms are

$$\dot{\mathbf{x}}(k+1) = \dot{\mathbf{x}}(k)$$
$$\mathbf{x}(k+1) = 2\mathbf{x}(k) - \mathbf{x}(k-1).$$

Two frames are needed to form a prediction, and since distance changes linearly in time, this is referred to as the *linear* predictor. For the constant acceleration case ($\frac{\partial^3 \mathbf{x}}{\partial t^3} = 0$):

$$\ddot{\mathbf{x}}(k+1) = \ddot{\mathbf{x}}(k)$$
$$\mathbf{x}(k+1) = 3\mathbf{x}(k) - 3\mathbf{x}(k-1) + \mathbf{x}(k-2).$$

Three frames are needed for a prediction, and since distance changes quadratically in time, this is referred to as the *quadratic* predictor.

Figure 2.15 compares overall tracker efficiency with and without a predictor in terms of the average number of pixels searched per forced match. An 11×11 search window and a 5×5 prediction refinement window[5] are used, so the upper and lower bounds on this value are 121 and 25. Prediction clearly limits the search substantially, reducing the average search area from around 120 to around 30 (linear predictor). The lower limit of 25 is not reached since new points require full search when they first appear, and the predictor obviously fails occasionally. Apart from speeding up the matching process, prediction has minimal effect on the actual matches[6]. This differs from many other prediction schemes, where the number of unmatched corners grows in the absence of prediction (due to large uncertainty). Uncertainty is thus contained effectively by forcing the unmatched corners in I_{t-1} to find "virtual" partners.

The two predictors are compared by computing their percentage of successful predictions (i.e. forced matches accepted without further search beyond the prediction refinement

---

[5]This allows a prediction error of 2 pixels in either direction.

[6]The only significant change from the non–prediction case is the downgrading of some strong matches to "compromise matches" (see [128]).

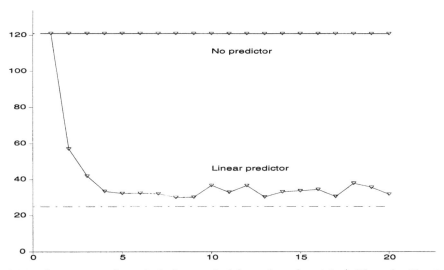

Figure 2.15: *Average number of pixels searched for a forced match (with and without predic-tion).*

window). Figure 2.16 shows results for the "Curl" sequence; both filters perform well here, because the motion is small and fairly uniform. One might expect the quadratic predictor to perform better in general since it subsumes the linear one, and since only pure translations in the world generate straight image trajectories (general 3D motion introduces curvature). Interestingly, though, the linear predictor is often better because small inter–frame motion generates locally linear trajectories. Furthermore, the motion is small relative to noise and quantisation errors, so second order temporal derivatives have a detrimental effect on per-formance of the quadratic filter.

2.5.3   Trajectory maintenance

Each corner has a record describing its general details (e.g. when it first appeared and was last sighted) and its frame–specific details (e.g. position, confidence in the match, type of match). The image locations at successive time slices constitute the trajectory. Maintaining this database involves various subtasks. First, all corners in I_1 are automatically instantiated (assigned "blank" records) during bootup; thereafter, intruders are instantiated dynamically. Second, corners are *retired* when they disappear permanently from sight (due to occlusion or exiting the field of view). The retirement decision is based on the number of elapsed frames since the corner was last spotted. This pruning is necessary to contain the size of the database. Other factors leading to a corner being retired include the merging of its path with that of another corner, or its identification as a weak corner. Finally, new corner positions are entered in the appropriate records and, where possible, the predictor is invoked.

Figure 2.17 shows this operating over twenty frames and illustrates the division of matches into strong and forced ones. The terms "left" and "right" corners refer to the number of

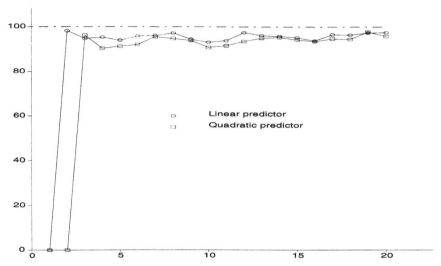

Figure 2.16: *Percentage of good estimates with linear vs quadratic predictors ("Curl" sequence).*

corners *actually extracted* from I_{t-1} and I_t respectively; hence, the number of right corners becomes the number of left corners for the next frame. These values are fairly constant over time, though obviously vary as new scene structure becomes visible and current scene structure is occluded.

The upper bound on the number of strong matches is the number of corners in the "right" image (I_t). After several frames, when there is adequate overlap in the corner points being extracted in successive frames, the number of strong matches stabilises relative to this upper bound, suggesting that a fixed percentage of corners are very robust. The number of forced matches rises due to the unmatched corners that accumulate over time; this stabilises once retirement kicks in. There is necessarily a "lag" here since time is needed to make a confident decision about a point having disappeared.

The number of corners actually *matched* (the sum of strong and forced matches) exceeds the number extracted from the "left" image since the forced matches that have accumulated from previous frames must also be matched. This is shown by the total database size (triangles), which grows initially for the first few frames and then reaches an approximate equilibrium (once retirement starts to offset instantiation).

2.5.4   Results

Figure 2.18(b) shows trajectories from the "Curl" sequence obtained over several frames. Also shown are the corners constituting these trajectories, with and without forced matches (Figures 2.18(c) and (d)). The forced matches clearly fill in the gaps when a corner disappears temporarily.

Figures 2.19 and 2.20 give equal–length trajectories for different image sequences obtained

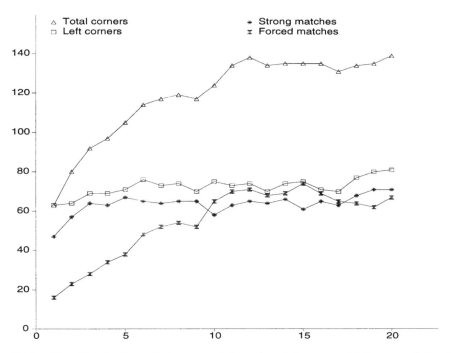

Figure 2.17: *The distribution of strong and forced matches over 20 frames of the "Curl" sequence (constant velocity predictor).*

over several frames. Figure 2.19 shows a simple calibration grid (moving camera), Richard (bespectacled) nodding his head downwards before a cluttered background, Larry and Phil nodding and shaking their heads (two independent motions), and Clair moving her head in a circular motion. Figure 2.20 shows Mike translating away from the camera along the corridor on a wheeled chair (towards the focus of expansion), a highway traffic scene filmed from a moving car (infra–red image), and Larry translating his upper body parallel to the image plane. The trajectories clearly indicate where the motion occurs in the image. The problem of false corners is also apparent (e.g. in Figure 2.20(a) Mike's arm forms a false corner with the vertical pillar, leading to an inconsistent trajectory), confirming the need for outlier rejection techniques.

Finally, for many applications involving stationary cameras (e.g. videophones), it is useful to identify the background corners. This requires analysis of the corner's velocity history, i.e. computing the mean ($\bar{s}$) and standard deviation (σ_s) of its speed over m frames,

$$\bar{s} = \frac{1}{m}\sum_{i=1}^{m} s_i, \quad \sigma_s = \sqrt{\frac{\sum_{i=1}^{m}(s_i - \bar{s})^2}{m}},$$

where $s_i = \sqrt{u_i^2 + v_i^2}$ is the speed and (u, v) is the image velocity vector. The criteria for classification as a stationary point are small $\bar{s}$ and small σ_s (see Figure 2.20(d)).

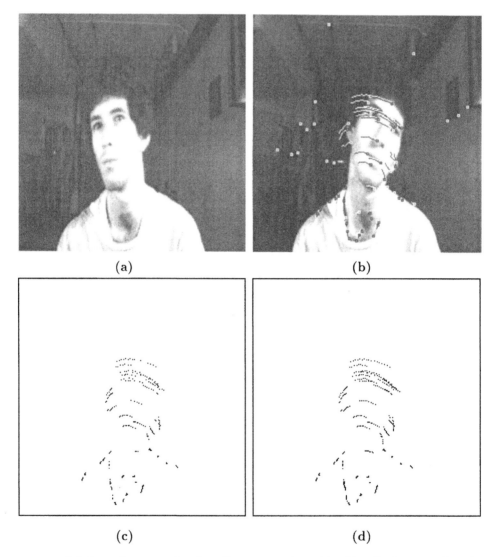

(a)   (b)

(c)   (d)

Figure 2.18: *(a) First frame in the "Curl" sequence (25 Hz); (b) 20ᵗʰ frame with 8–frame trajectories (true length) superimposed. Markers show final corner positions; (c)(d) Corners comprising the trajectories without and with forced matches (respectively). The trajectories have equal length (in number of frames).*

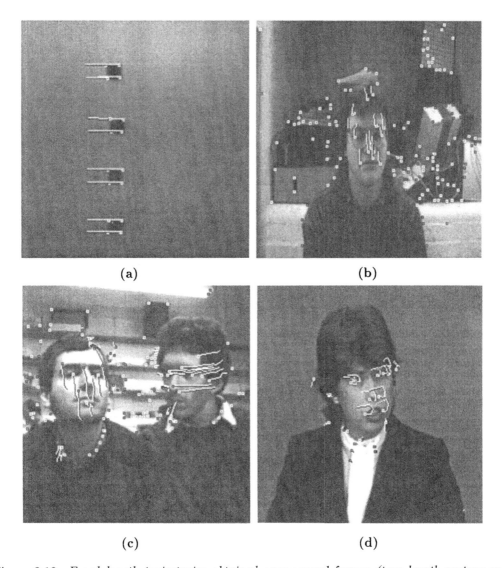

(a)   (b)

(c)   (d)

Figure 2.19: *Equal–length trajectories obtained over several frames (true length vectors superimposed on final frame, markers show final corner positions): (a) "Calibration grid"; (b) "Richard"; (c) "Larry & Phil"; (d) "Clair".*

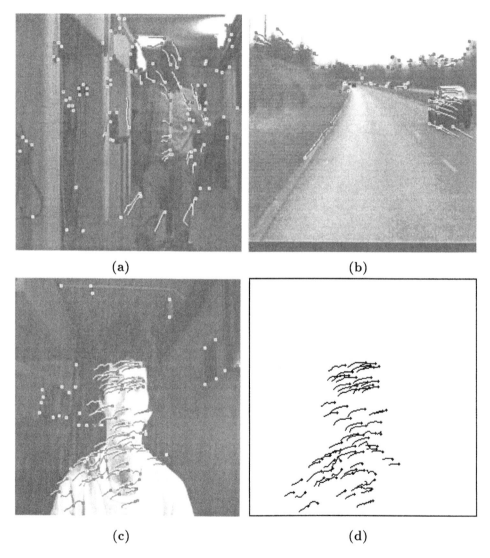

(a)   (b)

(c)   (d)

Figure 2.20: *Equal–length trajectories obtained over several frames (true–length vectors, markers show final positions): (a) "Mike"; (b) "FIR" (cooled infra–red); (c) "Trans"; (d) "Trans" with stationary points removed.*

2.5.5 Relation to previous work

The DROID system [26] broke new ground in matching and tracking corner features. Our system has much in common with DROID: we too use a bottom–up approach and allocate a predictor per feature. However, there are also several important differences. First, DROID assumed that an observer moved through a static (hence rigid) world; our tracker caters for (possibly non–rigid) objects moving independently of the camera. Secondly, DROID estimated and tracked the 3D positions of (static) features, using accurate ego–motion estimates to resolve the depth–speed ambiguity. This approach is impossible in our case since the objects move. Our tracker thus works entirely in the image plane, leaving 3D interpretation to the higher–level routines.

Third, DROID matched its corners by projecting the uncertainty region around the 3D feature's estimated position into the image plane, and seeking corners inside this "validation gate". When multiple (or no) corners fell inside this sausage–like region, the match was abandoned. We use our correlation metric to *force* matches when they aren't found and to resolve ambiguities. Moreover, instead of only matching the predictions to the new positions, we revert to the original data when the predictions fail.

Fourth, DROID used the intensity and its gradients at the corner location (I, I_x, I_y) as corner attributes for match verification; we use the correlation metric which checks relative (rather than absolute) similarity. Finally, DROID used a Kalman filter (per point) to track and predict; we have found that simpler filters (cf. Equation (2.3)) work satisfactorily in the absence of a deterministic motion model. The same class of filters was used by Li et al. [86], who used adaptive coefficients. However, accurate prediction was far more crucial to their system since they matched their new data to their predictions. Reviews of other motion estimation techniques for long image sequences can be found in [4, 134].

2.6 Conclusions

This chapter has presented an image–based object tracker which utilises low–level "corner" features. These corners are stable, well–localised beacons afforded by the image. The bottom–up approach has the advantages of generality and opportunism, and the system is demonstrably useful in many application domains (not just those whose scenes have "physical" corners). The matcher–tracker uses local operations and tracks each corner independently. Temporal integration overcomes the problems of "flashing" corners, noise, and occlusion and disocclusion of scene structure. Uncertainty is contained by assigning *forced* matches to unmatched points, and simple predictors speed up the matching process significantly. Normalised cross–correlation of local image structure gives match confidences, and is also used to verify and force matches. The system degrades gracefully when predictors fail by reverting to the original image data. The final image trajectories give a strong impression of "what motion occurs where" in the image.

There are several directions for further research to pursue. Ideally, the corner detection parameters should be set automatically. For instance, the edge threshold E could be computed by sampling the image for an edge strength distribution. Beardsley et al. [16] describe progress towards automatically updating such parameters based on matching success. Parallel implementation of the corner tracker would also be desirable, and recent progress towards towards this goal has been reported in [123].

Chapter 3

The affine camera and affine structure

3.1 Introduction

In order to compute 3D information from an image, a camera model must be defined. Orthographic and scaled orthographic projection are widely used in computer vision to model the imaging process [18, 55, 66, 79, 145, 151, 153]. They provide a good approximation to the perspective projection model (the ideal pinhole camera) when the field of view is small and when the variation in depth of the scene along the line of sight is small compared to its average distance from the camera [144] (Figure 3.1). More importantly, they expose the ambiguities that arise when perspective effects diminish. In such cases, it is not only *advantageous* to use these simplified models but also *advisable* to do so, for by explicitly incorporating these ambiguities into the algorithm, one avoids computing parameters that are inherently ill–conditioned [55].

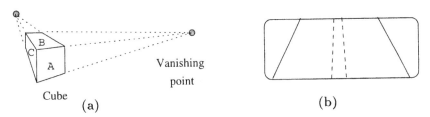

Figure 3.1: *Perspective projection preserves parallel lines when the object is relatively shallow and the field of view is small: (a) Face A is more parallelogram–like than faces B and C, since it has a smaller depth variation; (b) Road markings viewed through a windscreen show that parallelism is distorted less for a narrow field of view (dashed lines) than for a wide one (solid lines).*

The *affine camera*, introduced by Mundy and Zisserman [98], generalises the orthographic, scaled orthographic and para–perspective models. It is the natural projection of a 3D affine space to a 2D affine image. For example, parallelism is preserved, so that parallel lines in the scene project to parallel lines in the image. An advantage of the affine camera is that it is an *uncalibrated* scaled orthographic camera and therefore requires no calibration parameters, such as focal length, aspect ratio and principal point. This enables the identification of quantities that can be computed under parallel projection without calibration, such as affine epipolar geometry (Chapter 5) and new views of an object (Chapter 8). Moreover, when calibration *is* needed, the precise stage at which it must be introduced into the computation can be determined, e.g. aspect ratio is required to compute rigid motion parameters (Chapter 7). This approach echoes the "stratification" philosophy of Koenderink and van Doorn [79].

It is well known that two distinct affine images of a 3D scene permit the recovery of *affine structure* (scene structure up to an arbitrary 3D affine transformation) [79]. However, a weakness of many existing algorithms is their use of "local coordinate frames"; by relying on a minimal subset of the valid data, whose appropriate selection is itself problematical and computationally demanding, such approaches forfeit the advantages that accrue from using *all* the available features, including improved noise immunity and the ability to identify outliers. This chapter therefore makes the following contributions:

- The affine camera is related to other familiar models, and shown to subsume the orthographic, scaled orthographic and para–perspective camera models (Section 3.2). The equations of its stereo geometry are also derived (Section 3.3).

- The literature on affine structure using a local coordinate frame (LCF) is reviewed, and the main results are placed in a common framework (Section 3.4).

- A new geometric interpretation of the problem is presented (Section 3.5), using a "concatenated image space" (*CI space*). This enables affine structure to be computed using *all* available points and *without* an explicit LCF, thereby providing noise immunity and obviating the difficult "frame selection" task.

3.2   Camera models

Six camera models are considered here: the projective, perspective, affine, para–perspective, weak perspective (scaled orthographic) and orthographic cameras. The projective camera is the most general of these, and the orthographic camera the least (see Figure 3.4).

3.2.1   The projective camera

A camera projects a 3D world point $\mathbf{X} = (X, Y, Z)^{\top}$ onto a 2D image point $\mathbf{x} = (x, y)^{\top}$. The general mapping from $\mathcal{P}^3$ to $\mathcal{P}^2$ can be written in terms of a projection matrix $\mathbf{T} = [T_{ij}]$,

$$\begin{bmatrix} x_1 \\ x_2 \\ x_3 \end{bmatrix} = \begin{bmatrix} T_{11} & T_{12} & T_{13} & T_{14} \\ T_{21} & T_{22} & T_{23} & T_{24} \\ T_{31} & T_{32} & T_{33} & T_{34} \end{bmatrix} \begin{bmatrix} X_1 \\ X_2 \\ X_3 \\ X_4 \end{bmatrix}, \tag{3.1}$$

where (x_1, x_2, x_3) and (X_1, X_2, X_3, X_4) are homogeneous coordinates related to $\mathbf{x}$ and $\mathbf{X}$ by $(x, y) = (x_1/x_3, x_2/x_3)$ and $(X, Y, Z) = (X_1/X_4, X_2/X_4, X_3/X_4)$. Mundy and Zisserman [98] termed this a *projective camera*. Since scale is arbitrary for homogeneous coordinates, only the *ratios* of the elements T_{ij} are important, so $\mathbf{T}$ has only 11 independent degrees of freedom. Equation (3.1) places no restriction on the coordinate systems in which $\mathbf{X}$ and $\mathbf{x}$ are measured: neither frame has to be orthogonal, and the two frames need not be aligned. It is convenient to decompose $\mathbf{T}$ as follows [42, 89]:

$$\mathbf{T} = \mathbf{C}\,\mathbf{P}\,\mathbf{G} = \begin{bmatrix} C_{11} & C_{12} & C_{13} \\ C_{21} & C_{22} & C_{23} \\ 0 & 0 & C_{33} \end{bmatrix} \begin{bmatrix} 1 & 0 & 0 & 0 \\ 0 & 1 & 0 & 0 \\ 0 & 0 & 1 & 0 \end{bmatrix} \begin{bmatrix} G_{11} & G_{12} & G_{13} & G_{14} \\ G_{21} & G_{22} & G_{23} & G_{24} \\ G_{31} & G_{32} & G_{33} & G_{34} \\ G_{41} & G_{42} & G_{43} & G_{44} \end{bmatrix}. \tag{3.2}$$

The 3×3 matrix $\mathbf{C}$ accounts for intrinsic camera parameters and represents a 2D affine transformation[1] (hence $C_{31} = C_{32} = 0$). It encodes camera calibration and has a variable number of unknowns (usually up to five), depending on the sophistication of the camera model. We assume there is no shear in the camera axes and use four parameters,

$$\mathbf{C} = \begin{bmatrix} f\xi & 0 & o_x \\ 0 & f & o_y \\ 0 & 0 & 1 \end{bmatrix}, \tag{3.3}$$

where ξ is the camera aspect ratio, f the focal length, and (o_x, o_y) the principal point (where the optic axis intersects the image plane). The camera is said to be "calibrated" when $\mathbf{C}$ is known. The 3×4 matrix $\mathbf{P}$ performs the projection operation, and the 4×4 matrix $\mathbf{G}$ accounts for extrinsic camera parameters, encoding the relative position and orientation between the world and camera coordinate systems.

The projective camera generalises *perspective* (or *central*) projection, reducing to the familiar pinhole camera when the camera and world coordinate frames are related by a rigid transformation (6 degrees of freedom),

$$\mathbf{X}^c = \mathbf{R}\,\mathbf{X} + \mathbf{D}. \tag{3.4}$$

Here, $\mathbf{X}$ is the coordinate in the world frame, $\mathbf{X}^c$ is the corresponding coordinate in the camera frame, $\mathbf{R}$ is a 3×3 rotation matrix with rows $\{\mathbf{R}_1^\top, \mathbf{R}_2^\top, \mathbf{R}_3^\top\}$, and $\mathbf{D} = (D_x, D_y, D_z)^\top$ is a translation vector representing the origin of the world frame. Consequently,

$$\mathbf{G} = \begin{bmatrix} \mathbf{R} & \mathbf{D} \\ \mathbf{0}^\top & 1 \end{bmatrix}$$

and the perspective form of $\mathbf{T}$ (using Equation (3.3)) is

$$\mathbf{T}_p = \begin{bmatrix} f\xi\mathbf{R}_1^\top + o_x\mathbf{R}_3^\top & f\xi D_x + o_x D_z \\ f\mathbf{R}_2^\top + o_y\mathbf{R}_3^\top & f D_y + o_y D_z \\ \mathbf{R}_3^\top & D_z \end{bmatrix}.$$

Image and world coordinates are thus related by

$$\mathbf{x} = f \begin{bmatrix} \xi(\mathbf{R}_1 \cdot \mathbf{X} + D_x)/(\mathbf{R}_3 \cdot \mathbf{X} + D_z) \\ (\mathbf{R}_2 \cdot \mathbf{X} + D_y)/(\mathbf{R}_3 \cdot \mathbf{X} + D_z) \end{bmatrix} + \begin{bmatrix} o_x \\ o_y \end{bmatrix}.$$

---

[1]In fact, $\mathbf{C}$ can be written as an upper triangular matrix with no loss of generality [42, 57].

A simple example, with the camera and world frames aligned ($\mathbf{R} = \mathbf{I}_3$ and $\mathbf{D} = \mathbf{0}$), unity aspect ratio ($\xi = 1$) and the principal point at $(0,0)$, gives

$$\mathbf{T}_p = \begin{bmatrix} f & 0 & 0 & 0 \\ 0 & f & 0 & 0 \\ 0 & 0 & 1 & 0 \end{bmatrix} \quad \text{and} \quad \begin{bmatrix} x \\ y \end{bmatrix} = \frac{f}{Z^c} \begin{bmatrix} X^c \\ Y^c \end{bmatrix}. \tag{3.5}$$

This is the familiar camera–centred perspective model, with each point scaled by its individual depth and all projection rays converging to the optic centre. Figure 3.3 illustrates the 1D case, where the "image" is a line rather than a plane, and Figure 3.2(a) shows the 2D case, where the intersection of the ray star with the image plane generates the image. Even though the perspective model is itself a simplification of the true projection mechanism [62] (it ignores radial distortion, etc.), the fact that it is a *non–linear* transformation of scene coordinates renders the structure and motion equations difficult to solve. Moreover, when perspective effects are small, the structure and motion equations can become ill–conditioned [55].

3.2.2   The weak perspective camera

Equation (3.4) relates the camera and world coordinate frames by a rigid transformation. The depth of a point $\mathbf{X}_i$ measured along the line of sight in the camera frame is then $Z_i^c = \mathbf{R}_3 \cdot \mathbf{X}_i + D_z$, with the centroid of the point set denoted $\mathbf{X}_{ave}$. When the camera field of view is small and the depth variation of the object $\Delta Z_i^c = Z_i^c - Z_{ave}^c = \mathbf{R}_3 \cdot (\mathbf{X}_i - \mathbf{X}_{ave})$ is small compared to the average distance of the object from the camera Z_{ave}^c, the individual depths Z_i^c may be approximated by Z_{ave}^c. This gives a *weak perspective* or *scaled orthographic* camera:

$$\begin{bmatrix} x_1 \\ x_2 \\ x_3 \end{bmatrix} = \mathbf{C} \begin{bmatrix} \mathbf{R}_1 \cdot \mathbf{X} + D_x \\ \mathbf{R}_2 \cdot \mathbf{X} + D_y \\ Z_{ave}^c \end{bmatrix} = \mathbf{C} \begin{bmatrix} \mathbf{R}_1^\mathsf{T} & D_x \\ \mathbf{R}_2^\mathsf{T} & D_y \\ \mathbf{0}^\mathsf{T} & Z_{ave}^c \end{bmatrix} \begin{bmatrix} X_1 \\ X_2 \\ X_3 \\ X_4 \end{bmatrix},$$

whence

$$\mathbf{T}_{wp} = \mathbf{C} \begin{bmatrix} 1 & 0 & 0 & 0 \\ 0 & 1 & 0 & 0 \\ 0 & 0 & 0 & 1 \end{bmatrix} \begin{bmatrix} \mathbf{R} & \mathbf{D} \\ \mathbf{0}^\mathsf{T} & Z_{ave}^c \end{bmatrix}. \tag{3.6}$$

The $\mathbf{P}$ matrix above differs from that in Equation (3.2) since Z_i^c has been replaced by the constant Z_{ave}^c. In image and world coordinates,

$$\mathbf{x} = \frac{f}{Z_{ave}^c} \begin{bmatrix} \xi \mathbf{R}_1^\mathsf{T} \\ \mathbf{R}_2^\mathsf{T} \end{bmatrix} \mathbf{X} + \frac{f}{Z_{ave}^c} \begin{bmatrix} \xi D_x \\ D_y \end{bmatrix} + \begin{bmatrix} o_x \\ o_y \end{bmatrix} = \mathbf{M}_{wp}\mathbf{X} + \mathbf{t}_{wp}, \tag{3.7}$$

where $\mathbf{M}_{wp}$ is a 2×3 matrix whose rows are the uniformly scaled rows of a rotation matrix[2], and $\mathbf{t}_{wp}$ is a 2–vector giving the projection of the origin of the world coordinate frame ($\mathbf{X}$

---

[2]An *orthographic camera* arises when the magnification f/Z_{ave}^c is unity (Figures 3.3 and 3.2(b)).

$= 0$). A simple example of a weak perspective camera is $\mathbf{R} = \mathbf{I}_3$, $\mathbf{D} = \mathbf{0}$, $\xi = 1$ and $(o_x, o_y) = (0, 0)$, whence

$$\mathbf{T}_{wp} = \begin{bmatrix} f & 0 & 0 & 0 \\ 0 & f & 0 & 0 \\ 0 & 0 & 0 & Z_{ave} \end{bmatrix} \quad \Rightarrow \quad \begin{bmatrix} x_i \\ y_i \end{bmatrix} = \frac{f}{Z_{ave}^c} \begin{bmatrix} X_i^c \\ Y_i^c \end{bmatrix}. \tag{3.8}$$

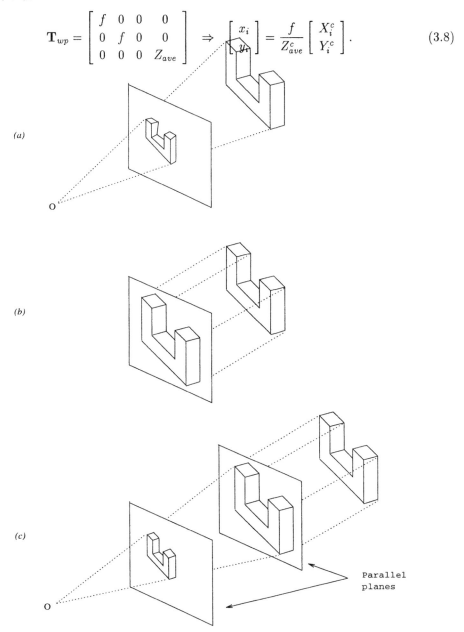

Figure 3.2: *Camera models: (a) Perspective (all light rays pass through a single projection point O); (b) Orthographic (all light rays are parallel, with the optic centre O at infinity); (c) Weak perspective (combined orthographic and perspective projection). For (b) and (c), parallel lines in the scene remain parallel in the image, which isn't true for (a).*

Equation (3.8) is the perspective equation (3.5) with Z_{ave}^c substituted for Z_i^c. The weak perspective camera therefore combines orthographic and perspective projection (Figures 3.3 and 3.2(c)): points are first projected orthographically onto the average depth plane $Z^c = Z^c_{ave}$ and then projected perspectively from this fronto–parallel plane onto the image. The latter operation simply introduces a scale factor, accounting for changes in image size when an object looms towards, or recedes from, the camera.

To derive the conditions for validity of the weak perspective camera approximation, consider a world point $\mathbf{X}^c$ with depth $Z^c = Z^c_{ave} + \Delta Z^c$, and expand the perspective projection equation (3.5) about Z^c_{ave} using a Taylor series:

$$\mathbf{x} = \frac{f}{Z^c_{ave} + \Delta Z^c} \begin{bmatrix} X^c \\ Y^c \end{bmatrix} = \frac{f}{Z^c_{ave}} \left(1 - \frac{\Delta Z^c}{Z^c_{ave}} + \left(\frac{\Delta Z^c}{Z^c_{ave}} \right)^2 - \cdots \right) \begin{bmatrix} X^c \\ Y^c \end{bmatrix} \qquad (3.9)$$

When $|\Delta Z^c| \ll Z^c_{ave}$, only the zero–order term remains, giving Equation (3.8). A useful rule of thumb requires Z_{ave} to exceed $|\Delta Z|$ by an order of magnitude [144], i.e. $Z^c_{ave} \geq 10\,|\Delta Z^c|$. The absolute error in image point position is then

$$\mathbf{x}_{err} = \mathbf{x}_{persp} - \mathbf{x}_{wp} = -\frac{\Delta Z^c}{Z^c_{ave}} \frac{f}{Z^c} \begin{bmatrix} X^c \\ Y^c \end{bmatrix}, \qquad (3.10)$$

showing that a small field of view (X^c/Z^c and Y^c/Z^c) and small depth variation ($\Delta Z^c/Z^c_{ave}$) contribute to validity of the model. The errors are clearly not uniform across the image.

3.2.3 The para–perspective camera

In the weak perspective case, projection of the scene point onto the average depth plane occurs parallel to the optic axis. The *para–perspective* camera [8] generalises this by projecting parallel to an *arbitrary* (but fixed) projection direction. Since the average depth plane remains parallel to the image plane, the perspective projection stage simply introduces a scale factor (as for the weak perspective model). The 1D case takes the form (Figure 3.3)

$$x_{pp} = \frac{f}{Z^c_{ave}} (X^c - \Delta Z^c \cot \theta),$$

where θ denotes the angle between the projection direction and the positive X–axis, and $\Delta Z^c = Z^c - Z^c_{ave}$. In the 2D case, the projection direction is described by two angles (θ_x, θ_y), where θ_x lies in the X–Z plane (θ in Figure 3.3) and θ_y is the equivalent angle in the Y–Z plane. Factoring in camera calibration parameters and the rigid transformation between the camera and world coordinate frames gives

$$\mathbf{T}_{pp} = \mathbf{C} \begin{bmatrix} 1 & 0 & -\cot \theta_x & \cot \theta_x \\ 0 & 1 & -\cot \theta_y & \cot \theta_y \\ 0 & 0 & 0 & 1 \end{bmatrix} \begin{bmatrix} \mathbf{R} & \mathbf{D} \\ \mathbf{0}^\top & Z^c_{ave} \end{bmatrix}, \qquad (3.11)$$

a more general form of the expressions in [8]. In terms of image and world coordinates,

$$\begin{aligned} \mathbf{x} &= \frac{f}{Z^c_{ave}} \begin{bmatrix} \xi \mathbf{R}^\top_1 - \xi \cot \theta_x \mathbf{R}^\top_3 \\ \mathbf{R}^\top_2 - \cot \theta_y \mathbf{R}^\top_3 \end{bmatrix} \mathbf{X} + \frac{f}{Z^c_{ave}} \begin{bmatrix} \xi D_x - \xi \cot \theta_x D_z \\ D_y - \cot \theta_y D_z \end{bmatrix} + \begin{bmatrix} f\xi \cot \theta_x + o_x \\ f \cot \theta_y + o_y \end{bmatrix} \\ &= \mathbf{M}_{pp} \mathbf{X} + \mathbf{t}_{pp}, \end{aligned} \qquad (3.12)$$

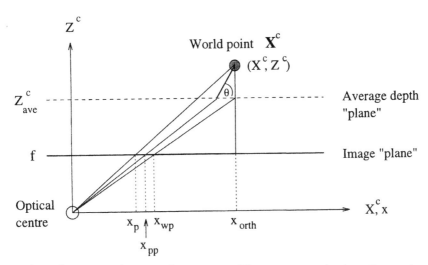

Figure 3.3: *One–dimensional image formation. The image is the line $Z^c = f$. For x_p (perspective), projection is along the ray connecting the world point $\mathbf{X}^c$ to the optic centre. For x_{orth} (orthographic), projection is perpendicular to the image. For x_{pp} (para–perspective), $\mathbf{X}^c$ is first projected onto the average depth plane at angle θ, and then projected perspectively onto the image plane; x_{wp} (weak perspective) is a special case of x_{pp} with $\theta = 90°$ (i.e. orthographic projection onto the average depth plane).*

where $\mathbf{M}_{pp}$ is a 2×3 matrix and $\mathbf{t}_{pp}$ is a 2–vector. A simple example of a para–perspective camera is $\mathbf{R} = \mathbf{I}_3$, $\mathbf{D} = \mathbf{0}$, $\xi = 1$ and $(o_x, o_y) = (0, 0)$:

$$
\mathbf{T}_{pp} = \begin{bmatrix} 1 & 0 & -\cot\theta_x & Z^c_{ave}\cot\theta_x \\ 0 & 1 & -\cot\theta_y & Z^c_{ave}\cot\theta_y \\ 0 & 0 & 0 & Z^c_{ave}/f \end{bmatrix} \Rightarrow \begin{bmatrix} x_i \\ y_i \end{bmatrix} = \frac{f}{Z^c_{ave}}\begin{bmatrix} X^c_i - \Delta Z^c_i \cot\theta_x \\ Y^c_i - \Delta Z^c_i \cot\theta_y \end{bmatrix}.
$$

The variable projection direction is generally taken parallel to the ray connecting the optic centre to the object centroid, e.g. $\theta_x = \arctan(X^c_{ave}/Z^c_{ave})$. This camera is a better approximation to the perspective model than is the weak perspective camera, but it is also more complex, requiring additional calibration information (e.g. the principal point, which isn't needed in the weak perspective case) and the angles θ_x and θ_y.

3.2.4   The affine camera

An *affine camera* has the same form as Equations (3.6) and (3.11), but has no constraints on the matrix elements other than $T_{31} = T_{32} = T_{33} = 0$, i.e.

$$
\mathbf{T}_{aff} = \begin{bmatrix} T_{11} & T_{12} & T_{13} & T_{14} \\ T_{21} & T_{22} & T_{23} & T_{24} \\ 0 & 0 & 0 & T_{34} \end{bmatrix}. \tag{3.13}
$$

This is a special case of the projective camera in Equation (3.1) and has eight degrees of freedom. It corresponds to a projective camera with its optical center on the plane at infinity;

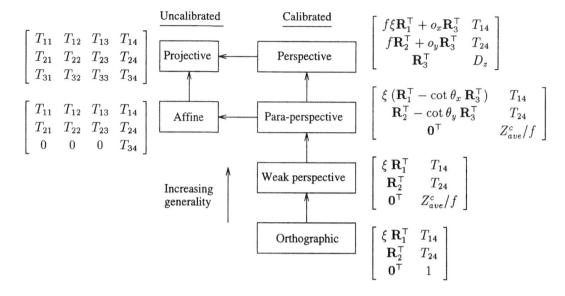

Figure 3.4: *Hierarchy of cameras and their* **T** *matrices.*

consequently, all projection rays are parallel. In terms of image and world coordinates, the affine camera is written

$$\mathbf{x} = \mathbf{MX} + \mathbf{t}, \tag{3.14}$$

where $\mathbf{M} = [M_{ij}]$ is a 2×3 matrix (with elements $M_{ij} = T_{ij}/T_{34}$) and $\mathbf{t} = (T_{14}/T_{34}, T_{24}/T_{34})^{\mathsf{T}}$ is a 2–vector. This clearly generalises the weak perspective and para–perspective cameras. A key property of the affine camera is that it *preserves parallelism*: lines that are parallel in the world remain parallel in the image. The proof is simple: two parallel world lines $\mathbf{X}_1(\lambda) = \mathbf{X}_a + \lambda\mathbf{U}$ and $\mathbf{X}_2(\mu) = \mathbf{X}_b + \mu\mathbf{U}$ project to the image lines $\mathbf{x}_1(\lambda) = (\mathbf{MX}_a + \mathbf{t}) + \lambda\mathbf{MU}$ and $\mathbf{x}_2(\mu) = (\mathbf{MX}_b + \mathbf{t}) + \mu\mathbf{MU}$, which are clearly parallel.

The affine camera covers the composed effects of: (i) a 3D *affine* transformation between world and camera coordinate systems; (ii) parallel projection onto the image plane; and (iii) a 2D affine transformation of the image. It therefore generalises the orthographic, scaled orthographic and para–perspective models in two ways. First, *non–rigid* deformation of the object is permitted by the 3D affine transformation. Second, calibration is unnecessary (unlike in Equations (3.6) and (3.11), where $\mathbf{C}$ is needed to enforce the rotation constraint).

An affine camera may therefore be thought of as an *uncalibrated weak perspective camera*. It is extremely useful in this role, for although Euclidean measurements (e.g. angles and distances) are only meaningful with a calibrated camera, various affine measurements are still well–defined without requiring arduous and often ill–conditioned calibration (e.g. parallelism, ratios of lengths in parallel directions, ratios of areas on parallel planes [20]). Such properties are often sufficient for vision tasks. For instance, affine epipolar geometry can be determined without camera calibration (see Chapter 5); distances only enter the computation when noise must be minimised (cf. Section 5.4).

3.3 Affine stereo/motion equations

Having examined a single affine camera, we now turn to the case of two affine cameras, which arises due to stereo viewing or relative motion between camera and scene.

3.3.1 Scene transformation

The affine camera retains its form when the scene undergoes a 3D affine transformation. To see why, consider a world point $\mathbf{X}_i$ projected by an affine camera $\{\mathbf{M}, \mathbf{t}\}$ to the image point $\mathbf{x}_i$, i.e.

$$\mathbf{x}_i = \mathbf{M}\mathbf{X}_i + \mathbf{t}. \tag{3.15}$$

Let the scene (or camera) then move according to

$$\mathbf{X}'_i = \mathbf{A}\mathbf{X}_i + \mathbf{D}, \tag{3.16}$$

where $\mathbf{X}'_i$ is the new world position, $\mathbf{A}$ is a 3×3 matrix and $\mathbf{D}$ is a 3–vector. This *scene transformation* encodes relative motion between the camera and the world as a 3D affine transformation (12 degrees of freedom, not necessarily a rigid motion). The new world point $\mathbf{X}'_i$ then projects to $\mathbf{x}'_i = (x'_i, y'_i)^T$, where

$$\mathbf{x}'_i = \mathbf{M}\mathbf{X}'_i + \mathbf{t} = \mathbf{M}\left(\mathbf{A}\mathbf{X}_i + \mathbf{D}\right) + \mathbf{t} = \mathbf{M}\mathbf{A}\mathbf{X}_i + (\mathbf{M}\mathbf{D} + \mathbf{t}) = \mathbf{M}'\,\mathbf{X}_i + \mathbf{t}'. \tag{3.17}$$

This can be interpreted as a second affine camera $\{\mathbf{M}', \mathbf{t}'\}$ observing the original scene, with $\{\mathbf{M}', \mathbf{t}'\}$ accounting for changes in both the extrinsic *and* intrinsic parameters (i.e. pose *and* calibration). The form of the affine camera is thus preserved.

3.3.2 Relative coordinates

An important advantage of the affine camera model is that *relative coordinates* cancel out translation effects, and this will be used frequently in subsequent computations. If $\mathbf{X}_0$ is designated a reference point (or *origin*), then vector differencing in the scene gives

$$\mathbf{\Delta X} = \mathbf{X} - \mathbf{X}_0 \quad \text{and} \quad \mathbf{\Delta X}' = \mathbf{X}' - \mathbf{X}'_0 = \mathbf{A}\,\mathbf{\Delta X},$$

which are clearly independent of $\mathbf{D}$. More importantly, in the *image*, registering the points gives

$$\mathbf{\Delta x} = \mathbf{x} - \mathbf{x}_0 = \mathbf{M}\,\mathbf{\Delta X} \quad \text{and} \quad \mathbf{\Delta x}' = \mathbf{x}' - \mathbf{x}'_0 = \mathbf{M}'\,\mathbf{\Delta X} = \mathbf{M}\mathbf{A}\,\mathbf{\Delta X}, \tag{3.18}$$

which are again independent of $\mathbf{D}$, $\mathbf{t}$ and $\mathbf{t}'$. This cancellation relies crucially on linearity and is not possible in general under perspective projection.

3.3.3 Point motion

It is useful to relate a point in one image to its position in the other image and to the intrinsic and extrinsic camera parameters. If $\mathbf{M}$ is partitioned as $(\mathbf{B} \mid \mathbf{b})$, where $\mathbf{B}$ is a (non-singular) 2×2 matrix and $\mathbf{b}$ a 2×1 vector. then Equation (3.14) becomes

$$\mathbf{x}_i = \mathbf{B} \begin{bmatrix} X_i \\ Y_i \end{bmatrix} + Z_i\, \mathbf{b} + \mathbf{t}. \tag{3.19}$$

Similarly, if $\mathbf{M}'$ is partitioned into $(\mathbf{B}' \mid \mathbf{b}')$, Equation (3.17) becomes

$$\mathbf{x}_i' = \mathbf{B}' \begin{bmatrix} X_i \\ Y_i \end{bmatrix} + Z_i\, \mathbf{b}' + \mathbf{t}'. \tag{3.20}$$

Eliminating the world coordinates $(X_i, Y_i)^\top$ between these two equations yields the desired relation,

$$\mathbf{x}_i' = \mathbf{\Gamma}\, \mathbf{x}_i + Z_i\, \mathbf{d} + \boldsymbol{\varepsilon}, \tag{3.21}$$

with $\mathbf{\Gamma} = \mathbf{B}'\, \mathbf{B}^{-1}$, $\mathbf{d} = \mathbf{b}' - \mathbf{\Gamma b}$ and $\boldsymbol{\varepsilon} = \mathbf{t}' - \mathbf{\Gamma t}$. Quantities $\mathbf{\Gamma}$, $\mathbf{d}$ and $\boldsymbol{\varepsilon}$ depend only on the cameras and the relative motion; they are independent of scene structure. Inverting Equation (3.21) gives the expression for $\mathbf{x}_i$ in I_1:

$$\mathbf{x}_i = \mathbf{\Gamma}^{-1}(\mathbf{x}_i' - \boldsymbol{\varepsilon}) - Z_i\, \mathbf{\Gamma}^{-1}\mathbf{d} \tag{3.22}$$

These equations are extremely important, and will be discussed in more detail in Chapter 5 with regard to epipolar lines.

3.4 Affine structure using local coordinate frames

Koenderink and van Doorn [79] showed constructively that 3D scene structure can be recovered up to an arbitrary 3D affine transformation from two distinct affine views, without requiring any 3D knowledge or camera calibration. Their scheme did, however, require an object–centred local coordinate frame (LCF), or "perceptual frame".

This section reviews recent research on the LCF–based *affine structure* problem and provides a framework that encompasses the two–frame solutions of Koenderink and van Doorn [79], Quan and Mohr [118], and Zisserman et al. [35, 98, 173]. These algorithms are then generalised to the m–view case.

3.4.1 Local coordinate frames

Consider four non–coplanar[3] scene points $\mathbf{X}_0 \ldots \mathbf{X}_3$, with $\mathbf{X}_0$ the *reference point* or *origin* (Figure 3.5). Define three *axis* vectors $\mathbf{E}_j$ ($j = 1 \ldots 3$) centred on $\mathbf{X}_0$, which are linearly independent and thus span $\mathcal{R}^3$. We call $\{\mathbf{E}_1, \mathbf{E}_2, \mathbf{E}_3\}$ a *spanning set* or *local coordinate frame* (LCF). Each of the n vectors $\mathbf{X}_i$ can then be expressed as a linear combination of these "axes"

$$\mathbf{X}_i - \mathbf{X}_0 = \alpha_i\, \mathbf{E}_1 + \beta_i\, \mathbf{E}_2 + \gamma_i\, \mathbf{E}_3, \quad i = 0 \ldots n-1,$$

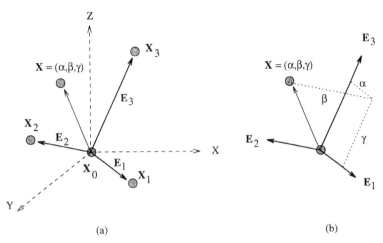

Figure 3.5: *Affine coordinates: (a) Four non–coplanar points on the object (X_1, X_2, X_3 and origin X_0) define a set of axes in terms of which other points X_i can be assigned affine coordinates $(\alpha_i, \beta_i, \gamma_i)$; (b) The coordinates are formally defined by parallel projection (since parallelism is an affine property).*

where $(\alpha_i, \beta_i, \gamma_i)^T$ are the affine coordinates of $\mathbf{X}$ in the coordinate system defined by $\{\mathbf{E}_1, \mathbf{E}_2, \mathbf{E}_3\}$. Now suppose $\mathbf{X}_i$ undergoes the motion transformation $\mathbf{X'} = \mathbf{AX} + \mathbf{D}$. Then

$$\mathbf{X}_i' - \mathbf{X}_0' = \mathbf{A}\,\mathbf{X}_i - \mathbf{A}\,\mathbf{X}_0 = \mathbf{A}\,(\mathbf{X}_i - \mathbf{X}_0) = \alpha_i\,\mathbf{A}\,\mathbf{E}_1 + \beta_i\,\mathbf{A}\,\mathbf{E}_2 + \gamma_i\,\mathbf{A}\,\mathbf{E}_3.$$

The axes $\mathbf{E}_j$ become $\mathbf{E}_j' = \mathbf{A}\,\mathbf{E}_j$, giving

$$\Delta\mathbf{X}_i \;=\; \alpha_i\,\mathbf{E}_1 + \beta_i\,\mathbf{E}_2 + \gamma_i\,\mathbf{E}_3 \tag{3.23}$$
$$\Delta\mathbf{X}_i' \;=\; \alpha_i\,\mathbf{E}_1' + \beta_i\,\mathbf{E}_2' + \gamma_i\,\mathbf{E}_3' \tag{3.24}$$

Thus, although the spanning set changes from $\{\mathbf{E}_1, \mathbf{E}_2, \mathbf{E}_3\}$ to $\{\mathbf{E}_1', \mathbf{E}_2', \mathbf{E}_3'\}$, the (α, β, γ) coordinate of each point *within* that frame remain the same. The affine coordinates are thus *independent* of the frame, and directly encode the point geometry.

Importantly, the notion of selecting an object–centred reference frame and assigning each feature a 3D affine coordinate (α, β, γ) within that frame, also holds in the *image plane* under affine projection [79]. From Equation (3.18), $\Delta\mathbf{x} = \mathbf{M}\,\Delta\mathbf{X}$ and $\Delta\mathbf{x'} = \mathbf{M}\mathbf{A}\,\Delta\mathbf{X}$. Substituting from Equations (3.23) and (3.24) gives [98]

$$\Delta\mathbf{x}_i \;=\; \mathbf{x}_i - \mathbf{x}_0 = \alpha_i\,\mathbf{e}_1 + \beta_i\,\mathbf{e}_2 + \gamma_i\,\mathbf{e}_3 \tag{3.25}$$
$$\Delta\mathbf{x}_i' \;=\; \mathbf{x}_i' - \mathbf{x}_0' = \alpha_i\,\mathbf{e}_1' + \beta_i\,\mathbf{e}_2' + \gamma_i\,\mathbf{e}_3' \tag{3.26}$$

where $\mathbf{e}_j = \mathbf{M}\mathbf{E}_j$ and $\mathbf{e}_j' = \mathbf{M'}\mathbf{E}_j = \mathbf{M}\mathbf{A}\mathbf{E}_j$. The image axis vectors $\mathbf{e}_j$ and $\mathbf{e}_j'$ are the projections of the world axis vectors $\mathbf{E}_j$ and $\mathbf{E}_j'$. They are 2D vectors lying in the image plane and are thus directly measurable. For instance, a simple affine frame is one defined by

---

[3]The methods will indicate if the points are in fact planar, by having deficient rank.

the 4 points themselves[4]: $\{\mathbf{E}_1, \mathbf{E}_2, \mathbf{E}_3\} = \{\mathbf{\Delta X}_1, \mathbf{\Delta X}_2, \mathbf{\Delta X}_3\}$. The image LCF's are then $\{\mathbf{e}_1, \mathbf{e}_2, \mathbf{e}_3\} = \{\mathbf{\Delta x}_1, \mathbf{\Delta x}_2, \mathbf{\Delta x}_3\}$ and $\{\mathbf{e}'_1, \mathbf{e}'_2, \mathbf{e}'_3\} = \{\mathbf{\Delta x}'_1, \mathbf{\Delta x}'_2, \mathbf{\Delta x}'_3\}$.

Notice that Equations (3.25) and (3.26) describe the image structure using *three* image axes, which is counter–intuitive; after all, *two* axes suffice to describe 2D position, and one generally aims for minimal descriptions. However, the additional image axis permits the *3D affine coordinates* $(\alpha_i, \beta_i, \gamma_i)$ to be computed. Note also that it is only possible to recover 3D positions *relative* to the 3D frame; $\mathbf{A}$ and $\mathbf{D}$, which fix this frame, are *not* recovered. It is therefore said that "3D scene structure is extracted up to an arbitrary 3D affine transformation"; if $\mathbf{X}_{rec}$ denotes the recovered 3D coordinate (α, β, γ) and $\mathbf{X}_{euc}$ the true Euclidean position, then

$$\mathbf{X}_{euc} = \mathbf{A}\,\mathbf{X}_{rec} + \mathbf{D}$$

for some (unknown) non–singular 3×3 matrix $\mathbf{A}$ and 3–vector $\mathbf{D}$.

3.4.2   Affine structure from m views

Suppose n features appear in m distinct views with known correspondence $(n \geq 5, m \geq 2)$, where $\mathbf{x}_i(k)$ denotes the ith point in view k. Four features $\{\mathbf{X}_0, \mathbf{X}_1, \mathbf{X}_2, \mathbf{X}_3\}$ are chosen as the affine basis, with the proviso that the frame is non–coplanar and that no two axes are collinear in every image. The axis vectors are thus $\mathbf{e}_j(k) = \mathbf{x}_j(k) - \mathbf{x}_0(k)$ $(j = 1 \ldots 3)$ and each point gives $2m$ equations in the 3 unknowns $(\alpha_i, \beta_i, \gamma_i)$,

$$\begin{bmatrix} \mathbf{\Delta x}_i(1) \\ \mathbf{\Delta x}_i(2) \\ \vdots \\ \mathbf{\Delta x}_i(m) \end{bmatrix} = \begin{bmatrix} \mathbf{e}_1(1) & \mathbf{e}_2(1) & \mathbf{e}_3(1) \\ \mathbf{e}_1(2) & \mathbf{e}_2(2) & \mathbf{e}_3(2) \\ \vdots & \vdots & \vdots \\ \mathbf{e}_1(m) & \mathbf{e}_2(m) & \mathbf{e}_3(m) \end{bmatrix} \begin{bmatrix} \alpha_i \\ \beta_i \\ \gamma_i \end{bmatrix}, \tag{3.27}$$

with $\mathbf{\Delta x}_i(k)$ measured directly from the images. The redundancy in these equations suggests a least squares solution, minimising the cost function

$$\epsilon(\alpha_i, \beta_i, \gamma_i) = \sum_{k=1}^{m} \sum_{i=1}^{n-1} |\mathbf{\Delta x}_i(k) - \alpha_i\,\mathbf{e}_1(k) - \beta_i\,\mathbf{e}_2(k) - \gamma_i\,\mathbf{e}_3(k)|^2. \tag{3.28}$$

As shown in Figure 3.6, ϵ sums the squared image distance between the observed location and the location given by the computed affine coordinates (using the specified axes). It is convenient to write Equation (3.27) as

$$\mathbf{v}_i = \mathbf{L}\,\mathbf{s}_i, \tag{3.29}$$

where $\mathbf{v}_i$ is a $2m$–vector containing the observations, $\mathbf{L}$ a $2m \times 3$ matrix containing the affine basis, and $\mathbf{s}_i$ a 3–vector containing the affine structure. The associated error expression is

$$\epsilon(\mathbf{s}_i) = \sum_{i=1}^{n-1} |\mathbf{v}_i - \mathbf{L}\mathbf{s}_i|^2, \tag{3.30}$$

---

[4]This was the frame used by Quan and Mohr [118] and Mundy and Zisserman [98].

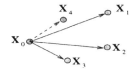

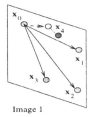

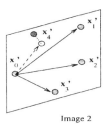

Image 1

Image 2

Figure 3.6: *Two–frame example (m = 2). Four non–coplanar points* $\{\mathbf{X}_0, \mathbf{X}_1, \mathbf{X}_2, \mathbf{X}_3\}$ *define the image axes and the affine coordinates of any other point* $\mathbf{X}_4$ *are computed directly from the two images (dashed arrow), so as to minimise the image distance (dotted line) between the observed and computed points (solid and open circles respectively).*

and the full system for n points is then

$$\mathbf{V} = \mathbf{L}\,\mathbf{S}, \tag{3.31}$$

with $\mathbf{V} = [\mathbf{v}_1 \mid \mathbf{v}_2 \mid \cdots \mid \mathbf{v}_{n-1}]$ a $2m \times (n-1)$ matrix. The unknown $3 \times (n-1)$ matrix $\mathbf{S} = [\mathbf{s}_1 \mid \mathbf{s}_2 \mid \cdots \mid \mathbf{s}_{n-1}]$ is thus determined by the pseudo–inverse,

$$\mathbf{S} = (\mathbf{L}^{\mathsf{T}}\,\mathbf{L})^{-1}\,\mathbf{L}^{\mathsf{T}}\,\mathbf{V}. \tag{3.32}$$

The complete algorithm[5] is given in Figure 3.7 and Figure 3.8 shows an example where the affine structure of a wire–frame face is computed using two images. The two view solution ($m = 2$) is a special case of the m–view algorithm, and reduces to the approach taken in [98, 118]. Four reference points are selected as the LCF, and the affine coordinates of the remaining points are computed. Choosing new image axes then generates new views of the face (Figures 3.8(c) and (d)). Figure 3.9(c) and (d) show the results when the simple triangle–based texture mapping scheme of [162] is performed on the new views.

3.4.3   Rank considerations

The redundancy in Equation (3.31) allows a check on the validity of the affine projection model: $\mathbf{V}$ should have maximum rank three [145] since both $\mathbf{L}$ and $\mathbf{S}$ have maximum rank three (by the laws of matrix algebra, rank($\mathbf{LS}$) $\leq$ rank($\mathbf{L}$) and rank($\mathbf{LS}$) $\leq$ rank($\mathbf{S}$)). This redundancy was neatly stated by Poggio [111], who noted that "1.5 snapshots are sufficient" to recover the structure, which is clear from Equations (3.25) and (3.26).

---

[5]This technique was independently derived by Weinshall and Tomasi [159]; however, they never stated explicitly what the minimisation criterion was (namely Equations (3.28) and (3.30)).

Task

Given n corresponding image points in m distinct views $(n \geq 4, m \geq 2)$, with $\mathbf{x}_i(k)$ the designated non–coplanar affine basis $(i = 0 \ldots 3, \ k = 1 \ldots m)$, compute the affine structure of the point set.

Algorithm

1. Define $\boldsymbol{\Delta}\mathbf{x}_i(k) = \mathbf{x}_i(k) - \mathbf{x}_0(k)$ and

$$
\mathbf{L} =
\begin{bmatrix}
\mathbf{e}_1(1) & \mathbf{e}_2(1) & \mathbf{e}_3(1) \\
\mathbf{e}_1(2) & \mathbf{e}_2(2) & \mathbf{e}_3(2) \\
\vdots & \vdots & \vdots \\
\mathbf{e}_1(m) & \mathbf{e}_2(m) & \mathbf{e}_3(m)
\end{bmatrix}
=
\begin{bmatrix}
\boldsymbol{\Delta}\mathbf{x}_1(1) & \boldsymbol{\Delta}\mathbf{x}_2(1) & \boldsymbol{\Delta}\mathbf{x}_3(1) \\
\boldsymbol{\Delta}\mathbf{x}_1(2) & \boldsymbol{\Delta}\mathbf{x}_2(2) & \boldsymbol{\Delta}\mathbf{x}_3(2) \\
\vdots & \vdots & \vdots \\
\boldsymbol{\Delta}\mathbf{x}_1(m) & \boldsymbol{\Delta}\mathbf{x}_2(m) & \boldsymbol{\Delta}\mathbf{x}_3(m)
\end{bmatrix}.
$$

2. Compute $\text{rank}(\mathbf{L})$ (see Section 3.4.3) and stop unless $\text{rank}(\mathbf{L}) = 3$ (within the bounds of noise).

3. Compute the affine coordinates for each point i:

$$
\mathbf{s}_i =
\begin{bmatrix}
\alpha_i \\
\beta_i \\
\gamma_i
\end{bmatrix}
= (\mathbf{L}^\top \mathbf{L})^{-1} \mathbf{L}^\top
\begin{bmatrix}
\boldsymbol{\Delta}\mathbf{x}_i(1) \\
\boldsymbol{\Delta}\mathbf{x}_i(2) \\
\vdots \\
\boldsymbol{\Delta}\mathbf{x}_i(m)
\end{bmatrix}
\qquad i = 4 \ldots n - 1.
$$

Figure 3.7: m–view affine structure algorithm (using a LCF).

These rank relations are useful in identifying the causes of rank deficiency in $\mathbf{V}$, which have not previously been investigated. There are two possible reasons why rank $(\mathbf{L})=2$. First, if the object is planar, the third axis vectors $\{\mathbf{e}_3, \mathbf{e}_3'\}$ are redundant and can be expressed as linear combinations of the other two axes (e.g. $\mathbf{e}_3 = \alpha_3 \mathbf{e}_1 + \beta_3 \mathbf{e}_2$). There are then only two independent *columns* in $\mathbf{L}$, and the structure can be correctly recovered by using *two* image axes. Second, if the relative camera–object motion results in a pure affine transformation in the image plane, $\mathbf{x}_i' = \boldsymbol{\Gamma} \mathbf{x}_i + \boldsymbol{\varepsilon}$ (where $\boldsymbol{\Gamma}$ and $\boldsymbol{\varepsilon}$ are constant), then $\mathbf{e}_i' = \boldsymbol{\Gamma} \mathbf{e}_i$ and there are only two independent *rows* in $\mathbf{L}$. This occurs, for instance, when there is pure translation parallel to the image plane or when rotation occurs only about the optic axis. In these cases, the object *appears* to be planar (even if it isn't), and whatever structure can be extracted from the available views will be extracted using two axis vectors. The case of $\text{rank}(\mathbf{L})=1$ occurs if the three image axes are collinear.

Similarly, $\text{rank}(\mathbf{S})=2$ if the object is planar, and $\text{rank}(\mathbf{S})=1$ if the points are collinear. When $\text{rank}(\mathbf{V})$ *exceeds* 3, and this cannot be attributed to noise, then a fundamental assumption has been violated, e.g. the camera model is invalid (there are perspective effects) or there are independent motions in the world.

There are several ways to compute $\text{rank}(\mathbf{V})$. For instance, if $p = \min\{2m, n - 1\}$ and $\mathbf{V}$

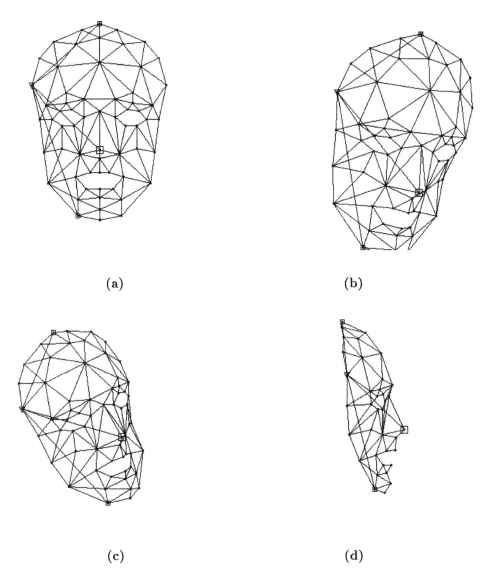

(a)   (b)

(c)   (d)

Figure 3.8: *LCF–based affine structure demonstrated on a wire–frame model (WFM): (a)(b) Two input images (known correspondence) enable computation of 3D affine structure (affine frame marked by squares, with triangle denoting origin); (c)(d) New views are generated by specifying only a new affine frame. 3D structure has clearly been recovered.*

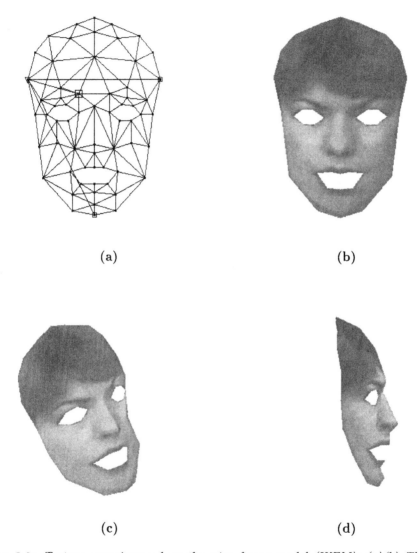

(a)   (b)

(c)   (d)

Figure 3.9: *Texture superimposed on the wire–frame model (WFM): (a)(b) The texture is initially obtained by manually fitting the WFM; (c)(d) The texture is mapped to a new view "one triangle at a time" using bilinear interpolation and the appropriate 2D affine transform [162].*

has rank r, then its smallest $p–r$ singular values should be zero. (Let $\mathbf{V}$'s singular values be $\{\mu_1 \ldots \mu_p\}$, arranged in decreasing order.) In practice, noise in the data inflates the rank, and it is hard to determine the true value of r, since the redundant singular values will be "small", not zero. Tomasi and Kanade [145] suggested using the ratio μ_3/μ_4 to ascertain whether their system had rank 3. Although our experiments have shown that this approach does identify the rank=4 case fairly reliably, the combination of noise, minor perspective effects and small motions makes it difficult to differentiate between the rank=2 and rank=3 cases (e.g. using μ_2/μ_3). An alternative method for directly testing the matrix rank (based on a statistical noise model and a χ^2 test) is thus given in Section 4.4.

3.4.4   Relation to previous work

Having established a framework for affine structure, we now relate it to previous work. Koenderink and van Doorn [79] employed a different local coordinate system from that in Section 3.4.1. They used three world points $\{\mathbf{X}_0, \mathbf{X}_1, \mathbf{X}_2\}$ to define a reference plane π_r and to establish two axes of the affine world frame, i.e. $\{\mathbf{E}_1, \mathbf{E}_2\} = \{\mathbf{\Delta X}_1, \mathbf{\Delta X}_2\}$ with origin $\mathbf{X}_0$. The third axis $\mathbf{E}_3$ was then the vector parallel to $\mathbf{k}$ connecting $\mathbf{X}_3$ to π_r, with $\mathbf{k}$ the *direction of viewing in the first frame* (Figure 3.10). The γ coordinate therefore measured the distance from $\mathbf{X}_i$ to π_r along the optic axis (i.e. "depth"), relative to the reference distance $\gamma = 1$ defined by $\mathbf{X}_3$.

Since the projection of $\mathbf{E}_3$ into I_1 was degenerate ($\mathbf{e}_3 = \mathbf{ME}_3 = \mathbf{Mk} = 0$), γ was indeterminate in I_1 and only *two* basis vectors $\mathbf{e}_1$ and $\mathbf{e}_2$ were necessary there. Thus, α and β could be calculated from I_1 alone:

$$\mathbf{\Delta x}_i = \alpha_i\, \mathbf{e}_1 + \beta_i\, \mathbf{e}_2.$$

In I_2, $\mathbf{E}_3$ was no longer degenerate ($\mathbf{e}_3' = \mathbf{ME}_3' = \mathbf{MAk}$). Using α, β, $\mathbf{e}_1'$ and $\mathbf{e}_2'$, Koenderink and van Doorn predicted where each point would appear in I_2 assuming it lay *on* π_r, namely $\hat{\mathbf{x}}_i' = \mathbf{x}_0' + \alpha_i\mathbf{e}_1' + \beta_i\mathbf{e}_2'$. This corresponded to the projection of the 3D location $\hat{\mathbf{X}}_i$ satisfying $\gamma_i = 0$ (the "trace" or "piercing point" [118]). The vector joining this piercing point to the observed position $\mathbf{x}_i' = \mathbf{x}_0' + \alpha_i\mathbf{e}_1' + \beta_i\mathbf{e}_2' + \gamma_i\mathbf{e}_3'$ then determined γ_i:

$$\mathbf{x}_i' - \hat{\mathbf{x}}_i' = \mathbf{\Delta x}_i' - \alpha_i\mathbf{e}_1' - \beta_i\mathbf{e}_2' = \gamma_i\mathbf{e}_3'.$$

Furthermore, since all these "disparity vectors" had to be parallel (to $\mathbf{e}_3'$), this provided a check on the validity of the affine assumption.

Koenderink and van Doorn's choice of $\mathbf{E}_3 = \mathbf{k}$ is inferior in several respects to $\mathbf{E}_3 = \mathbf{\Delta X}_3$. First, the spanning sets $\{\mathbf{\Delta X}_1, \mathbf{\Delta X}_2, \mathbf{k}\}$ and $\{\mathbf{\Delta X}_1', \mathbf{\Delta X}_2', \mathbf{Ak}\}$ *combine* structure and motion effects; $\mathbf{E}_1$, $\mathbf{E}_2$, $\mathbf{E}_1'$ and $\mathbf{E}_2'$ are structure–dependent, while $\mathbf{E}_3$ and $\mathbf{E}_3'$ encode camera pose and relative motion. By contrast, the spanning set with $\{\mathbf{E}_3, \mathbf{E}_3'\} = \{\mathbf{\Delta X}_3, \mathbf{\Delta X}_3'\}$ encodes only *structure,* with motion represented implicitly. The latter is more general and has the advantage of viewpoint independence [98, 118]. Second, the use of $\{\mathbf{E}_3, \mathbf{E}_3'\} = \{\mathbf{k}, \mathbf{Ak}\}$ leads to an uneven error distribution amongst the affine coordinates, since γ depends on α and β, "biasing" the solution in favour of the first view. By contrast, Equation (3.25)

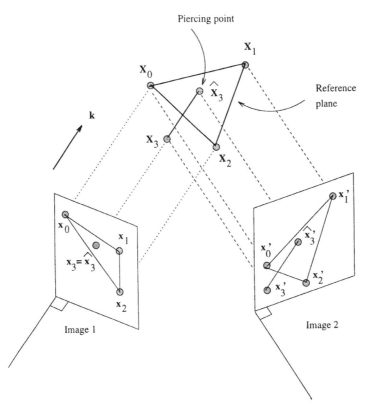

Figure 3.10: *Koenderink and van Doorn's affine structure construction, which uses* $\mathbf{E}_3 = \mathbf{k}$. *An alternative basis vector would be* $\mathbf{E}_3 = \mathbf{X}_3 - \mathbf{X}_0$.

weights the two views equally and avoids this anisotropy of error. These drawbacks do not detract from the theory, but are important considerations in a robust implementation.

Weinshall and Tomasi [159] examined the m–view case and introduced a method for incrementally updating structure as new views appeared, i.e. a sequential method rather than a batch solution. Two frames provided the initial structure estimate, whereafter the updating process began. Their solution is in fact a recursive form of Equation (3.30), obtained from the Kalman filter equations.

3.5   Affine structure without local coordinate frames

The algorithm in Section 3.4 required the explicit choice of a LCF, and this has three drawbacks: it is difficult to define criteria (apart from non–coplanarity) for automatic selection of the four basis points; any error in the basis points directly affects the entire solution; and the basis points have to be changed regularly [121] since they are "ephemeral" (due to occlusions, limitations of corner detectors, and the like). It is therefore desirable to eliminate the need for a LCF and instead utilise *all* available points. The algorithm presented here automatically computes a LCF which is not only defined by the entire set of points (rather than a selected few), but also remains *implicit* in the computation.

The algorithm builds on the work of Tomasi and Kanade [145], who computed rigid structure from m views under scaled orthography ($m \geq 3$). Their scheme is extended to the affine case ($m \geq 2$), and a new representation (the *concatenated image space*) is introduced, providing a novel geometric interpretation of the problem and showing how noise models may be incorporated in a principled way. The two–view case is investigated first to establish notation and illustrate the idea in a geometrically simpler situation, followed by the general m–view case.

3.5.1   Two–view formulation

Consider n static scene points seen in two distinct images, where the cameras $\{\mathbf{M}, \mathbf{t}\}$ and $\{\mathbf{M}', \mathbf{t}'\}$ and the scene $\mathbf{X}_i$ are unknown[6]. Equations (3.15) and (3.17) give

$$\begin{bmatrix} \mathbf{x}_i \\ \mathbf{x}'_i \end{bmatrix} = \begin{bmatrix} \mathbf{M} \\ \mathbf{M}' \end{bmatrix} \mathbf{X}_i + \begin{bmatrix} \mathbf{t} \\ \mathbf{t}' \end{bmatrix},$$

and a least squares formulation is adopted (as in Section 3.4.2), to minimise a cost function over the camera parameters and affine structure:

$$\epsilon_{tk}\left(\mathbf{M}, \mathbf{M}', \mathbf{t}, \mathbf{t}', \mathbf{X}_i\right) = \sum_{i=0}^{n-1} |\mathbf{x}_i - \mathbf{M}\,\mathbf{X}_i - \mathbf{t}\,|^2 + \sum_{i=0}^{n-1} |\mathbf{x}'_i - \mathbf{M}'\,\mathbf{X}_i - \mathbf{t}'\,|^2 . \tag{3.33}$$

Reid [121] showed that this is in fact the expression minimised by Tomasi and Kanade [145], hence the tk subscript. This expression sums the point–to–point image distances between the observed locations ($\mathbf{x}_i$ and $\mathbf{x}'_i$) and the image projections of the computed scene structure $\mathbf{X}_i$ using the computed cameras (Figure 3.11). It is a sensible quantity to minimise since it involves the exact number of degrees of freedom in the system, and since the noise originates in the image plane (where the observations are made).

It is instructive to contrast ϵ_{tk} with the LCF–based expression in Equation (3.28), whose equivalent two–frame form is

$$\epsilon(\alpha_i, \beta_i, \gamma_i) = \sum_{i=1}^{n-1} |\Delta \mathbf{x}_i - \alpha_i\,\mathbf{e}_1 - \beta_i\,\mathbf{e}_2 - \gamma_i\,\mathbf{e}_3|^2 + \sum_{i=1}^{n-1} |\Delta \mathbf{x}'_i - \alpha_i\,\mathbf{e}'_1 - \beta_i\,\mathbf{e}'_2 - \gamma_i\,\mathbf{e}'_3|^2 .$$

Whereas ϵ uses four designated basis points to define the frame (and assumes these basis points to be noise–free), ϵ_{tk} uses *all* the points and caters for errors in any of them.

We now express ϵ_{tk} in the **V–L–S** notation of Section 3.4. Let $\bar{\mathbf{x}}$, $\bar{\mathbf{x}}'$ and $\bar{\mathbf{X}}$ be centroids of the datasets $\{\mathbf{x}_i\}$, $\{\mathbf{x}'_i\}$ and $\{\mathbf{X}_i\}$ respectively, and minimise Equation (3.33) directly over $\mathbf{t}$ and $\mathbf{t}'$, giving $\mathbf{t} = \bar{\mathbf{x}} - \mathbf{M}\,\bar{\mathbf{X}}$ and $\mathbf{t}' = \bar{\mathbf{x}}' - \mathbf{M}'\,\bar{\mathbf{X}}$. Substitute these offsets in the above equations and write $\Delta \mathbf{x}_i = \mathbf{x}_i - \bar{\mathbf{x}}$ etc., giving

$$\begin{bmatrix} \Delta \mathbf{x}_i \\ \Delta \mathbf{x}'_i \end{bmatrix} = \begin{bmatrix} \mathbf{M} \\ \mathbf{M}' \end{bmatrix} \Delta \mathbf{X}_i \tag{3.34}$$

---

[6]The $\{\mathbf{M}, \mathbf{t}, \mathbf{X}\}$ notation is used here instead of the $\{\mathbf{e}_1, \mathbf{e}_2, \mathbf{e}_3, \alpha, \beta, \gamma\}$ notation of Section 3.4, to avoid a specific affine basis.

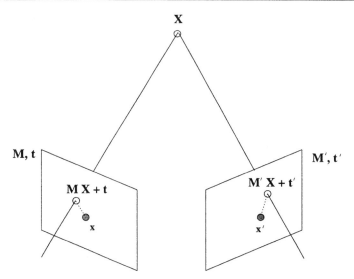

Figure 3.11: *The minimisation expression ϵ_{tk}, summing the image distance between the computed point (open circle) and the observed point (solid circle).*

and

$$\epsilon_{tk}\left(\mathbf{M}, \mathbf{M}', \mathbf{X}_i\right) = \sum_{i=0}^{n-1} |\mathbf{\Delta}\mathbf{x}_i - \mathbf{M}\,\mathbf{\Delta}\mathbf{X}_i|^2 + \sum_{i=0}^{n-1} |\mathbf{\Delta}\mathbf{x}_i' - \mathbf{M}'\,\mathbf{\Delta}\mathbf{X}_i|^2 . \qquad (3.35)$$

The point–set is thus registered with respect to its *centroid* rather than a designated point $\mathbf{X}_0$ (as in Section 3.4). Equation (3.34) is then written as $\mathbf{v}_i = \mathbf{L}\mathbf{s}_i$, where $\mathbf{v}_i$ is the *concatenated image vector* containing the registered projections of scene point $\mathbf{X}_i$ into the two images, $\mathbf{L}$ is the 4×3 matrix containing the two camera matrices ($\mathbf{M}$ and $\mathbf{M}'$), and $\mathbf{s}_i$ is the 3D affine structure vector. However, whereas previously $\mathbf{L}$ was *known* (the LCF was specified), it must now be *computed* along with $\mathbf{s}_i$. Equation (3.35) thus becomes

$$\epsilon_{tk}\left(\mathbf{L}, \mathbf{S}\right) = \sum_{i=0}^{n-1} |\mathbf{v}_i - \mathbf{L}\mathbf{s}_i|^2 . \qquad (3.36)$$

The full system of equations is again[7] $\mathbf{V} = \mathbf{L}\mathbf{S}$ (cf. Equation (3.31)), with $\mathbf{V}$ the $4 \times n$ matrix $[\mathbf{v}_0 \mid \mathbf{v}_1 \mid \cdots \mid \mathbf{v}_{n-1}]$, $\mathbf{S}$ the $3 \times n$ matrix $[\mathbf{s}_0 \mid \mathbf{s}_1 \mid \cdots \mid \mathbf{s}_{n-1}]$ and

$$\epsilon_{tk}\left(\mathbf{L}, \mathbf{S}\right) = \text{Trace}\left[\left(\mathbf{V} - \mathbf{L}\mathbf{S}\right)^{\top}\left(\mathbf{V} - \mathbf{L}\mathbf{S}\right)\right]. \qquad (3.37)$$

The task is thus to compute $\mathbf{L}$ and $\mathbf{S}$, given $\mathbf{V}$. Note that $\mathbf{L}$ and $\mathbf{S}$ cannot be recovered uniquely (they are a product), so additional constraints will have to be imposed (see later).

3.5.2   Singular value decomposition

Equation (3.37) is minimised by means of singular value decomposition (SVD), a brief introduction to which is given below (further details can be found in Strang [138]). SVD can

---

[7]Here, $\mathbf{V}$ and $\mathbf{S}$ have n columns (versus $n{-}1$ columns in Section 3.4.2), since registration is now with respect to the centroid (a virtual point) rather than an actual point. Naturally, the matrices still only have $n{-}1$ *independent* columns, as before.

be shown to decompose a general $M \times N$ matrix $\mathbf{V}$ into two matrices $\mathbf{L}^\star$ and $\mathbf{S}^\star$,

$$\mathbf{V} = \mathbf{L}^\star \mathbf{S}^\star,$$

where $\mathbf{L}^\star$ is an $M \times M$ orthogonal matrix with columns $\boldsymbol{\ell}_i$ ($i = 1 \dots M$) and $\mathbf{S}^\star$ is an $M \times N$ matrix with mutually orthogonal rows. The $\boldsymbol{\ell}_i$ vectors form an *orthonormal basis* and are arranged in order of decreasing singular values[8]. Let $p = \min\{M, N\}$ (the maximum rank of $\mathbf{V}$) and define r (where $0 < r < p$). Then $\mathbf{L}^\star$ and $\mathbf{S}^\star$ can be partitioned as

$$\mathbf{V} = \begin{bmatrix} \mathbf{L} & \mathbf{L}^\perp \end{bmatrix} \begin{bmatrix} \mathbf{S} \\ \mathbf{S}^\perp \end{bmatrix} = \mathbf{L}\mathbf{S} + \mathbf{L}^\perp \mathbf{S}^\perp, \tag{3.38}$$

where $\mathbf{L}$ is the $M \times r$ matrix $[\boldsymbol{\ell}_1 \mid \boldsymbol{\ell}_2 \mid \cdots \mid \boldsymbol{\ell}_r]$ and $\mathbf{L}^\perp$ is the $M \times (M - r)$ matrix $[\boldsymbol{\ell}_{r+1} \mid \cdots \mid \boldsymbol{\ell}_M]$. The $\mathbf{S}$ and $\mathbf{S}^\perp$ matrices, with respective dimensions $r \times N$ and $(M - r) \times N$, encode the components of $\mathbf{v}_i$ along the $\boldsymbol{\ell}$"axes". If $\text{rank}(\mathbf{V}) = r$, then $\mathbf{S}^\perp = \mathbf{0}$, $\mathbf{L}$ is the *column space* of $\mathbf{V}$ and $\mathbf{L}^\perp$ the *left null space* of $\mathbf{V}$. If $\text{rank}(\mathbf{V}) > r$, then $\mathbf{S}^\perp \neq \mathbf{0}$ and $\mathbf{L}\mathbf{S}$ is the *best rank–r approximation* to $\mathbf{V}$ [120], minimising Trace $[(\mathbf{V} - \mathbf{L}\mathbf{S})^\top (\mathbf{V} - \mathbf{L}\mathbf{S})]$.

In the two–view case, then, where $(M, N) = (4, n)$, a rank–three system is required (with $\mathbf{L}$ and $\mathbf{S}$ respectively 4×3 and $3 \times n$ matrices), i.e. $r = 3$. To solve for $\mathbf{L}$ and $\mathbf{S}$, then, SVD is performed on the noisy measurement matrix $\mathbf{V}$ and the three largest singular values determine $\mathbf{L}$ and $\mathbf{S}$.

This solution generalises that of Tomasi and Kanade [145] whose idea, in effect, was better than they themselves realised: they didn't make their minimisation criterion explicit, and they failed to note that their solution contained the core principles of affine structure. Thus, while they solved for *scaled Euclidean* structure (requiring at least *three* views), the system clearly has full rank when *two* views are present, so *affine* structure can be recovered.

As noted in [145], the decomposition of $\mathbf{V}$ into $\mathbf{L}$ and $\mathbf{S}$ is not unique. In fact, if $\mathbf{A}$ is any invertible 3×3 matrix, the matrices $\mathbf{L}\mathbf{A}$ and $\mathbf{A}^{-1}\mathbf{S}$ also give a valid decomposition of $\mathbf{V}$, since $(\mathbf{L}\mathbf{A})(\mathbf{A}^{-1}\mathbf{S}) = \mathbf{L}(\mathbf{A}\mathbf{A}^{-1})\mathbf{S} = \mathbf{L}\mathbf{S}$. This matrix $\mathbf{A}$ is actually the arbitrary affine transformation matrix of Section 3.4.1 that fixes the true 3D structure. Two views do not provide sufficient constraint to solve for $\mathbf{A}$ although three views do[9], explaining why at least three views are needed to compute scaled Euclidean structure.

3.5.3   Concatenated image space

This section provides a geometric interpretation of the affine structure problem. If $\mathbf{L}$ is decomposed into its three column vectors, $\mathbf{L} = [\boldsymbol{\ell}_1 \mid \boldsymbol{\ell}_2 \mid \boldsymbol{\ell}_3]$, then the equation $\mathbf{v}_i = \mathbf{L}\mathbf{s}_i$ can be written as

$$\mathbf{v}_i = \Delta X_i \, \boldsymbol{\ell}_1 + \Delta Y_i \, \boldsymbol{\ell}_2 + \Delta Z_i \, \boldsymbol{\ell}_3. \tag{3.39}$$

---

[8]The singular values are the positive square roots of the eigenvalues of $\mathbf{V}\mathbf{V}^\top$ and $\mathbf{V}^\top\mathbf{V}$.

[9]Let row i of the $2m \times 3$ matrix $\mathbf{L}$ be $\mathbf{m}_i^\top$, giving the final rows $\mathbf{m}_i^\top \mathbf{A}$. For rigid motion (Euclidean structure), each row–pair belongs to a scaled rotation matrix, and without loss of generality, the first rotation matrix can be set to $\mathbf{I}_3$, i.e. $\mathbf{A}^\top \mathbf{m}_1 = \mathbf{i}$ and $\mathbf{A}^\top \mathbf{m}_2 = \mathbf{j}$ (6 equations). Each remaining pair of rows gives two equations, e.g. $\mid \mathbf{A}^\top \mathbf{m}_3 \mid^2 = \mid \mathbf{A}^\top \mathbf{m}_4 \mid^2$ (i.e. $\mathbf{m}_3^\top \mathbf{A}\mathbf{A}^\top \mathbf{m}_3 = \mathbf{m}_4^\top \mathbf{A}\mathbf{A}^\top \mathbf{m}_4$) and $(\mathbf{A}^\top \mathbf{m}_3) \cdot (\mathbf{A}^\top \mathbf{m}_4) = \mathbf{m}_3^\top \mathbf{A}\mathbf{A}^\top \mathbf{m}_4 = 0$. Thus, $2m$ rows give $6 + 2(m - 1) = 2m + 4$ equations in the 9 unknown elements of $\mathbf{A}$, requiring $m \geq 3$.

The 4–vector $\mathbf{v}_i$ is clearly a linear combination of the three column vectors, and lies on a *hyperplane* π in the 4–dimensional "concatenated image space" (or *CI space*)[10]. This hyperplane is spanned by the three columns of $\mathbf{L}$; its *orientation* depends solely on the *motion* of the camera, while the distribution of points *within* the hyperplane depends solely on the *scene structure* (Figure 3.12(a)). The CI space is therefore divided into *two* vector subspaces, one spanning π and one spanning the remaining dimensions. These two subspaces are mutually orthogonal: the subspace spanning π is $\mathbf{L}$, and the orthogonal subspace is $\mathbf{L}^\perp$. In the two–view case, $\mathbf{L}^\perp$ is a single vector $\boldsymbol{\ell}_4$ (normal to π).

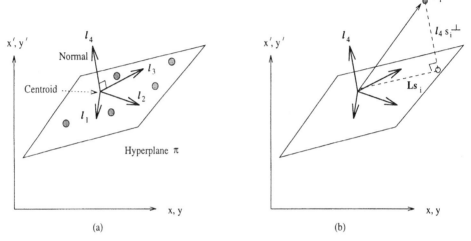

(a)   (b)

Figure 3.12: *The 4D CI space* (x, y, x', y') *for two images: (a) Noise–free vectors* $\mathbf{v}_i$ *lie on the hyperplane* π, *spanned by vectors* $\boldsymbol{\ell}_1$, $\boldsymbol{\ell}_2$ *and* $\boldsymbol{\ell}_3$. *Note that* $\mathbf{v}_i$ *is defined with respect to the centroid of the 4D data. The orthogonal subspace is simply the hyperplane normal* $\boldsymbol{\ell}_4$; *(b) Noise displaces* $\mathbf{v}_i$ *from* π *and the best estimate of* $\mathbf{s}_i$ *is obtained by orthogonal projection onto* π *(assuming isotropic independent Gaussian noise).*

Given the points $\mathbf{v}_i$ in CI space, then, the task is to find a best–fitting hyperplane π. So far, only the noise–free case has been considered, where $\mathbf{v}_i$ lies exactly on π. In practice, noise displaces $\mathbf{v}_i$ from π (Figure 3.12(b)) and a "best" hyperplane must be found. The previous, LCF–based approach (Section 3.4) effectively defined π using four designated points (the affine basis), with no regard to the quality of fit for the remaining points. A better approach is to use *all* the points to compute π. The optimal minimisation criterion then depends on the image noise distribution, which determines the noise distribution in CI space and hence specifies the covariances of $\mathbf{v}_i$.

For example, suppose the image noise is zero–mean, isotropic and Gaussian. It follows that the noise distribution in CI space is *also* zero–mean, isotropic and Gaussian, so the covariance matrix $E\{(\mathbf{v}_i - \mathbf{L}\mathbf{s}_i)(\mathbf{v}_j - \mathbf{L}\mathbf{s}_j)^\top\}$ equals $\delta_{ij}\sigma^2\mathbf{I}_4$ (where σ is the standard deviation, δ_{ij} the Kronecker delta product and $\mathbf{I}_4$ the 4×4 identity matrix). The optimal hyperplane

---

[10]A hyperplane is defined by one linear constraint (in this case $\mathbf{v}_i \cdot \boldsymbol{\ell}_4 = 0$), so has dimension one less than the space in which it is embedded. Thus, π is a 3D linear subspace. This is an alternative statement of the "rank three" principle of Tomasi and Kanade [145].

is then found by orthogonal regression in the 4D space, i.e. by minimising the sum of the squared perpendicular 4D distances between $\mathbf{v}_i$ and π. This is equivalent to minimising the component of $\mathbf{v}_i$ in the *orthogonal* subspace, which is precisely what SVD accomplishes.

SVD therefore *implicitly* assumes a zero–mean, independent, isotropic, Gaussian noise distribution on the residuals $\mathbf{v}_i - \mathbf{L}\mathbf{s}_i$ (and hence in the images). In general, however, σ may differ from image to image (leading to non–uniform diagonal elements in the covariance matrix), and different projections of a single feature may have correlated noise (leading to non–zero off-diagonal elements). A more general noise model is therefore[11]

$$E\{\mathbf{v}_i - \mathbf{L}\mathbf{s}_i\} = \mathbf{0}, \quad E\{(\mathbf{v}_i - \mathbf{L}\mathbf{s}_i)\,(\mathbf{v}_j - \mathbf{L}\mathbf{s}_j)^\top\} = \delta_{ij}\,\mathbf{\Lambda}.$$

Here, *different weights* are assigned to the components of the residual vector, attaching more importance (higher weighting) to more reliable components (so the minimisation tries harder to reduce the error in that component). Effectively, then, a weighting matrix $\mathbf{U}$ has been introduced, giving the weighted sum of squares problem

$$\sum_{i=0}^{n-1} |\mathbf{U}(\mathbf{v}_i - \mathbf{L}\mathbf{s}_i)|^2 = \sum_{i=0}^{n-1}(\mathbf{v}_i - \mathbf{L}\mathbf{s}_i)^\top \mathbf{\Lambda}^{-1}\,(\mathbf{v}_i - \mathbf{L}\mathbf{s}_i) \rightarrow \min,$$

where $\mathbf{\Lambda}^{-1} = \mathbf{U}^\top\mathbf{U}$ is the inverse covariance matrix [138]. The larger the weighting, the greater the confidence in the measurement (hence the smaller its variance/covariance). The change in solution due to $\mathbf{U}$ has the geometric interpretation of *altering the distance measure* in CI space; rather than *Euclidean distance* $|\mathbf{v}_i - \mathbf{L}\mathbf{s}_i|$, a *weighted distance* $|\mathbf{U}(\mathbf{v}_i - \mathbf{L}\mathbf{s}_i)|$ is used. This changes lengths and inner products, altering the perpendicularity property and redefining "closest". Only an orthogonal weighting matrix (e.g. isotropic noise) leaves the original Euclidean distance measure intact.

Once π has been determined, its orientation defines the cameras and their motions, and the projection of $\mathbf{v}_i$ onto π defines the structure $\mathbf{s}_i$. That is, $\mathbf{s}_i$ is the point *on* π closest to $\mathbf{v}_i$. Apart from the proviso that ℓ_1, ℓ_2 and ℓ_3 span π, they may be chosen arbitrarily. Since the choice obviously affects the computed scene structure, $\mathbf{s}_i$ can only be recovered up to a 3D affine transformation (which maps one valid spanning set of π into another).

3.5.4   Affine structure from m views

It is straightforward to extend the cost function ϵ_{tk} to m views. Let $\mathbf{x}_i(k)$ denote the projection of point i into image k, and $\{\mathbf{M}(k), \mathbf{t}(k)\}$ denote the camera in view k, giving

$$\mathbf{x}_i(k) = \mathbf{M}(k)\,\mathbf{X}_i + \mathbf{t}(k), \quad i = 1 \ldots n-1, \quad k = 1 \ldots m.$$

The system of equations $\mathbf{V} = \mathbf{L}\mathbf{S}$ is thus

$$\begin{bmatrix} \mathbf{\Delta x}_0(1) & \mathbf{\Delta x}_1(1) & \cdots & \mathbf{\Delta x}_{n-1}(1) \\ \mathbf{\Delta x}_0(2) & \mathbf{\Delta x}_1(2) & \cdots & \mathbf{\Delta x}_{n-1}(2) \\ \vdots & \vdots & & \vdots \\ \mathbf{\Delta x}_0(m) & \mathbf{\Delta x}_1(m) & \cdots & \mathbf{\Delta x}_{n-1}(m) \end{bmatrix} = \begin{bmatrix} \mathbf{M}(1) \\ \mathbf{M}(2) \\ \vdots \\ \mathbf{M}(m) \end{bmatrix} \begin{bmatrix} \mathbf{\Delta X}_0 & \mathbf{\Delta X}_1 & \cdots & \mathbf{\Delta X}_{n-1} \end{bmatrix}$$

$$(3.40)$$

---

[11]This model still assumes that the residuals for *different* features (namely $\mathbf{v}_i - \mathbf{L}\mathbf{s}_i$ and $\mathbf{v}_j - \mathbf{L}\mathbf{s}_j$) are independent, and thus have uncorrelated noise.

where $\mathbf{V}$ and $\mathbf{L}$ are respectively $2m \times n$ and $2m \times 3$ matrices, and the associated cost function is

$$\epsilon_{tk}(\mathbf{L}, \mathbf{S}) = \sum_{k=1}^{m} \sum_{i=0}^{n-1} |\, \mathbf{\Delta x}_i(k) - \mathbf{M}(k)\, \mathbf{\Delta X}_i(k)\,|^2 = \sum_{i=0}^{n-1} |\, \mathbf{v}_i - \mathbf{L s}_i\,|^2 \,. \tag{3.41}$$

Here, the vector $\mathbf{v}_i$ is formed by concatenating the m images of point i (after registration with respect to their centroids). As before, SVD is used to compute $\mathbf{L}$ and $\mathbf{S}$; all the relations in Section 3.5.2 hold, with $(M, N, r) = (2m, n, 3)$. The final algorithm is summarised in Figure 3.13.

The CI space interpretation has $\mathbf{v}_i$ lying in a 3D linear subspace π; however, π can no longer be termed a "hyperplane" since it now lies in a $2m$–dimensional CI space. The three $2m$–vectors $\boldsymbol{\ell}_1$, $\boldsymbol{\ell}_2$ and $\boldsymbol{\ell}_3$ span π, and the orthogonal subspace $\mathbf{L}^\perp$ has dimension $2m - 3$. The fact that π has three dimensions requires the $2m$–dimensional CI space to have at least three dimensions; that is, $2m \geq 3$. Thus, at least two images ($m \geq 2$) are required to reconstruct the scene (up to a 3D affine transformation).

Task

Given m distinct views of n non–coplanar scene points ($n \geq 4, m \geq 2$), compute the affine structure of the point set.

Algorithm

1. Compute the centroids $\bar{\mathbf{x}}(k)$ ($k = 1 \ldots m$). Define $\mathbf{\Delta x}_i(k) = \mathbf{x}_i(k) - \bar{\mathbf{x}}(k)$ and

$$\mathbf{V} = \begin{bmatrix} \mathbf{\Delta x}_0(1) & \mathbf{\Delta x}_1(1) & \cdots & \mathbf{\Delta x}_{n-1}(1) \\ \mathbf{\Delta x}_0(2) & \mathbf{\Delta x}_1(2) & \cdots & \mathbf{\Delta x}_{n-1}(2) \\ \vdots & \vdots & & \vdots \\ \mathbf{\Delta x}_0(m) & \mathbf{\Delta x}_1(m) & \cdots & \mathbf{\Delta x}_{n-1}(m) \end{bmatrix}.$$

2. Perform singular value decomposition on $\mathbf{V}$, and use the three largest singular values to write $\mathbf{V} = \mathbf{L S}$, where $\mathbf{L}$ is a $2m \times 3$ matrix and $\mathbf{S}$ a $3 \times n$ matrix. The ith column of $\mathbf{S}$, $\mathbf{s}_i$, contains the affine coordinate of point i, while the columns of $\mathbf{L}$, $\{\boldsymbol{\ell}_1, \boldsymbol{\ell}_2, \boldsymbol{\ell}_3\}$, encode the implicit LCF used (concatenated through all m views).

Figure 3.13: m–view affine structure algorithm (no LCF).

3.5.5 Relation to previous work

In their landmark paper, Tomasi and Kanade [145] formulated the rank–3 principle and used SVD to determine rigid structure and motion parameters under scaled orthography. Our modifications to their scheme (which are in fact simplifications) extend it to the affine case and have been described in Sections 3.5.1 and 3.5.2. This scheme will also be further discussed in Chapters 7 and 8.

A noteworthy contribution to the n–point problem was made by Harris [55], who tackled the two–frame problem using rigid motion and scaled orthographic projection. The affine version of his cost function is

$$\epsilon_h\left(\mathbf{\Gamma}, \mathbf{d}, \boldsymbol{\varepsilon}, Z_i\right) = \sum_{i=0}^{n-1} |\mathbf{x}'_i - \mathbf{\Gamma}\,\mathbf{x}_i - Z_i\,\mathbf{d} - \boldsymbol{\varepsilon}|^2, \tag{3.42}$$

which is simply the least squares form of Equation (3.21). It measures the distance in I_2 between the observed location $\mathbf{x}'_i$ and the location predicted by the computed image motion parameters ($\mathbf{\Gamma}$, $\boldsymbol{\varepsilon}$ and $\mathbf{d}$), computed depth Z_i and observed location $\mathbf{x}_i$. Like ϵ_{tk}, ϵ_h sums point–to–point image distances and is minimised over both camera parameters and affine structure. The remainder of this section analyses ϵ_h, relates it to ϵ_{tk} and shows why ϵ_h is unsuitable.

First, ϵ_h can be simplified by minimising over $\boldsymbol{\varepsilon}$, giving $\boldsymbol{\varepsilon} = \bar{\mathbf{x}}' - \mathbf{\Gamma}\,\bar{\mathbf{x}} - \bar{Z}\,\mathbf{d}$. Resubstitution yields

$$\epsilon_h\left(\mathbf{\Gamma}, \mathbf{d}, Z_i\right) = \sum_{i=0}^{n-1} |\Delta\mathbf{x}'_i - \mathbf{\Gamma}\,\Delta\mathbf{x}_i - \Delta Z_i\,\mathbf{d}|^2. \tag{3.43}$$

Now, from Equations (3.19), (3.20) and (3.35),

$$\epsilon_{tk} = \sum_{i=0}^{n-1} \left|\Delta\mathbf{x}_i - \mathbf{B}\begin{bmatrix}\Delta X_i \\ \Delta Y_i\end{bmatrix} - \Delta Z_i\,\mathbf{b}\right|^2 + \sum_{i=0}^{n-1} \left|\Delta\mathbf{x}'_i - \mathbf{B}'\begin{bmatrix}\Delta X_i \\ \Delta Y_i\end{bmatrix} - \Delta Z_i\,\mathbf{b}'\right|^2,$$

and when the first term is set to zero (i.e. there is assumed to be *no error* in the first view),

$$\begin{bmatrix}\Delta X_i \\ \Delta Y_i\end{bmatrix} = \mathbf{B}^{-1}\left(\Delta\mathbf{x}_i - \Delta Z_i\,\mathbf{b}\right). \tag{3.44}$$

Substitution into ϵ_{tk} then gives

$$\epsilon_{tk} = \sum_{i=0}^{n-1} |\Delta\mathbf{x}'_i - \mathbf{B}'\mathbf{B}^{-1}\left(\Delta\mathbf{x}_i - \Delta Z_i\,\mathbf{b}\right) - \Delta Z_i\,\mathbf{b}'|^2 = \sum_{i=0}^{n-1} |\Delta\mathbf{x}'_i - \mathbf{\Gamma}\,\Delta\mathbf{x}_i - \Delta Z_i\,\mathbf{d}|^2 = \epsilon_h.$$

Thus, ϵ_h is a special case of ϵ_{tk}, arising when the first image is trusted completely and all the errors are assumed to occur in I_2. The advantage of ϵ_h is its greater simplicity, since the dimension of the fit is reduced from a 4D space to a 2D space. That is, minimisation is only over x' and y'; there are no residual components in the x and y directions because those fits are exact. However, ϵ_h has three major drawbacks. First, the distribution of errors between the views is uneven, leading to a grossly anisotropic (and unrealistic) noise distribution in CI space. Second, it is possible that no solution will be found (since the residual in x and y is forced to zero). Third, there is no straightforward extension of ϵ_h to more than two images. These weaknesses make ϵ_{tk} the preferred cost function.

3.6 Conclusions

This chapter has provided the necessary background to the affine camera and has investigated methods for recovering affine structure. Two m–view frameworks have been proposed, one using a specified four–point LCF and one using the full point–set (with an implicit LCF). Experimental results given in Chapter 8 (where transfer is discussed) confirm the expected superiority of the second framework, which also plays an important role in the clustering scheme of Chapter 4.

A novel interpretation of the affine structure and motion problem has also been given, in terms of a *concatenated image space* (CI space). The concatenated image vectors $\mathbf{v}_i$ have been shown to lie on a 3D linear subspace in a high–dimensional space, in accordance with the familiar "rank three" principle. This interpretation proves useful in the chapters on affine epipolar geometry and affine transfer (Chapters 5 and 8 respectively).

Chapter 4

Clustering using maximum affinity spanning trees

4.1 Introduction

Once the corner tracker has generated a set of image trajectories, the next task is to group these points into putative objects. The practice of classifying objects into sensible groupings is termed "clustering", and is fundamental to many scientific disciplines. This chapter presents a novel clustering technique that groups points together on the basis of their affine structure and motion. The system copes with sparse, noisy and partially incorrect input data, and with scenes containing multiple, independently moving objects undergoing general 3D motion. The key contributions are as follows:

- A graph theory framework is employed (in the spirit of [119]) using maximum affinity spanning trees (MAST's), and the clusters are computed by a *local, parallel* network, with each unit performing simple operations. The use of such networks has long been championed by Ullman, who has used them to fill in subjective contours [150], compute apparent motion [151] and detect salient curves [132].

- Clustering occurs over multiple frames, unlike the more familiar two–frame formulations (e.g. [3, 80, 134]).

- A *graduated motion analysis scheme* extends the much–used simplistic image motion models, e.g. grouping on the basis of parallel and equal image velocity vectors (as in [80, 134]) is only valid for a fronto–parallel plane translating parallel to the image. The layered complexity of our models utilises full *3D* information where available, but doesn't use a more complex model than is required.

- The termination criteria (to control cluster growth) are based on sound statistical noise models, in contrast to many heuristic measures and thresholds (e.g. [119, 134]).

The abstract problem of organising data according to perceived similarities is considered first: Section 4.2 formulates the problem in graph theory terms and Section 4.3 describes our clustering philosophy. The algorithm is then tailored to the structure and motion domain: Section 4.4 defines the relevant affinity measures and Section 4.5 explains how to halt cluster growth. Implementation details are provided in Section 4.6, with results on synthetic and real data given in Section 4.7.

4.2   Maximum affinity spanning trees

Consider an image with N points, which form the universal point–set $\mathcal{U} = \{p_1, p_2, \ldots, p_N\}$. Each point p_i possesses a set of properties (e.g. shape, colour, brightness, position, speed, length, etc.) and "attractive forces" (or *affinities*) are computed between these points, based on some similarity function. The affinity[1] between p_i and p_j is denoted by a_{ij} or $a(\ell_{ij})$, and is transmitted via a "virtual" link ℓ_{ij} (Figure 4.1(a)). The task is then, on the basis of these affinities, to partition $\mathcal{U}$ into Q disjoint, non–empty point–sets (or *clusters*) $\mathcal{C}_1, \mathcal{C}_2, \ldots, \mathcal{C}_Q$ $(Q \leq N)$, so that

$$\mathcal{U} = \mathcal{C}_1 \cup \mathcal{C}_2 \cup \cdots \cup \mathcal{C}_Q,$$

where Q is not known *a priori*. This section introduces the maximum affinity spanning tree (MAST) and shows how to compute it. Section 4.2.1 summarises the relevant graph theory background and Section 4.2.2 outlines the basic MAST generation algorithm. Sections 4.2.3 and 4.2.4 then investigate how to speed up parallel MAST generation by utilising the decisions made by neighbouring processors.

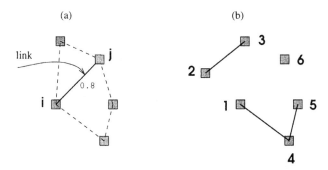

Figure 4.1: *(a) The points p_i and p_j are connected by link ℓ_{ij} with affinity $a_{ij} = 0.8$; (b) The graph, $\mathcal{G}$, has 6 points and 3 links.*

4.2.1   A graph theory primer

In the terminology of graph theory [108, 166], the system of points, links and affinities described above is a *weighted graph* $\mathcal{G}$; the points are *vertices*, the links are *edges* and the affinity values are *edge weights*. The points are distinct, so $\mathcal{G}$ is said to be *labelled*. The point–set associated with $\mathcal{G}$ is denoted $\mathcal{P}$, with finite cardinality $|\mathcal{P}| = N$. If $\mathcal{P}$ is a proper subset of the universal point–set $\mathcal{U}$, then $(\mathcal{U} - \mathcal{P})$ denotes the complement of $\mathcal{P}$ (i.e. the points "outside" $\mathcal{G}$).

The graph $\mathcal{G}$ is defined as a finite set of two–element sets $\{p_i, p_j\}$, each an unordered pair of distinct elements of $\mathcal{P}$ (i.e. $p_i \neq p_j$ if $i \neq j$). Thus $\mathcal{G}$ is a subset of the Cartesian product space $\mathcal{P} \times \mathcal{P}$. A link ℓ_{ij} is some element $\{p_i, p_j\} \in \mathcal{G}$ joining p_i to p_j (or equivalently p_j to p_i, since $\mathcal{G}$ is *undirected*):

$$\ell_{ij} = \{p_i, p_j\}. \tag{4.1}$$

---

[1]Here, the term "affinity" means "attraction"; it has no relation to the affine camera.

For instance, the graph in Figure 4.1(b) is

$$\mathcal{G} = \{\{p_1, p_4\}, \{p_2, p_3\}, \{p_4, p_5\}\} = \{\ell_{14}, \ell_{23}, \ell_{45}\}.$$

Points p_i and p_j are the *end–points* of ℓ_{ij}, and ℓ_{ij} is *incident* on these two points. The number of links in $\mathcal{G}$ is given by its cardinality $|\mathcal{G}|$. The *null* graph $\emptyset$ consists of *isolated* points and contains no links (i.e. $\mathcal{G} = \{\}$, though $\mathcal{P}$ is non–empty). A *complete* graph $\mathcal{K}_N$ has a link between every pair of points in $\mathcal{P}$, giving the maximum number of links $N(N-1)/2$.

Two points in $\mathcal{P}$ are *neighbours* if they are directly joined by a link. The neighbours of p_a form the set $\Gamma(p_a)$ (or simply Γ_a), a subset of $\mathcal{P}$. The point–to–set mapping Γ therefore takes an element of $\mathcal{P}$ to a subset of $\mathcal{P}$:

$$\Gamma_a = \{p_b | \exists \{p_a, p_b\} \in \mathcal{G}\}. \tag{4.2}$$

For instance, the graph in Figure 4.1(b) has the neighbour sets $\Gamma_1 = \{p_4\}$, $\Gamma_2 = \{p_3\}$, $\Gamma_3 = \{p_2\}$, $\Gamma_4 = \{p_1, p_5\}$, $\Gamma_5 = \{p_4\}$ and $\Gamma_6 = \{\}$. The neighbours of a point–set $\mathcal{P}$ are the combined neighbours of the individual points, excluding those points already in $\mathcal{P}$:

$$\Gamma(\mathcal{P}) = \{p_b | \exists \{p_a, p_b\} \in \mathcal{G}, p_a \in \mathcal{P}, p_b \notin \mathcal{P}\}. \tag{4.3}$$

A point in $\mathcal{P}$ lies in the *span* $\mathcal{S}$ of $\mathcal{G}$, denoted $\mathcal{S}(\mathcal{G})$, if at least one link is incident on it, i.e. if it is joined to at least one other point in $\mathcal{G}$. Formally, p_i is in $\mathcal{S}(\mathcal{G})$ if it participates in an element of $\mathcal{G}$:

$$\mathcal{S}(\mathcal{G}) = \{p \mid \exists \ell \in \mathcal{G}, p \in \ell\}. \tag{4.4}$$

The span has (finite) cardinality $|\mathcal{S}|$ and we say that "$\mathcal{G}$ spans $\mathcal{S}$". Evidently $\mathcal{S} \subseteq \mathcal{P}$, with all isolated points excluded from $\mathcal{S}$. Thus, Figure 4.1(b) has $\mathcal{G} = \{\ell_{14}, \ell_{23}, \ell_{45}\}$, $\mathcal{P} = \{p_1, p_2, p_3, p_4, p_5, p_6\}$ and $\mathcal{S} = \{p_1, p_2, p_3, p_4, p_5\}$. The null graph spans the empty set (i.e. $|\mathcal{S}(\emptyset)| = 0$) while the complete graph spans the entire point–set (i.e. $|\mathcal{S}(\mathcal{K}_N)| = N$).

The affinity measure is a function $a : \mathcal{G} \rightarrow \mathcal{R}^1$ where $a(\{p_i, p_j\})$ is the affinity of p_i for p_j; this will also be written as $a(\ell_{ij})$ or simply a_{ij}. The *affinity score* $a(\mathcal{G})$ is the sum of the affinities of $\mathcal{G}$'s links,

$$a(\mathcal{G}) = \sum_{\ell \in \mathcal{G}} a(\ell). \tag{4.5}$$

Thus, the graph in Figure 4.2(b) has $a(\mathcal{G}) = 0.7 + 0.9 + 0.6 = 2.2$. A *subgraph* $\mathcal{H}$ of $\mathcal{G}$ is obtained from $\mathcal{G}$ by removing a number of points and/or links from $\mathcal{G}$, i.e. $\mathcal{H} \subseteq \mathcal{G}$.

Two points p_a and p_b in $\mathcal{G}$ are *connected* if some *path* (a sequence of links) leads from p_a to p_b. That is, if p_a and p_b are points of $\mathcal{G}$, then p_a connects p_b if and only if

- $\{p_a, p_b\} \in \mathcal{G}$, or

- $\exists p_c \in \mathcal{P}$ such that $\{p_a, p_c\} \in \mathcal{G}$ and p_c connects p_b.

If the path returns to the starting point (i.e. p connects p), it is termed a *cycle*. Two connected points are said to be in the same *component* of the graph. When every point in $\mathcal{G}$ is connected to every other point, the *graph is connected* (has only one component). In Figure 4.1(b), p_1 and p_5 are connected but the graph $\mathcal{G}$ isn't. A *tree* $\mathcal{T}$ is a connected graph (with point–set $\mathcal{P}$) containing no cycle. Thus,

- there is precisely one path between any two points of $\mathcal{T}$;

- $\mathcal{T}$ has $(N-1)$ links, where $N = |\mathcal{P}|$ is the number of points;

- the addition of any new link creates exactly one cycle;

- each link is a *bridge* between connected components; if removed, no path remains between its endpoints.

Finally, a *spanning tree* $\mathcal{T}_s$ of $\mathcal{G}$ is a connected, acyclic subgraph spanning the same point–set as $\mathcal{G}$. Thus, $\mathcal{T}_s$ is a subgraph of $\mathcal{G}$ which is a tree, and its span $\mathcal{S}(\mathcal{T}_s)$ equals $\mathcal{P}$. This represents a minimal collection of links which preserves the connectedness of the graph, and leads to an important definition:

Definition 1 *A* **maximum affinity spanning tree** *(MAST)* $\mathcal{M}$ *is a spanning tree for which the affinity score (the sum of affinities of $\mathcal{M}$'s links) is maximum.*

Such a MAST $\mathcal{M}$ provides a solution to the well–known *connector problem*: given N vertices and the distances between them, find which edges to include so that (a) there exists a path between every pair of vertices, and (b) the total distance is a minimum. This problem can be posed in terms of road construction, water mains, gas pipes, electrical wire connections, and so on. The MAST defined above has many different names in the literature, among them maximum/minimum weight spanning trees, maximal/minimal spanning trees, economy trees, shortest spanning trees and shortest connection networks [117]. The maximisation and minimisation problems may be interchanged freely.

Importantly, $\mathcal{G}$ need not have a *unique* MAST; there may be links with equal affinities (called *ties*), in which case a choice between equally valid candidates must be made. Nonetheless, all MAST's of $\mathcal{G}$ have the same (maximum) affinity score (Figure 4.2).

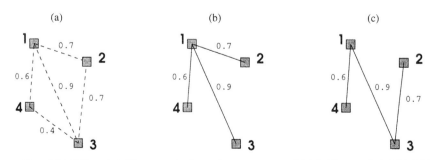

Figure 4.2: *Tie MAST's: (a) The graph $\mathcal{G}$ with $a_{12} = a_{23}$; (b)(c) Two valid MAST's, both with (maximum) affinity score 2.2.*

4.2.2 MAST generation

We now examine how to construct a MAST for $\mathcal{G}$. Many algorithms have been proposed, notably by Kruskal [82] and Prim [117], and a good overview of the various techniques can be found in [49]. One simple algorithm due to Kruskal [82] is as follows:

1. Sort the links in order of decreasing affinity.

2. Accept the maximum affinity link in the sorted list provided it doesn't form a closed loop with any previously chosen link. The spans of the connected subgraphs define the clusters.

3. Remove the accepted link from the list. Stop if all points are connected, else return to step 2.

An alternative way to construct the identical MAST is to start at *any point* $p_r \in \mathcal{P}$ (the *root* point) and successively add the *maximum affinity link* available to the evolving tree $\mathcal{T}$. Thus, by making the optimal decision at each step, an optimal tree eventually obtains [117]. This algorithm is due to Prim and is the one we employ (for reasons given later). The remainder of this section introduces our notation and provides a worked example.

Recall that the affinity measure a_{ij} encodes the mutual attraction between a pair of points p_i and p_j. Conventionally, this similarity function is symmetric ($a_{ij} = a_{ji}$) and bounded ($a_{min} \leq a_{ij} \leq a_{max}$), with large a values indicating strong mutual attraction and small a values indicating a lack of affinity (rather than repulsion). We "reserve" the extreme values a_{max} and a_{min} to indicate "self–affinity" ($a_{ii} = a_{max}$) and missing links respectively (see later). The affinities may be arranged in a symmetric *affinity matrix* $\mathbf{H} = [a_{ij}]$ (also termed a *distance/proximity table*), whose rows and columns index the different points:

$$\mathbf{H} = \begin{bmatrix} a_{max} & a_{12} & \cdots & a_{1N} \\ a_{21} & a_{max} & & a_{2N} \\ \vdots & & \ddots & \vdots \\ a_{N1} & a_{N2} & \cdots & a_{max} \end{bmatrix}$$

Point i therefore has an *affinity vector* $\mathbf{a}_i = (a_{i1}, a_{i2}, \ldots, a_{iN})$, the ith row of $\mathbf{H}$, encoding the affinity of p_i for each of its neighbours. Although constructing such a matrix suggests that $\mathcal{G}$ is complete (i.e. that every point is directly joined to every other one), incomplete graphs are represented by assigning the value a_{min} to non–existent links.

Let $\mathcal{M}_r$ represent the MAST grown from the root point p_r. While under construction (i.e. in the process of "evolving"), this MAST will span a subset of $\mathcal{P}$. We denote by $\mathcal{M}_r[k]$ the evolving MAST after k iterations, so $\mathcal{M}_r[0] = \emptyset$ and $\mathcal{M}_r[k] = \mathcal{M}_r$. The span of $\mathcal{M}_r[k]$ is denoted $\mathcal{P}_r[k]$, so $\mathcal{P}_r[0] = \{p_r\}$ and $\mathcal{P}_r[k] = \mathcal{P}$. A *tree vector* $\mathbf{t}_r = (t_{r1}, t_{r2}, \ldots, t_{rN})$, with $a_{min} \leq t_{rj} \leq a_{max}$ ($j = 1 \ldots N$), is introduced to record the affinities between $\mathcal{M}_r$ and *its* neighbours (the points not yet incorporated). Membership of a point p_j in $\mathcal{M}_r$ is indicated by $t_{rj} = a_{max}$. Initially, the MAST only spans the root point p_r, so $\mathbf{t}_r[0] = \mathbf{a}_r$. Thus, the only a_{max} element in $\mathbf{t}_r[0]$ is t_{rr}.

The MAST then grows by incorporating that point p_n which has the largest affinity component in $\mathbf{t}_r$, i.e.

$$n = \arg_{j=1...N} \max \{t_{rj}\}, \quad t_{rn} \neq a_{max}, \quad t_{rn} \neq a_{min}.$$

The condition $t_{rn} < a_{max}$ restricts the search to points not already in the tree, so that $p_n \in (\mathcal{P} - \mathcal{P}_r[k])$. The condition $t_{rn} > a_{min}$ further limits the search to a "neighbourhood" $\mathcal{N}_r$, excluding from consideration the points for which it has no affinity. Once p_n has been incorporated, the new tree vector is given by

$$t_{rj} \leftarrow \max (t_{rj}, a_{nj}), \quad j = 1 \ldots N,$$

or more succinctly

$$\mathbf{t}_r[k+1] \leftarrow \mathbf{t}_r[k] \, \circledM \, \mathbf{a}_n,$$

where $\circledM$ is a maximisation operator[2]. Because $a_{nn} = a_{max}$, it follows that $t_{rn} = a_{max}$, confirming membership of p_n in $\mathcal{M}_r$. The neighbour set $\mathcal{N}_r$ will also change once p_n has been added, since new neighbours may be introduced via the acquired point. In the case of a tie (i.e. more than one neighbour has the maximum affinity value in $\mathbf{t}_r$), the choice of p_n is arbitrary. Growth continues until all components of $\mathbf{t}_r$ have value a_{max}, by which time $\mathcal{M}_r$ spans $\mathcal{P}$. Since the MAST contains no cycles and one link is added at each step, precisely $(N-1)$ steps (or *iterations*) are required to determine $\mathcal{M}_r$. The algorithm is summarised in Figure 4.3 (and the proof can be found in [45, 117]).

Prim's algorithm has two distinct advantages over other algorithms [51, 117]. First, it avoids complicated checks for cycles and connectedness. Second, no matter how large the graph, only two vectors are required at any stage: the current tree vector $\mathbf{t}_r$ and the affinity vector $\mathbf{a}_n$ of the new point. The algorithm has complexity $O(N^2)$, since $N-1$ steps are needed to grow $\mathcal{M}_r$, and at each step the number of elementary operations (e.g. comparisons) is of order N. For sparse graphs where the number of links is relatively small ($|\mathcal{G}| \ll N(N-1)/2$), the complexity can be reduced to $O(|\mathcal{G}| \log N)$ by using a heap to select the best point at each step [49]. Yao [169] further reduced the complexity for sparse graphs to $O(|\mathcal{G}| \log \log N)$ by partitioning the links incident on each point after sorting them.

---

[2]To define the properties of the $\circledM$ operator, consider the N–vectors $\mathbf{p}$, $\mathbf{q}$ and $\mathbf{r}$ whose components lie in the range $(a_{min}; a_{max})$. Then $\mathbf{p} \circledM \mathbf{q} = (\max (p_1, q_1); \max (p_2, q_2); \cdots ; \max (p_N, q_N))$, and it follows that $\mathbf{p} \circledM \mathbf{q} = \mathbf{q} \circledM \mathbf{p}$ (commutativity), $(\mathbf{p} \circledM \mathbf{q}) \circledM \mathbf{r} = \mathbf{p} \circledM (\mathbf{q} \circledM \mathbf{r})$ (associativity) and $\mathbf{p} \circledM \mathbf{p} = \mathbf{p}$ (idempotence). Commutativity is important for symmetry, while associativity and idempotence ensure that the final tree vector is invariant to the order in which points are processed. The identity vector, $\mathbf{0}$, is defined as the N–vector $(a_{min}, a_{min}, \ldots, a_{min})$, i.e. $\mathbf{p} \circledM \mathbf{0} = \mathbf{p}$.

Task

Given a graph $\mathcal{G}$ with point–set $\mathcal{P}$ and affinity matrix $\mathbf{H} = [a_{ij}]$ (where $a_{min} \leq a_{ij} \leq a_{max}$), construct a MAST $\mathcal{M}_r$ starting from point p_r $(1 \leq r \leq N)$, where $N = |\mathcal{P}|$.

Algorithm

1. Set $\mathbf{t}_r[0] \leftarrow \mathbf{a}_r$.

2. For $k = 1 \ldots N - 1$:

   (a) Determine the new point p_n to acquire, where

   $$n = \underset{j=1\ldots N}{\arg} \max \{t_{rj}\}, \quad a_{min} \leq t_{rn} \leq a_{max}.$$

   (b) Incorporate p_n into the evolving MAST vector:

   $$\mathbf{t}_r[k] \leftarrow \mathbf{t}_r[k-1] \; Ⓜ \; \mathbf{a}_n.$$

Figure 4.3: MAST algorithm (due to Prim [117]).

Prim's algorithm is demonstrated on the graph in Figure 4.4, where $a_{max} = 1$ and $a_{min} = 0$. The affinity matrix is[3]

$$\mathbf{H} = \begin{bmatrix} \mathbf{a}_1 \\ \mathbf{a}_2 \\ \mathbf{a}_3 \\ \mathbf{a}_4 \\ \mathbf{a}_5 \\ \mathbf{a}_6 \end{bmatrix} = \begin{bmatrix} 1 & 0.7 & 0.4 & 0 & 0 & 0.9 \\ 0.7 & 1 & 0.5 & 0.3 & 0 & 0 \\ 0.4 & 0.5 & 1 & 0.8 & 0 & 0 \\ 0 & 0.3 & 0.8 & 1 & 0.4 & 0.6 \\ 0 & 0 & 0 & 0.4 & 1 & 0.6 \\ 0.9 & 0 & 0 & 0.6 & 0.6 & 1 \end{bmatrix}$$

and the root point is p_2. Thus, $\mathbf{t}_2[0] = \mathbf{a}_2 = (0.7, 1, 0.5, 0.3, 0, 0)$. The largest element in $\mathbf{a}_2$ (ignoring 0's and 1's) is $a_{21} = 0.7$, so p_1 is selected and $\mathcal{M}_2$ is updated according to $\mathbf{t}_2[1] \leftarrow \mathbf{t}_2[0] \; Ⓜ \; \mathbf{a}_1 = (1, 1, 0.5, 0.3, 0, 0.9)$. The next selection is p_6 $(t_{26} = 0.9)$, so $\mathbf{t}_2[2] \leftarrow \mathbf{t}_2[1] \; Ⓜ \; \mathbf{a}_6$. A tie now occurs between p_4 and p_5 $(t_{24} = t_{25} = 0.6)$; p_4 is chosen arbitrarily, then p_3 and finally p_5. The evolution of the MAST is illustrated in Figure 4.4, with $\mathbf{t}_2$ shown below each stage. The alternative tree, arising from the choice of p_5 rather than p_4 at step 3, generates an identical MAST in this example, though the order of formation is different (namely $\ell_{21}, \ell_{16}, \ell_{65}, \ell_{64}, \ell_{34}$). The final affinity score is 3.6.

4.2.3   Cooperative evolution

The clustering algorithm given later in Section 4.3 requires MAST's to be grown in parallel from every point in $\mathcal{G}$. An obvious solution is simply to replicate the algorithm in Figure 4.3 for every point in the graph; we term this the *parallel Prim* algorithm. However,

---

[3]Note that $\mathbf{a}_i$ and $\mathbf{t}_i$ are *row–vectors*.

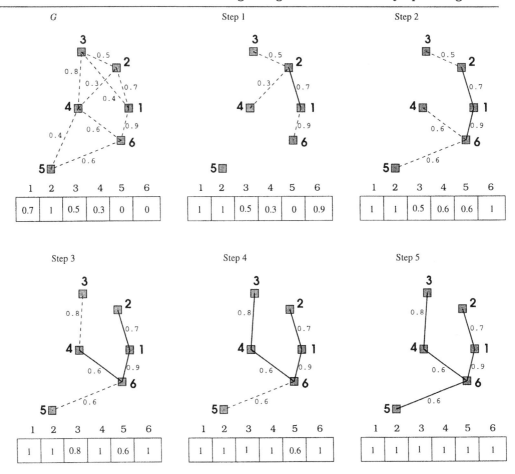

Figure 4.4: *A graph $\mathcal{G}$ (affinities shown on dotted lines) and the evolving MAST $\mathcal{M}_2$ (grown from p_2). The tree vector $\mathbf{t}_2$ is shown below each graph. The solid lines denote the evolving tree and for steps 1–5, the dotted lines show the best links from this evolving tree to the remaining points.*

this "isolationist" approach (with each point oblivious to the other MAST's being grown simultaneously around it) is inefficient, and significant computational savings result from examining the MAST's of neighbouring points.

To illustrate the concept, consider growing simultaneous MAST's from p_3 and p_4 in the graph $\mathcal{G}$ of Figure 4.5(a), which has

$$\begin{bmatrix} \mathbf{a}_3 \\ \mathbf{a}_4 \end{bmatrix} = \begin{bmatrix} 0.8 & 0 & 1 & 0.7 & 0 \\ 0 & 0 & 0.7 & 1 & 0.9 \end{bmatrix}.$$

The tree vectors $\mathbf{t}_i$ are initialised to the affinity vectors $\mathbf{a}_i$, and the best neighbour is chosen for each evolving MAST. On the first iteration[4], $\mathcal{M}_3 \to p_1$ and $\mathcal{M}_4 \to p_5$, giving Figures 4.5(b)

---

[4]The notation $\mathcal{M}_i \to p_j$ means that the ith evolving MAST chooses the jth point.

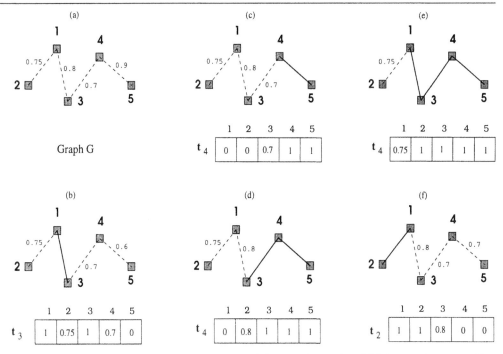

Figure 4.5: *Illustration of the trust concept: (a) Initial graph; (b)(c) Simultaneous first iteration growth of MAST's from root points p_3 and p_4 respectively; (d)(e) Second and third iterations for $\mathcal{M}_4$; (f) First iteration growth from p_2.*

and 4.5(c):

$$\left[\begin{array}{c} t_3[1] \\ t_4[1] \end{array} \right] = \left[\begin{array}{c} t_3[0] \; \textcircled{M} \; a_1 \\ t_4[0] \; \textcircled{M} \; a_5 \end{array} \right] = \left[\begin{array}{ccccc} 1 & 0.75 & 1 & 0.7 & 0 \\ 0 & 0 & 0.7 & 1 & 1 \end{array} \right].$$

The next acquisition of $\mathcal{M}_4$ is p_3 (Figure 4.5(d)), and the question under consideration is whether $\mathcal{M}_3$'s previous choice (in acquiring p_1) is also now optimal with respect to $\mathcal{M}_4$. It clearly is, for $\mathcal{M}_4$ acquires p_1 anyhow on the next iteration (Figure 4.5(e)).

Theorem 1 (in Appendix A) proves for the general case that "trusting one's neighbours" gives the identical solution to growing the N MAST's independently. That is, *a MAST fares no worse (in the affinity score sense) by trusting its neighbour's choices than if it grows in the normal way, augmenting its span by a single point at each iteration.* Thus, when the new point p_n is incorporated into the evolving MAST $\mathcal{M}_r$, the information embedded within p_n's own MAST $\mathcal{M}_n$ greatly reduces $\mathcal{M}_r$'s workload, speeding up the overall algorithm. When t_r acquires p_n, then, the update equation is

$$t_r[k] \leftarrow t_r[k-1] \; \textcircled{M} \; t_n[k-1],$$

rather than $t_r[k] \leftarrow t_r[k-1] \; \textcircled{M} \; a_n$.

Of course, it is possible that the information contained within $t_n[k-1]$ provides no new information beyond that already contained within a_n. An example of this is the MAST grown from p_2 in Figure 4.5(f): on the first iteration $\mathcal{M}_2 \rightarrow p_1$, and on the second iteration $\mathcal{M}_2 \rightarrow p_3$. Here, $\mathcal{M}_3[1]$ (Figure 4.5(b)) overlaps with $\mathcal{M}_2[1]$ (in point p_1) and hence provides no new acquisitions to $\mathcal{M}_2[2]$ other than p_3 itself. Equally, though, nothing has been lost by using $\mathbf{t}_n[k-1]$ rather than $\mathbf{a}_n$.

The maximum computational saving arises when $\mathcal{M}_r$ and $\mathcal{M}_n$ have mutually exclusive point–sets, i.e. $\mathcal{S}(\mathcal{M}_r) \cap \mathcal{S}(\mathcal{M}_n) = \emptyset$ (Figure 4.6(a)). Since each parallel MAST selects only one point on each iteration[5] (its "best neighbour"), the maximum growth of $\mathcal{M}_r$ is governed by a binary law; at best, the size of $\mathcal{M}_r$ doubles on each iteration. On the jth step, then, $\mathcal{M}_r$ acquires at most 2^{j-1} new points. After M iterations, the maximum cardinality of the MAST's span is

$$|\mathcal{S}(\mathcal{M}_r)|_{\max} = 1 + \sum_{j=1}^{M} 2^{j-1} = 2^M,$$

which includes the root point p_r. Under optimum conditions, then, 10 iterations would be sufficient to span 1024 points! The minimum computational saving occurs when the trees overlap entirely, except for a single link (Figure 4.6(b)). This case yields only one new point p_n (the rest are already in $\mathcal{M}_r$), and gives the same result as normal one–step growing (where $\mathbf{a}_n$ is used instead of $\mathbf{t}_n[k-1]$). After M iterations, the minimum cardinality of the MAST's span is

$$|\mathcal{S}(\mathcal{M}_r)|_{\min} = 1 + \sum_{i=1}^{M} 1 = M + 1,$$

inclusive of p_r. Thus, the maximum potential gain in number of points acquired over the previous method is $2^{j-1}-1$ on the jth step.

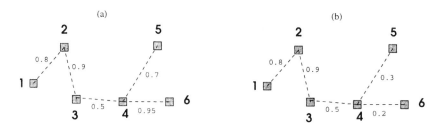

Figure 4.6: *(a) Maximum gain when there is no overlap between $\mathcal{P}_r$ and $\mathcal{P}_n$ (disjoint sets). $\mathcal{M}_1$ grows to p_2 and then p_3, while $\mathcal{M}_4$ grows to p_5 and then p_6. When $\mathcal{M}_1$ then acquires p_4, it gains p_5 and p_6 too; (b) Minimum gain (overlapping sets). $\mathcal{M}_1$ grows to p_2 and p_3, while $\mathcal{M}_4$ grows to p_3 and then p_2. Now when $\mathcal{M}_1$ acquires p_4, it only gets one new point (p_4).*

Importantly, the idempotency property of ⓜ ensures that no special processing is needed to cope with overlapping spans, e.g. if $\mathbf{t}_1 = \mathbf{a}_1$ ⓜ $\mathbf{a}_2$ ⓜ $\mathbf{a}_3$ and $\mathbf{t}_2 = \mathbf{a}_2$ ⓜ $\mathbf{a}_3$ ⓜ $\mathbf{a}_4$, then

$$\mathbf{t}_1 \;ⓜ\; \mathbf{t}_2 = \mathbf{a}_1 \;ⓜ\; (\mathbf{a}_2 \;ⓜ\; \mathbf{a}_2) \;ⓜ\; (\mathbf{a}_3 \;ⓜ\; \mathbf{a}_3) \;ⓜ\; \mathbf{a}_4 = \mathbf{a}_1 \;ⓜ\; \mathbf{a}_2 \;ⓜ\; \mathbf{a}_3 \;ⓜ\; \mathbf{a}_4,$$

as required.

---

[5]Obviously, though, it may *acquire* more than one point.

4.2.4   The "trust thy neighbour" algorithm

Before presenting the final algorithm for parallel evolving MAST's, it is necessary to introduce the concept of *hibernation*. The fact that the simultaneously evolving MAST's acquire a *variable* number of points on each iteration (rather than just a single point as in the parallel Prim algorithm) leads to differently sized MAST's at any given instant. This causes synchronisation difficulties later when MAST's must be compared to test for clusters. Consider, as an example, the graph in Figure 4.7. After one iteration,

$$
\begin{bmatrix} t_1[1] \\ t_2[1] \\ t_3[1] \\ t_4[1] \\ t_5[1] \end{bmatrix}
=
\begin{bmatrix}
1 & 1 & 0.7 & 0.5 & 0.3 \\
1 & 1 & 0.7 & 0.5 & 0.3 \\
0.8 & 1 & 1 & 0.6 & 0.3 \\
0.5 & 0.7 & 1 & 1 & 0 \\
0.8 & 1 & 0.7 & 0 & 1
\end{bmatrix} .
$$

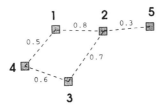

Figure 4.7: *An example illustrating why hibernation is necessary (see text). Here, $a_{min} = 0$ and $a_{max} = 1$.*

Then $\mathcal{M}_1 \rightarrow p_3$, $\mathcal{M}_2 \rightarrow p_3$, $\mathcal{M}_3 \rightarrow p_1$, $\mathcal{M}_4 \rightarrow p_2$ and $\mathcal{M}_5 \rightarrow p_1$, giving

$$
\begin{bmatrix} t_1[2] \\ t_2[2] \\ t_3[2] \\ t_4[2] \\ t_5[2] \end{bmatrix}
=
\begin{bmatrix}
1 & 1 & 1 & 0.6 & 0.3 \\
1 & 1 & 1 & 0.6 & 0.3 \\
1 & 1 & 1 & 0.6 & 0.3 \\
1 & 1 & 1 & 1 & 0.3 \\
1 & 1 & 0.7 & 0.5 & 1
\end{bmatrix}
$$

Thus, t_4 *already* spans four points while the other tree vectors span only three. The solution to this problem is to force any tree that has grown quicker than the minimum rate to "rest" for several iterations until the others catch up. We term this *hibernation*, and point out that it in no way reduces the gains in efficiency that have been made – it is far cheaper for a MAST to acquire (say) 25 new points in one go and then rest for 24 iterations, than to do 25 separate calculations, each of the same complexity as the single one. In the above example, then, $t_4[2]$ will not grow again until step 4.

The final algorithm is summarised in Figure 4.8.

4.3   Clustering concepts

A *cluster* is a set of points $\mathcal{C} \subseteq \mathcal{P}$ which are grouped together on the basis of some clustering criterion, and the graph theory paradigm provides a natural framework for defining and

Task

For an N–point graph $\mathcal{G}$ with point–set $\mathcal{P}$ and affinity matrix $\mathbf{H} = [a_{ij}]$ (where $a_{min} \leq a_{ij} \leq a_{max}$), construct a MAST for every point using parallel, evolving trees communicating with their neighbours.

Algorithm

1. Initialise $\mathbf{t}_r[0] \leftarrow \mathbf{a}_r$ for $r = 1 \ldots N$.

2. For $k = 1 \ldots N - 1$ (iteration number):

   (a) If p_r is hibernating ($r = 1 \ldots N$):

       • Decrement the hibernation counter $\mathtt{hib\_count}[r]$.

   (b) Else:

       • Determine the new point p_{n_r} for $\mathbf{t}_r$ to acquire:

       $$n_r = \mathop{\arg\max}_{j=1\ldots N} \{t_{rj}\}, \quad a_{min} \leq t_{rn_r} \leq a_{max}.$$

       • Incorporate p_{n_r} into the evolving MAST $\mathbf{t}_r$ ($r = 1 \ldots N$):

       $$\mathbf{t}_r[k] \leftarrow \mathbf{t}_r[k-1] \ \textcircled{M} \ \mathbf{t}_n[k-1].$$

       • Set $\mathtt{hib\_count}[r] \leftarrow$ number of new points acquired $- 1$.

Figure 4.8: The "trust thy neighbour" parallel MAST algorithm.

generating such clusters. Recall that the objective is to partition a point–set $\mathcal{P}$ into Q disjoint non–empty sets $\mathcal{C}_1, \mathcal{C}_2, \ldots, \mathcal{C}_Q$ ($Q \leq N$), that is $\mathcal{C}_i \neq \emptyset$ ($i = 1 \ldots Q$), $\mathcal{C}_i \cap \mathcal{C}_j = \emptyset$ ($i \neq j$) and $\mathcal{C}_1 \cup \cdots \cup \mathcal{C}_Q = \mathcal{P}$. The resulting clusters give a *partition* of $\mathcal{P}$.

This section examines what constitutes a suitable clustering criterion and how to compute clusters that satisfy it. The clustering criterion will be a function of the affinities, since these are the sole indicators of similarity between points. One simple criterion is a global threshold [69], i.e. delete all links whose affinities fall below a specified value a_0. The resulting "threshold graph" comprises isolated points and connected components, which define the clusters (Figure 4.9). This scheme is naturally sensitive to the choice of a_0, and an adjustable threshold would be preferable. For instance, one could cycle through a range of thresholds and select a_0 based on the stability of the resulting clusters. This has parallels with scale–space methods [167], but still remains a global technique.

The grouping criterion introduced in this chapter utilises MAST's, and the resulting scheme is inherently local, permitting variable thresholds in different regions of the graph. An optimum set of links connecting the points in the cluster (and containing no cycles) is generated as a natural byproduct. Section 4.3.1 reviews previous work, Section 4.3.2 presents the novel cluster definition, Section 4.3.3 outlines the clustering algorithm and Section 4.3.4

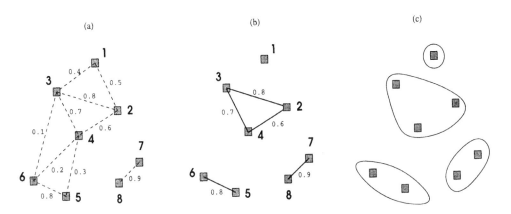

Figure 4.9: *Threshold clustering: (a) Graph $\mathcal{G}$; (b) Links remaining after applying the threshold $a_0 = 0.55$; (c) Resulting clusters.*

gives a worked example. Finally, Section 4.3.5 discusses how to enhance efficiency by once again "trusting one's neighbours".

4.3.1 Background and previous work

There exists a wide range of clustering techniques, differing greatly in the extent of their mathematical foundations. Indeed, many methods are defined only by an algorithm, without any established properties or specified optimisation criterion. A taxonomy of clustering algorithms [69] reveals two primary classes (Figure 4.10): *partitional methods,* which generate a single partition of the data, and *hierarchical methods,* which build a nested sequence of partitions. Partitional clustering is straightforward in theory: one selects a clustering criterion (e.g. square error [37]), evaluates it for all possible partitions, and picks the partition that optimises the criterion. In practice, it is difficult to select a criterion that successfully translates one's intuitive notion of a "cluster" into a reasonable mathematical formula. Moreover, the number of potential partitions is often astronomical even for moderately–sized data sets, making it infeasible to evaluate the criterion over all partitions [69]. Although progress has been made in addressing these problems (e.g. see [37, 69, 136]), the above drawbacks make partitional schemes unattractive.

Hierarchical clustering arranges the data into a series of partitions, using either *agglomerative* or *divisive* methods. An agglomerative algorithm starts with each node in an individual cluster (the disjoint clustering), and merges two or more of these singleton clusters to give a second partition. This merging process is then repeated, with the number of clusters decreasing until finally a single cluster remains, containing all the nodes (the conjoint clustering). A divisive algorithm performs the procedure in reverse, starting with the conjoint clustering; this is generally more computationally demanding [37, 136], so the agglomerative approach is chosen. The two most popular hierarchical agglomerative strategies are *complete–link* and *single–link* algorithms, and Johnson [72] and Zahn [170] identify the important features of these two schemes:

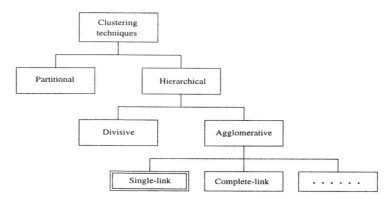

Figure 4.10: *Taxonomy of primary clustering schemes, placing hierarchical agglomerative single–link algorithms in context.*

- An explicit and intuitive description of the clusters is generated.

- The input consists solely of the affinity matrix and the clusters capture the inherent physical structure of the scene, without depending on arbitrary choices in the algorithm (such as the order in which points are scrutinised).

- The partition is relatively insensitive to small amounts of noise widely and randomly spread over the field.

Both methods have their appropriate domains of application and their key properties are briefly summarised below; in–depth discussions can be found in [37, 51, 69, 72]. Single–link algorithms are based on connectedness, leading to minimum path lengths among all pairs of nodes in the cluster, i.e. each cluster is a *maximally connected* subgraph. They therefore have a close relation to MAST's: in fact, if allowed to continue until all subsets are linked, the single–link algorithm generates a MAST. They have several desirable theoretical properties [69], e.g. they don't suffer from ambiguities due to ties (unlike their complete–link counterparts); however, they "chain" easily, since only a single link is needed to merge two large clusters.

Complete–link algorithms produce clusters in which all the nodes are connected to one another, i.e. every cluster is a *maximally complete* subgraph. Since completeness is a much stronger property than connectedness, the clusters are conservative and the growth of elongated clusters is discouraged (all points must be inter–related before forming a cluster). This method is thus most appropriate when clusters are expected to be compact and roughly equal in size; its disadvantage is a tendency to find structure when there is none, imposing meaningless groupings on the data set [69].

We choose single–link clustering for its simplicity, and overcome the chaining problem by sophisticated termination criteria (Section 4.5). Rashid's Lights system [119] used single–link cluster analysis in analysing Moving Light Displays (MLD's), but our system differs from his in several ways: whereas his method was divisive ("split"), ours is agglomerative ("merge"); whereas his method was sequential, ours is parallel, and whereas his criterion for separating clusters was ad hoc and empirically–based, our termination criteria have a sound statistical basis.

A useful picture of hierarchical clustering is provided by a *dendogram,* a special tree structure comprising layers of nodes. Each layer represents a partition of the data into clusters, with lines connecting nodes that are clustered. Figure 4.11(b) shows the single–link dendogram for the graph in (a). Cutting the dendogram horizontally creates a partition of the data. As with all hierarchical methods, cluster growth is monotonic: once formed, clusters can neither be dissolved nor overlap. This is due to the nesting property, whereby clusters in one partition are nested into the clusters of the next partition.

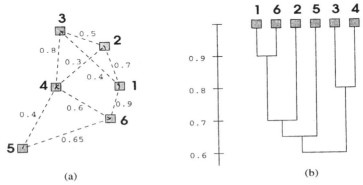

(a)   (b)

Figure 4.11: *Single–link clusters: (a) Graph $\mathcal{G}$; (b) Dendogram formed using Kruskal's algorithm described in Section 4.2.2 (e.g. ℓ_{16} is the strongest link, so $\{p_1, p_6\}$ forms the first cluster).*

Existing hierarchical agglomerative single–link algorithms are designed for a "single processor" which possesses global information about the graph. The simplest algorithm, which we term the *sequential algorithm,* builds on Kruskal's algorithm (Section 4.2.2); it iteratively chooses the largest link that doesn't form a closed loop with any previously chosen link, and the connected components define the clusters (as in Figure 4.9). The remainder of Section 4.3 shows that *identical* clusters are obtained by distributing the computation, with each node performing local operations in parallel.

4.3.2   Cluster definition

An "ideal" cluster $\mathcal{C}$ would be a group of points in which every point has of its own volition selected the others in the group. MAST's allow the discovery of such clusters, since a MAST $\mathcal{M}_r$ grown from a root point p_r evolves by successively incorporating the points to which it is most attracted. This observation suggests growing a MAST for *every point* in $\mathcal{P}$ and defining a cluster as follows:

Definition 2 *The k points $\{p_1, p_2, \ldots, p_k\}$ are defined to be a cluster $\mathcal{C}$ if and only if all of their k evolving MAST's $\{\mathcal{M}_1, \mathcal{M}_2, \ldots, \mathcal{M}_k\}$ span the same set of points.*

Note that only the *span* of each evolving MAST matters; the *links* are irrelevant (and may well differ between MAST's if there are tie affinities). The above cluster definition meshes elegantly with the MAST generation process; once k points have satisfied the above criterion, the growth of their k MAST's would be identical anyhow, since all have the same choices of affinities (e.g. see t_1 and t_2 in Section 4.2.4). It is therefore logical to assign a single common MAST to this cluster, effectively "shrinking" the group of points to a single point. We first illustrate the idea using the parallel Prim algorithm (where the MAST's grow independently and acquire only a single point on each iteration); the "trust thy neighbour" optimisations are described later in Section 4.3.5. The hierarchy of partitions is thus generated as follows:

1. Initialise N singleton clusters $C_i = \{p_i\}$ with MAST's $\mathcal{M}_i$ $(i = 1 \ldots N)$.

2. Let each MAST $\mathcal{M}_i$ acquire the point p_{ni} for which it has the largest affinity, so $\mathcal{S}(\mathcal{M}_i) \leftarrow \mathcal{S}(\mathcal{M}_i) \cup \{p_{ni}\}$. Update $\mathcal{M}_i$'s affinities for the points not yet acquired.

3. Check whether any MAST's share the same span. If so, the span becomes a new cluster, superseding the previous clusters of that span.

4. Stop when one global cluster remains (this will span $\mathcal{P}$, after N–1 iterations); otherwise, return to step 2 for another iteration.

Significantly, **Theorem 2** (in Appendix A) proves that this parallel clustering algorithm gives *identical clusters to a single–link agglomerative method*. Local clusters of points now form *simultaneously* in different spatial regions of the graph, with clusters of cardinality k being discovered on iteration $k - 1$. This cluster hierarchy is represented in a modified form of dendogram (Figure 4.12), which we term a *cardinality dendogram*. The scale on the left indicates the size k of the clusters formed at that step (or equivalently the step number $k+1$). This effectively "collapses" the traditional dendogram so that clusters of equal cardinality have equal ranking, and is better suited to parallel computation (since equal cardinality clusters form simultaneously).

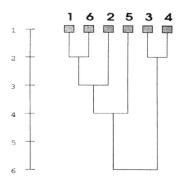

Figure 4.12: *Cardinality dendogram for the graph in Figure 4.11.*

A vital issue that remains is how to control the growth of these parallel MAST's; if they are permitted to grow fully, then a single global cluster will emerge after N–1 iterations, spanning $\mathcal{P}$. This is acceptable if one simply wants to generate the dendogram, but is obviously useless when actual groupings of the data are required. A *termination condition* is therefore needed to decide when the growth of a cluster should be halted. Thus, although

N–1 is the *upper bound* on the number of iterations (each MAST acquires one point per iteration unless stopped), the *actual* number of iterations will be much smaller. Section 4.5 addresses the selection of a suitable criterion. Once all MAST's have ceased growing, a forest[6] of connected components remains, and the clusters are the spans of these connected subgraphs.

4.3.3   The evolving MAST clustering algorithm

The clustering algorithm using parallel MAST's is given in Figure 4.13. Although this has been shown to generate the same clusters as the sequential single–link method, it clearly involves more computation. Indeed, it may seem strange to grow N MAST's in parallel when the same solution may be obtained by simply sorting the links once! Nonetheless, the new approach has important benefits.

First, when the affinity measure falls off with distance, distant points will have no direct affinity for one another, so each point need only be aware of its *local neighbourhood*. The parallel scheme can take advantage of this fact and use purely local operations to compute the desired clusters, without a single node having global knowledge. Naturally, as each MAST grows, its awareness of the global point–set gradually increases: it gains access to the neighbours of its neighbours, then to their neighbours and so on, until its growth is halted. In this way, each point obtains glimpses of the wider world purely on a "need–to–know" basis. Obviously, were all the MAST's to grow to full size, the benefits of this scheme would be lost, since each MAST would by then have global knowledge. In practice, MAST growth is halted by the termination condition so the MAST's are never globally aware.

Second, the computational cost can be greatly reduced by efficiently programming the local operations. The algorithm appears to have complexity $O(N^3)$, for there are N MAST's each with worst–case cost $O(N^2)$ (see Section 4.2.2). However, Section 4.3.5 will show how to reduce this cost by using the computations of neighbouring processors.

4.3.4   Example

Consider the example in Figure 4.14, with $a_{max} = 1$, $a_{min} = 0$ and the affinity matrix

$$\mathbf{H} = \begin{bmatrix} 1 & 0.5 & 0.4 & 0 & 0 & 0 & 0 & 0 \\ 0.5 & 1 & 0.8 & 0.6 & 0 & 0 & 0 & 0 \\ 0.4 & 0.8 & 1 & 0.7 & 0 & 0.1 & 0 & 0 \\ 0 & 0.6 & 0.7 & 1 & 0.3 & 0.2 & 0 & 0 \\ 0 & 0 & 0 & 0.3 & 1 & 0.8 & 0 & 0 \\ 0 & 0 & 0.1 & 0.2 & 0.8 & 1 & 0 & 0 \\ 0 & 0 & 0 & 0 & 0 & 0 & 1 & 0.9 \\ 0 & 0 & 0 & 0 & 0 & 0 & 0.9 & 1 \end{bmatrix}$$

---

[6]A forest is a graph with several connected components.

Task

Given a graph $\mathcal{G}$ with point–set $\mathcal{P}$ and affinity matrix $\mathbf{H} = [a_{ij}]$ (where $a_{min} \leq a_{ij} \leq a_{max}$), construct a cluster hierarchy using MAST's evolving in parallel.

Algorithm

1. Initialise $\mathbf{t}_r[0] \leftarrow \mathbf{a}_r$ for $r = 1 \ldots N$.

2. For $k = 1 \ldots N - 1$:

   (a) Determine the new point p_{n_r} for $\mathbf{t}_r$ to acquire $(r = 1 \ldots N)$, where

   $$n_r = \underset{j=1\ldots N}{\arg} \max \{t_{rj}\}, \quad a_{min} \leq t_{rn_r} \leq a_{max}.$$

   (b) Incorporate p_{n_r} into the evolving MAST $\mathbf{t}_r$ $(r = 1 \ldots N)$:

   $$\mathbf{t}_r[k] \leftarrow \mathbf{t}_r[k - 1] \,\textcircled{M}\, \mathbf{a}_n.$$

   (c) Check whether any tree vectors coincide (i.e. their MAST's span the same point–set); if so, combine them into a cluster and remove the individual tree vectors.

Figure 4.13: Evolving MAST clustering algorithm.

On the first iteration of parallel MAST growth, $\mathcal{M}_1 \rightarrow p_2$, $\mathcal{M}_2 \rightarrow p_3$, $\mathcal{M}_3 \rightarrow p_2$, $\mathcal{M}_4 \rightarrow p_3$, $\mathcal{M}_5 \rightarrow p_6$, $\mathcal{M}_6 \rightarrow p_5$, $\mathcal{M}_7 \rightarrow p_8$ and $\mathcal{M}_8 \rightarrow p_7$, giving the tree vectors:

$$
\begin{bmatrix} t_1[1] \\ t_2[1] \\ t_3[1] \\ t_4[1] \\ t_5[1] \\ t_6[1] \\ t_7[1] \\ t_8[1] \end{bmatrix} =
\begin{bmatrix}
1 & 1 & 0.8 & 0.6 & 0 & 0 & 0 & 0 \\
0.5 & 1 & 1 & 0.7 & 0 & 0.1 & 0 & 0 \\
0.5 & 1 & 1 & 0.7 & 0 & 0.1 & 0 & 0 \\
0.4 & 0.8 & 1 & 1 & 0.3 & 0.2 & 0 & 0 \\
0 & 0 & 0.1 & 0.3 & 1 & 1 & 0 & 0 \\
0 & 0 & 0.1 & 0.3 & 1 & 1 & 0 & 0 \\
0 & 0 & 0 & 0 & 0 & 0 & 1 & 1 \\
0 & 0 & 0 & 0 & 0 & 0 & 1 & 1
\end{bmatrix}.
$$

The equality of the tree vectors for $\mathcal{M}_2$ and $\mathcal{M}_3$ ($\mathbf{t}_2 = \mathbf{t}_3$) leads to the cluster $(p_2; p_3)$ and hence a joint tree $\mathcal{M}_{23}$. Similarly, $(p_5; p_6)$ and $(p_7; p_8)$ are clustered and combined into $\mathcal{M}_{56}$ and $\mathcal{M}_{78}$ respectively. Figure 4.14 illustrates the clusters formed after each iteration. Note that when checking for clusters, each tree need only check those neighbours which have a_{max} in its tree vector (i.e. those points which it has incorporated).

The updated trees now make their next choices, i.e. $\mathcal{M}_1 \rightarrow p_3$, $\mathcal{M}_{23} \rightarrow p_4$, $\mathcal{M}_4 \rightarrow p_2$

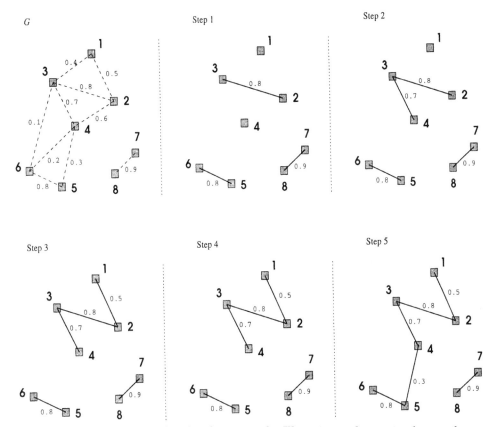

Figure 4.14: *Evolving clusters for the shown graph. There is no change in clusters from step 3 to step 4 (see text), and only 5 iterations are required (for an 8-point graph).*

and $\mathcal{M}_{56} \rightarrow p_4$ ($\mathcal{M}_{78}$ has no remaining choices so is terminated):

$$
\begin{bmatrix}
t_1[2] \\
t_{23}[2] \\
t_4[2] \\
t_{56}[2]
\end{bmatrix}
=
\begin{bmatrix}
1 & 1 & 1 & 0.7 & 0 & 0.1 & 0 & 0 \\
0.5 & 1 & 1 & 1 & 0.3 & 0.2 & 0 & 0 \\
0.5 & 1 & 1 & 1 & 0.3 & 0.2 & 0 & 0 \\
0 & 0.6 & 0.7 & 1 & 1 & 1 & 0 & 0
\end{bmatrix}.
$$

Cluster $(p_2; p_3)$ incorporates p_4, and growth resumes: $\mathcal{M}_1 \rightarrow p_4$, $\mathcal{M}_{234} \rightarrow p_1$ and $\mathcal{M}_{56} \rightarrow p_3$,

$$
\begin{bmatrix}
t_1[3] \\
t_{234}[3] \\
t_{56}[3]
\end{bmatrix}
=
\begin{bmatrix}
1 & 1 & 1 & 1 & 0.3 & 0.2 & 0 & 0 \\
1 & 1 & 1 & 1 & 0.3 & 0.2 & 0 & 0 \\
0.4 & 0.8 & 1 & 1 & 1 & 1 & 0 & 0
\end{bmatrix}.
$$

Cluster $(p_2; p_3; p_4)$ incorporates p_1, and the trees grow again: $\mathcal{M}_{1234} \rightarrow p_5$ and $\mathcal{M}_{56} \rightarrow p_2$,

$$
\begin{bmatrix}
t_{1234}[4] \\
t_{56}[4]
\end{bmatrix}
=
\begin{bmatrix}
1 & 1 & 1 & 1 & 1 & 0.8 & 0 & 0 \\
0.5 & 1 & 1 & 1 & 1 & 1 & 0 & 0
\end{bmatrix}.
$$

No new clusters can be formed here, so growth continues: $\mathcal{M}_{1234} \to p_6$ and $\mathcal{M}_{56} \to p_1$,

$$\begin{bmatrix} \mathbf{t}_{1234}[5] \\ \mathbf{t}_{56}[5] \end{bmatrix} = \begin{bmatrix} 1 & 1 & 1 & 1 & 1 & 1 & 0 & 0 \\ 1 & 1 & 1 & 1 & 1 & 1 & 0 & 0 \end{bmatrix}.$$

So $(p_1; p_2; p_3; p_4)$ finally merges with $(p_5; p_6)$, whereafter no further growth is possible. The final clusters are thus $\mathcal{C}_1 = \{p_1, p_2, p_3, p_4, p_5, p_6\}$ and $\mathcal{C}_2 = \{p_7, p_8\}$. Naturally, $\mathcal{C}_1$ needn't have grown so large; a termination condition could have prevented a merger (say) between $(p_1; p_2; p_3; p_4)$ and $(p_5; p_6)$. This issue is addressed in Section 4.5.

4.3.5   The grapevine algorithm

The parallel clustering algorithm in Figure 4.13 simply replicated Prim's MAST generation scheme for each point in the graph, and then performed checks for clusters. The MAST generation phase of this algorithm is clearly inefficient, for Section 4.2.3 showed how reliance on neighbouring processors reduces the workload substantially. This section proves that the same optimisations are valid for clustering. We first establish that the *identical* clusters emerge by trusting one's neighbours (i.e. the cardinality dendogram is preserved intact), and then outline the revised algorithm and present a worked example.

Section 4.2.3 argued that an evolving MAST is justified in adopting the whole of its neighbour's MAST since it would eventually adopt these points anyhow (given enough time). Our objective in growing MAST's, though, is not to form one large spanning tree of the graph $\mathcal{G}$ but rather to find clusters. It is therefore vital to verify that the revised algorithm doesn't "swamp" these desired clusters in its enthusiastic acquisition drive, overgrowing boundaries where the previous algorithm would have halted.

Theorem 3 (Appendix A) proves that the revised algorithm does simply enhance the efficiency of the "one step at a time" process; *the clustering solutions are identical*. The modifications to the algorithm are then identical to those made in Section 4.2.3, namely $\mathbf{t}_r$ is updated as $\mathbf{t}_r[k] \leftarrow \mathbf{t}_r[k-1] \, \circledM \, \mathbf{t}_n[k-1]$ (rather than $\mathbf{t}_r[k] \leftarrow \mathbf{t}_r[k-1] \, \circledM \, \mathbf{a}_n$), and hibernation variables are added. In other words, we simply append the check for clusters to the "trust thy neighbour" algorithm (see Figure 4.15). We term this the "grapevine algorithm" due to the "gossip" about desirable acquisitions that passes between the nodes.

We now revisit the example of Section 4.3.4. The first iteration is identical[7], while for the second iteration, the acquisition $\mathcal{M}_{56} \to \mathbf{t}_4$ introduces two new points into $\mathcal{M}_{56}$ (p_2 and p_3):

$$\begin{bmatrix} \mathbf{t}_1[2] \\ \mathbf{t}_{23}[2] \\ \mathbf{t}_4[2] \\ \mathbf{t}_{56}[2] \end{bmatrix} = \begin{bmatrix} 1 & 1 & 1 & 0.7 & 0 & 0.1 & 0 & 0 \\ 0.5 & 1 & 1 & 1 & 0.3 & 0.2 & 0 & 0 \\ 0.5 & 1 & 1 & 1 & 0.3 & 0.2 & 0 & 0 \\ 0.4 & 0.8 & 1 & 1 & 1 & 1 & 0 & 0 \end{bmatrix}$$

Tree $\mathcal{M}_{56}$ then hibernates for the third iteration, till the others catch up. On the fourth iteration, $\mathcal{M}_{1234} \to \mathbf{t}_5$ and $\mathcal{M}_{56} \to \mathbf{t}_2$, immediately giving

$$\begin{bmatrix} \mathbf{t}_{1234}[3] \\ \mathbf{t}_{56}[3] \end{bmatrix} = \begin{bmatrix} 1 & 1 & 1 & 1 & 1 & 1 & 0 & 0 \\ 1 & 1 & 1 & 1 & 1 & 1 & 0 & 0 \end{bmatrix},$$

---

[7]This is always true since $2^{i-1} = 1$ for $i = 1$, i.e. there is no gain in efficiency yet.

> Task
>
> Given an N–point graph $\mathcal{G}$ with point–set $\mathcal{P}$ and affinity matrix $\mathbf{H}$, construct a cluster hierarchy using parallel, evolving MAST's communicating with neighbouring processors.
>
> Algorithm
>
> Append to "Trust Thy Neighbour" MAST generation algorithm (Figure 4.8):
>
> 2 (c)   Check whether any tree vectors coincide; if so, combine them into a cluster and remove the individual tree vectors.

Figure 4.15: The grapevine clustering algorithm.

without requiring the extra step needed before. Note that the solutions are identical in terms of the clusters generated.

4.4   The affinity measures

The choice of an appropriate affinity measure is crucial to the success of a clustering algorithm [69]. Affinity measures are necessarily application–dependent, e.g. shape and colour will obviously be important attributes when sorting apples, bananas and oranges. Duda and Hart [37] provide a thorough discussion of clustering properties and affinity measures; the properties most appropriate for our domain are those encoding structure and motion. Unfortunately, many existing structure/motion–based clustering schemes cope only with simple image motions (e.g., [80, 134]), which greatly restricts their applicability. We achieve greater generality by incorporating *3D* information in the affinity measure, employing the concepts of affine structure (Chapter 3). The intuition behind our approach is to extract groups of points that maintain their structural integrity over the m views. This requires examining the "shape" of the point–set in each frame, rather than individual trajectories.

There are, however, obstacles to grouping points on the basis of 3D scene structure. First, *four* points are needed to define 3D affine structure (cf. Section 3.4.1), making a point–to–point affinity measure impossible. Bootstrapping is thus problematic, since the combinatorics involved in initially generating all possible five–point groups[8] are prohibitively large. Second, the approach violates the "least exertion philosophy", namely "don't use a more complicated structure–motion model than necessary". (In image coding, this is the bandwidth reduction principle, where the smallest possible number of parameters are used to explain scene changes.) After all, a full 3D affine frame is unnecessary for an object undergoing, say, pure image translation; a simple 2D frame suffices. Moreover, the algorithm can even *fail* on simpler motions, e.g. four points translating in the image plane cannot be grouped together if a five–point affinity measure is used!

---

[8]Four points define the affine frame; a fifth point is needed to form an invariant to assess the structure.

We therefore employ a *graduated clustering scheme,* starting with a simple motion interpretation and gradually increasing the complexity of the model as needed. There are many possible models: 2D translation, 2D Euclidean motion (translation, rotation and uniform scale), 2D affine motion, 3D fixed axis rotation, 3D Euclidean motion, 3D affine motion, 3D projective motion, and so on. We use a three–stage progression which is explained in Section 4.4.1. Section 4.4.2 defines the basic affinity measure while Sections 4.4.3–4.4.5 define the particular measures for the three chosen models.

4.4.1   Graduated motion analysis scheme

The following structure–motion models are used:

1. Rigid object undergoing fronto–parallel translation

   Each frame is formed by a 2D translation of the reference 2D shape (Figure 4.16(a)),

   $$\mathbf{x}_i(k) = \mathbf{P}_i + \mathbf{d}(k),$$

   where $\mathbf{x}_i(k)$ is the image position of point i at time k, $\mathbf{P}_i$ is the reference position for point i, and $\mathbf{d}(k)$ is the displacement in frame k (a 2–vector).

2. Rigid plane undergoing 3D affine motion transformation

   Each frame is formed by a 2D affine transform of the reference 2D shape (Figure 4.16(b)),

   $$\mathbf{x}_i(k) = \mathbf{B}(k)\,\mathbf{P}_i + \mathbf{d}(k),$$

   where $\mathbf{B}$ is a 2×2 matrix and $\{\mathbf{B}(k), \mathbf{d}(k)\}$ describes the 2D affine transform at time k of the points $\mathbf{P}_i$ (which lie on a plane).

3. General rigid object undergoing 3D affine motion transformation

   Each frame is formed by an affine camera (projected linear combination of the reference 3D affine structure, as in Figure 4.16(b) but with an extra point),

   $$\mathbf{x}_i(k) = \mathbf{M}(k)\,\mathbf{X}_i + \mathbf{d}(k),$$

   where $\mathbf{M}$ is a 3×2 matrix and $\mathbf{X}_i$ the 3D affine structure.

We define three centroids: the *space–centroid* of the N–point cluster in a single frame ($\bar{\mathbf{x}}(k) = \sum_{i=0}^{N-1} \mathbf{x}_i(k)/N$), the *time–centroid* of a single trajectory over m frames ($\bar{\mathbf{x}}_i = \sum_{k=1}^{m} \mathbf{x}_i(k)/m$), and the *space–time centroid* of all mN points ($\bar{\mathbf{x}} = \sum_{i=0}^{N-1} \sum_{k=1}^{m} \mathbf{x}_i(k)/mN$).

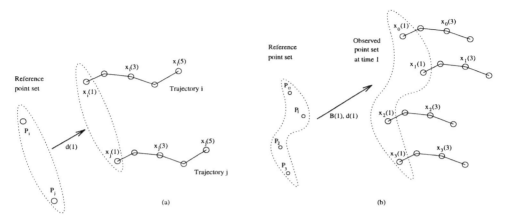

Figure 4.16: *Affinity measures for the graduated clustering scheme: (a) Pure image translation (at least two points required); (b) Planar object undergoing general 3D affine motion (at least four points required).*

4.4.2   Basic affinity measure

The affinity measure encodes the attraction between two sets of trajectories, comprising N_a and N_b trajectories respectively ($N_a, N_b \geq 1$), where $N = N_a + N_b$ and each trajectory spans m views. The measure a must: (i) be *symmetric* (i.e. $a(\ell_{ij}) = a(\ell_{ji})$), since the algorithm requires undirected graphs; (ii) be *bounded* (i.e. $a_{min} \leq a \leq a_{max}$); and (iii) attain its maximum a_{max} when the attraction is *strongest* (i.e. the similarity is greatest). All of the models in Section 4.4.1 can be formulated in terms of a noisy measurement matrix $\mathbf{V}$ of known rank (see later), whose best estimate $\hat{\mathbf{V}}$ is determined by singular value decomposition. A suitable "goodness of fit" expression to assess the quality of this estimate $\hat{\mathbf{V}}$ is [120]

$$a = \frac{\mu_1^2 + \cdots + \mu_p^2}{\mu_1^2 + \cdots + \mu_r^2},$$

where r is the actual rank of $\mathbf{V}$, p is its theoretical (desired) rank ($p \leq r$), and $\{\mu_1, \ldots, \mu_r\}$ are the r singular values in decreasing order. This function satisfies our requirements for an affinity measure, with a varying between 0 and 1 according to the quality of the SVD approximation ('1' representing a perfect match).

4.4.3   Model 1: Pure image translation

The reference points $\mathbf{P}_i$ and the displacements $\mathbf{d}(k)$ are determined by minimising

$$\epsilon_1(\mathbf{P}, \mathbf{d}) = \sum_{k=1}^{m} \sum_{i=0}^{N-1} \mid \mathbf{x}_i(k) - \mathbf{P}_i - \mathbf{d}(k) \mid^2.$$

After registering the points with respect to the space–centroids $\bar{\mathbf{x}}(k)$ and $\bar{\mathbf{P}}$, ϵ_1 becomes

$$\epsilon_1(\mathbf{P}) = \sum_{k=1}^{m} \sum_{i=0}^{N-1} \mid [\mathbf{x}_i(k) - \bar{\mathbf{x}}(k)] - [\mathbf{P}_i - \bar{\mathbf{P}}] \mid^2.$$

The solution is given by a singular value decomposition of the $2N \times m$ matrix

$$
\mathbf{V} = \begin{bmatrix}
\mathbf{x}_0(1) - \bar{\mathbf{x}}(1) & \mathbf{x}_0(2) - \bar{\mathbf{x}}(2) & \cdots & \mathbf{x}_0(m) - \bar{\mathbf{x}}(m) \\
\mathbf{x}_1(1) - \bar{\mathbf{x}}(1) & \mathbf{x}_1(2) - \bar{\mathbf{x}}(2) & \cdots & \mathbf{x}_1(m) - \bar{\mathbf{x}}(m) \\
\vdots & \vdots & & \vdots \\
\mathbf{x}_{N-1}(1) - \bar{\mathbf{x}}(1) & \mathbf{x}_{N-1}(2) - \bar{\mathbf{x}}(2) & \cdots & \mathbf{x}_{N-1}(m) - \bar{\mathbf{x}}(m)
\end{bmatrix} \tag{4.6}
$$

into a rank–1 approximation ($p = 1$), namely the $2N \times 1$ and $1 \times m$ matrices

$$
\mathbf{V} \approx \mathbf{LS} = \begin{bmatrix}
\mathbf{P}_0 - \bar{\mathbf{P}} \\
\mathbf{P}_1 - \bar{\mathbf{P}} \\
\vdots \\
\mathbf{P}_{N-1} - \bar{\mathbf{P}}
\end{bmatrix}
\begin{bmatrix} s_1 & s_2 & \cdots & s_m \end{bmatrix}.
$$

The single column vector in $\mathbf{L}$ has unit length and due to the centering operation, $\mathbf{V}$ and $\mathbf{L}$ have only $2(N-1)$ independent rows. This approximation therefore requires $m \geq 2$ and $N \geq 2$ (since $2(N-1) \geq 2$). The scalar values $\{s_1, s_2, \ldots, s_m\}$ should all be equal, since all $\mathbf{P}_i$'s have the same coefficient in ϵ_1. This equality is enforced by a variance measure[9]. A distance function, measured between the space–time centroids of the two trajectory sets ($\bar{\mathbf{x}}_a$ and $\bar{\mathbf{x}}_b$), discourages the acquisition of distant points. The final rank–1 affinity measure is thus

$$
a_1(\mathcal{C}_a, \mathcal{C}_b) = \frac{\mu_1^2}{\mu_1^2 + \cdots + \mu_r^2} \, e^{-|\bar{\mathbf{x}}_a - \bar{\mathbf{x}}_b|^2 / \sigma_d^2} \, e^{-\sum_{i=0}^{N-1}(s_i - \bar{s})^2 / \sigma_s^2} \tag{4.7}
$$

where σ_d and σ_s are Gaussian widths, and $r = \min\{2N, m\}$. This affinity function is bounded ($a_{1,min} = 0$ and $a_{1,max} = 1$), and a poor value in any property (large centroid separation, large disparity in s values, or poor shape correlation) influences the affinity negatively.

4.4.4   Model 2: Image affine transform

The planar structure $\mathbf{P}_i$ and 2D affine transformations $\{\mathbf{B}(k), \mathbf{d}(k)\}$ are determined by minimising

$$
\epsilon_2(\mathbf{P}, \mathbf{B}, \mathbf{d}) = \sum_{k=1}^{m} \sum_{i=0}^{N-1} |\, \mathbf{x}_i(k) - \mathbf{B}(k)\, \mathbf{P}_i - \mathbf{d}(k) \,|^2,
$$

or equivalently (after registration with respect to the space–centroids)

$$
\epsilon_2(\mathbf{P}, \mathbf{B}) = \sum_{k=1}^{m} \sum_{i=0}^{N-1} |\, [\mathbf{x}_i(k) - \bar{\mathbf{x}}(k)] - \mathbf{B}(k)\, [\mathbf{P}_i - \bar{\mathbf{P}}] \,|^2 .
$$

---

[9]This must be enforced explicitly since other, undesirable motions can generate a rank–1 matrix where s changes. For instance, the relative motion between a stationary point and a point moving along the direction of the line connecting them has the form $s_k(\mathbf{P}_i - \mathbf{P})$.

The solution is given by the rank–2 approximation to the $2m \times N$ matrix[10]

$$\mathbf{V} = \begin{bmatrix} \mathbf{x}_0(1) - \bar{\mathbf{x}}(1) & \mathbf{x}_1(1) - \bar{\mathbf{x}}(1) & \cdots & \mathbf{x}_{N-1}(1) - \bar{\mathbf{x}}(1) \\ \mathbf{x}_0(2) - \bar{\mathbf{x}}(2) & \mathbf{x}_1(2) - \bar{\mathbf{x}}(2) & \cdots & \mathbf{x}_{N-1}(2) - \bar{\mathbf{x}}(2) \\ \vdots & \vdots & & \vdots \\ \mathbf{x}_0(m) - \bar{\mathbf{x}}(m) & \mathbf{x}_1(m) - \bar{\mathbf{x}}(m) & \cdots & \mathbf{x}_{N-1}(m) - \bar{\mathbf{x}}(m) \end{bmatrix}, \tag{4.8}$$

whose singular value decomposition into $2m \times 2$ and $2 \times N$ matrices is:

$$\mathbf{V} \approx \mathbf{LS} = \begin{bmatrix} \mathbf{B}(1) \\ \mathbf{B}(2) \\ \vdots \\ \mathbf{B}(m) \end{bmatrix} \begin{bmatrix} \mathbf{P}_0 - \bar{\mathbf{P}} & \mathbf{P}_1 - \bar{\mathbf{P}} & \cdots & \mathbf{P}_{N-1} - \bar{\mathbf{P}} \end{bmatrix}.$$

The columns of $\mathbf{L}$ are mutually orthogonal unit vectors, the rows of $\mathbf{S}$ are mutually orthogonal, and $\mathbf{V}$ and $\mathbf{L}$ have only $N-1$ independent columns (due to the centering operation). Computing the rank–2 approximation requires $m \geq 2$ ($2m \geq 3$) and $N \geq 4$ ($N - 1 \geq 3$). The final affinity measure is similar to that of Equation (4.7), except that the approximation is now rank–2 (and $\mathbf{S}$ is unrestricted):

$$a_2(\mathcal{C}_a, \mathcal{C}_b) = \frac{\mu_1^2 + \mu_2^2}{\mu_1^2 + \cdots + \mu_r^2} \; e^{-|\bar{\mathbf{x}}_a - \bar{\mathbf{x}}_b|^2/\sigma_d^2} \tag{4.9}$$

4.4.5   Model 3: Projected 3D affine transform

The affinity measure used here is similar to Equation (4.9), but is based on the consistency of the *3D* affine structure (thus removing the planarity assumption). The affine shape $\mathbf{X}_i$ and transformations $\{\mathbf{M}(k), \mathbf{d}(k)\}$ are determined by minimising

$$\epsilon_3(\mathbf{X}, \mathbf{M}, \mathbf{d}) = \sum_{k=1}^{m} \sum_{i=0}^{N-1} |\mathbf{x}_i(k) - \mathbf{M}(k)\,\mathbf{X}_i - \mathbf{d}(k)|^2,$$

which becomes (after registration with respect to the space–centroids)

$$\epsilon_3(\mathbf{X}, \mathbf{M}) = \sum_{k=1}^{m} \sum_{i=0}^{N-1} |\,[\mathbf{x}_i(k) - \bar{\mathbf{x}}(k)] - \mathbf{M}(k)\,[\mathbf{X}_i - \bar{\mathbf{X}}]\,|^2.$$

The solution is given by the rank–3 approximation to the $2m \times N$ matrix

$$\mathbf{V} = \begin{bmatrix} \mathbf{x}_0(1) - \bar{\mathbf{x}}(1) & \mathbf{x}_1(1) - \bar{\mathbf{x}}(1) & \cdots & \mathbf{x}_{N-1}(1) - \bar{\mathbf{x}}(1) \\ \mathbf{x}_0(2) - \bar{\mathbf{x}}(2) & \mathbf{x}_1(2) - \bar{\mathbf{x}}(2) & \cdots & \mathbf{x}_{N-1}(2) - \bar{\mathbf{x}}(2) \\ \vdots & \vdots & & \vdots \\ \mathbf{x}_0(m) - \bar{\mathbf{x}}(m) & \mathbf{x}_1(m) - \bar{\mathbf{x}}(m) & \cdots & \mathbf{x}_{N-1}(m) - \bar{\mathbf{x}}(m) \end{bmatrix}, \tag{4.10}$$

---

[10]The matrix in Equation (4.6) was structured slightly differently to permit a rank–1 test. The form of Equation (4.8) *could* have been used with a rank–2 test and the proviso that $\mathbf{B}(1) = \mathbf{B}(2) = \cdots = \mathbf{B}(k) = \mathbf{I}_2$, but it is less elegant.

computed by singular value decomposition into $2m \times 3$ and $3 \times N$ matrices:

$$\mathbf{V} \approx \mathbf{LS} = \begin{bmatrix} \mathbf{M}(1) \\ \mathbf{M}(2) \\ \vdots \\ \mathbf{M}(m) \end{bmatrix} \begin{bmatrix} \mathbf{X}_0 - \bar{\mathbf{X}} & \mathbf{X}_1 - \bar{\mathbf{X}} & \cdots & \mathbf{X}_{N-1} - \bar{\mathbf{X}} \end{bmatrix}.$$

As before, the columns of $\mathbf{L}$ are mutually orthogonal unit vectors, the rows of $\mathbf{S}$ are mutually orthogonal, and $\mathbf{V}$ and $\mathbf{L}$ have only N–1 independent columns. Computing the rank–3 approximation requires $m \geq 2$ $(2m \geq 4)$ and $N \geq 5$ $(N - 1 \geq 4)$. The final affinity measure is:

$$a_3(\mathcal{C}_a, \mathcal{C}_b) = \frac{\mu_1^2 + \mu_2^2 + \mu_3^2}{\mu_1^2 + \cdots + \mu_r^2} \, e^{-|\bar{\mathbf{x}}_a - \bar{\mathbf{x}}_b|^2 / \sigma_d^2} \tag{4.11}$$

4.5 Termination criteria

As mentioned in Section 4.3, hierarchical agglomerative clustering schemes require a means of halting cluster growth, to prevent a single global cluster emerging. A *termination criterion* is therefore needed to assess the homogeneity of the grouped points. Thus, given the clusters $\mathcal{C}_a$ and $\mathcal{C}_b$, the task is to determine whether $\mathcal{C}_a \cup \mathcal{C}_b$ is a viable grouping, or whether the clusters have "grown too far".

A naive approach would be to simply threshold the affinity value; however, selecting a meaningful cut–off value is difficult. A more sophisticated approach is to use a *statistical noise model,* and if the variation in the joint cluster exceeds a specified confidence level (say 95%), the clusters are not merged. The noise model is assumed to be isotropic, additive, Gaussian image noise, making ϵ/σ^2 a χ^2 variable. If the χ^2 statistic for $\mathcal{C}_a \cup \mathcal{C}_b$ is excessively large, the merge is rejected and the growth of $\mathcal{C}_a$ and $\mathcal{C}_b$ halted. The degrees of freedom for the χ^2 tests (derived below) quantify the redundancy present in the observations.

4.5.1 Model 1

The image positions are perturbed by noise $\mathbf{w}$,

$$\mathbf{x}_i(k) = \mathbf{P}_i + \mathbf{d}(k) + \mathbf{w}_i(k),$$

where $\mathbf{w}$ is a zero–mean random variable $(E\{\mathbf{w}_i(k)\} = \mathbf{0})$, both temporally and spatially uncorrelated $(E\{\mathbf{w}_i(k)\,\mathbf{w}_j(k)\} = \delta_{ij}\,\sigma^2\,\mathbf{I}_2$ and $E\{\mathbf{w}_i(k)\,\mathbf{w}_i(\ell)\} = \delta_{k\ell}\,\sigma^2\,\mathbf{I}_2)$. The samples fill a $2N \times m$ matrix (see Equation (4.6)), of which $2(N-1)m$ elements are independent. The computed parameters fill $2N \times 1$ and $1 \times m$ matrices ($\mathbf{L}$ and $\mathbf{S}$ respectively); $\mathbf{L}$ has $2(N-1) - 1$ independent elements[11] and $\mathbf{S}$ has m independent elements. The degrees of freedom in the χ^2 variable ϵ_1/σ^2 are thus

$$d_1 = [2(N-1)m] - [2(N-1) - 1 + m] = 2mN - 3m - 2N + 3,$$

and d_1 must always exceed zero. For instance, when $m = 2$ and $N = 2$, then $d_1 = 1$. If ϵ_1/σ^2 then exceeds $\chi^2_{d_1, 95\%}$ (say), the merge is prohibited.

---

[11]The column is a unit vector and the row–pairs are centred (cf. Section 4.4.3)

4.5.2   Model 2

The noise–perturbed image positions are

$$\mathbf{x}_i(k) = \mathbf{B}(k)\,\mathbf{P}_i + \mathbf{d}(k) + \mathbf{w}_i(k),$$

and the samples fill a $2m \times N$ matrix, which has $2m(N-1)$ independent elements (see Equation (4.8)). The computed matrices are $\mathbf{L}$ $(2m \times 2)$ and $\mathbf{S}$ $(2 \times N)$, which have $2m(2)-3$ and $2(N-1)-1$ independent elements respectively[12]. The degrees of freedom in the χ^2 variable ϵ_2/σ^2 are thus

$$d_2 = [2m(N-1)] - [(4m-3) + (2N-3)] = 2mN - 6m - 2N + 6.$$

For instance, when $m = 2$ and $N = 4$, then $d_2 = 2$.

4.5.3   Model 3

The noise–perturbed image positions are

$$\mathbf{x}_i(k) = \mathbf{M}(k)\,\mathbf{X}_i + \mathbf{d}(k) + \mathbf{w}_i(k),$$

and the $2m \times N$ observation matrix has $2m(N-1)$ independent elements. The computed matrices are $\mathbf{L}$ $(2m \times 3)$ and $\mathbf{S}$ $(3 \times N)$, which have $2m(3)-6$ and $3(N-1)-3$ independent elements respectively[13]. The degrees of freedom in the χ^2 variable ϵ_3/σ^2 are thus

$$d_3 = [2m(N-1)] - [(6m-6) + (3N-6)] = 2mN - 8m - 3N + 12.$$

For example, when $m = 2$ and $N = 5$, then $d_3 = 1$.

4.6   Implementation

The three stages in the graduated clustering scheme are performed in sequence, i.e. the network first finds clusters satisfying Model 1, then Model 2, and finally Model 3. Each stage completes its growth fully before the next stage begins, with the final clusters of one stage (including singleton points which haven't yet been grouped) serving as the starting nodes for the following stage. This strategy ensures that clusters are always disjoint[14]. Each stage can therefore be considered a "pre–grouping step" for the next stage. The scheme is realised in a two–layer network (Figure 4.17):

- the first layer contains simple nodes, each representing an m–frame image trajectory;

---

[12]The two columns of $\mathbf{L}$ are mutually orthogonal unit vectors (3 constraints); the rows of $\mathbf{S}$ are mutually orthogonal (1 constraint) and are centred (2 constraints) (cf. Section 4.4.4).

[13]The three mutually orthogonal columns of $\mathbf{L}$ give 6 constraints; the centred rows in $\mathbf{S}$ along with their mutual orthogonality contribute another 6 (cf. Section 4.4.5).

[14]If unclustered, evolving MAST's were used as inputs to the next stage, the final clusters could span overlapping sets of points. Resolving the multiple ownership claims on a point would then demand sophisticated arbitration.

- the second layer contains compound nodes, which encode the MAST's (and eventually the final clusters).

Each node in the first layer (the *child*) has a corresponding *super–node* in the second layer (the *parent*) to maintain its personal MAST. A *cluster–node* is a special super–node supervising more than one child, and is formed when two or more super–nodes merge (in which case the MAST's of the children coincide). Figure 4.17 illustrates super–nodes and cluster–nodes for the example of Section 4.3.4.

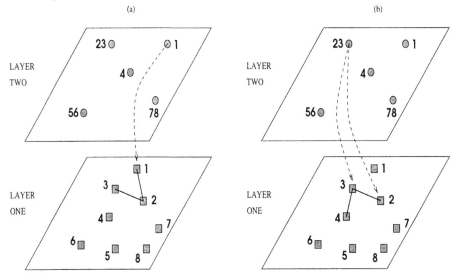

Figure 4.17: *The two–layer architecture for the example in Figure 4.14. Layer 1 contains simple nodes (squares) and layer 2 contains compound nodes (circles): (a) The super–node for p_1; (b) The cluster–node for (p_2, p_3). The states of their evolving MAST's at Step 2 are drawn on the first layer.*

4.6.1   Initialisation and basic cycle

Once the two–layer network has been created, each point p_i is assigned a set of neighbours. This establishes the initial graph $\mathcal{G}$, from which links will be selected. Section 4.3.3 noted the disadvantages of using a complete graph, where p_i is connected to every other point; *local neighbourhoods* are therefore used instead. One way to form these is to simply accept all points falling within a specified radius of p_i; however, this radius is an unwanted degree of freedom in the system, and its global nature leads to unbalanced neighbourhoods if point densities vary across the graph.

   A more elegant solution is to Delaunay triangulate the point–set [116] (Figure 4.18), with neighbours then defined as those points directly connected to p_i by a triangle side. Delaunay triangulation has several advantages: it is inherently local; it is independent of uniform scales, translations and rotations in the image plane; and it generates fewer connections in densely populated regions than the radius method. Although it does increase the connectivity of distant points, this effect (if undesirable) can be corrected for via a distance term in the affinity measure, as in Equations (4.7), (4.9) and (4.11).

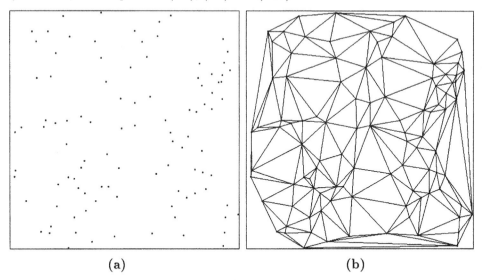

(a)   (b)

Figure 4.18: *A point–set (defined by the time–centroids of the trajectories) and its Delaunay triangulation (using the algorithm in [27]).*

All three stages follow the same basic control strategy. First, each node sets up its affinity vector **a** by calculating its attraction for the nodes falling within its spatial neighbourhood. Then a grow–merge–update cycle iterates until the final clusters for that stage emerge:

1. *Grow*:   Each non–hibernating compound node selects the best neighbour to acquire and updates its MAST vector **t**. If no neighbours remain (i.e. there are no options for expansion), the node's growth terminates.

2. *Merge*:   Each non–hibernating compound node checks its neighbours to see whether they can cluster; to do so, their MAST's must be identical and the termination criterion must approve the merge. If the merge is acceptable, one compound node (designated the "cluster–node") assumes responsibility for all the points in the cluster and the other compound nodes are destroyed; if the merge is unacceptable, the appropriate compound nodes have their growth halted.

3. *Update* :   The hibernation counters are updated (along with some other network maintenance variables).

Once all growth has ceased, the children of the remaining compound nodes (super–nodes and cluster–nodes) are the final clusters. The specifics of each stage are discussed below.

4.6.2   Stage 1 (Model 1)

The affinity measure used here is a_1 (Section 4.4.3) and the termination function is ϵ_1/σ^2 (Section 4.5.1). All clusters are initially singletons, so the affinities are computed for groups

of two trajectories. Once the network has run, *stationary clusters* are tested for, using
the criterion that both the mean speed of the points in the cluster and the variation of
these speeds must be small. Such clusters are then removed from consideration to improve
efficiency.

4.6.3   Stage 2 (Model 2)

The affinities are now recomputed using a_2 (Section 4.4.4), which requires the two compound
nodes being linked to jointly span at least four points; links not meeting this requirement
are removed (Figure 4.19(b)). The network then runs again, using the termination function
ϵ_2/σ^2 (Section 4.5.2). A removed link is reinstated during the computation as soon as the
compound nodes it links span more than three points (Figure 4.19(c)).

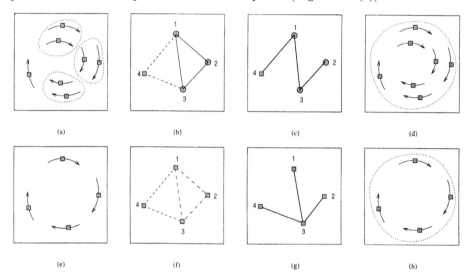

Figure 4.19: *Stage 2 clustering with a pure image rotation. Circles are cluster–nodes, squares
are singletons and dotted lines enclose clusters: (a) Input to Stage 2 (final clusters from Stage
1); (b) Initial Stage 2 graph using a_2 (links **14** and **34** are removed for linking fewer than 4
points); (c) MAST after Pass 1 (with link **14** reinstated after 1 clustered with 2 or 3); (d)
Final cluster from Stage 2 (correct); (e) Same example with fewer trajectories, so Stage 1
finds no clusters; (f) No a_2 links are possible, so pass 1 fails; (g)(h) Pass 2 finds the correct
solution using a_1 affinities and the Model 2 termination criterion.*

The clusters that finally emerge will not necessarily identify all the planar regions, since
some of the removed links may not have been reinstated. For instance, if points on a plane
π do not have sufficiently similar image trajectories for Stage 1 to partially cluster them,
then no point on π has a large enough neighbour to act as a catalyst for the cluster (Figure 4.19(e)). A second pass is therefore performed, using only the removed links which
weren't reinstated[15]. The affinity measure reverts to a_1 for this second pass, though the
termination condition remains ϵ_2/σ^2. Thus, points which possess some degree of attraction

---

[15]No other points are included in Pass 2 since they had the opportunity to incorporate the removed

for their neighbours (based on local similarity), albeit insufficient to satisfy the pure translation model, can still be tested for planarity. The termination condition tests these potential
clusters as soon as they span 4 or more points; clusters with fewer points are accepted on
trust, since they will anyhow be terminated later if they are invalid.

There are two remarks to make about this two–pass solution. First, it might appear
feasible to combine the a_1 and a_2 affinity measures in the same network: this would avoid
the need to remove any links (those linking fewer than four points could simply use the
a_1 measure), and would permit a single–pass solution. Unfortunately, two different affinity
measures would be competing against each other, and there is no principled way to compare
their values. Second, the two–pass solution still doesn't guarantee that all planar structures
will be found; the scheme still relies on the assumption that points belonging together will
exhibit some degree of local similarity in their trajectories. Section 4.7 demonstrates that
this is a perfectly reasonable assumption when, as in our application, the points are densely
distributed and the motions small.

4.6.4   Stage 3 (Model 3)

This stage duplicates the two–pass procedure of Stage 1, the only differences being that the
affinity measure is a_3 (Section 4.4.5), which requires 5 points, and the termination condition
is ϵ_3/σ^2 (Section 4.5.3).

4.7   Results

4.7.1   Synthetic data

Figure 4.18(a) shows a randomly generated 3D point-set containing two independently moving objects and projected onto a weak perspective camera. The image coordinates (in a
256×256 image) are perturbed by Gaussian noise with $\sigma = 0.5$ pixels. In Figure 4.20, the
objects translate in the image plane against a stationary background, and Stage 1 of the
algorithm successfully identifies the objects.

Figure 4.21 shows more general motions in the image plane, with the objects rotating and
translating against a moving background: the background points are clustered together after
Stage 1, and the two objects are correctly identified after Stage 2. (The pure translation
model obviously cannot segment the rotating objects; Stage 1 simply forms partial clusters
to be collected into a coherent whole by the more powerful affinity measure of Stage 2.)
Finally, Figure 4.22 shows the objects rotating and translating in 3D, along with the Stage
3 clusters.

---

points on Pass 1. Pass 2 simply caters for the possibility that the isolated points may form clusters among
themselves.

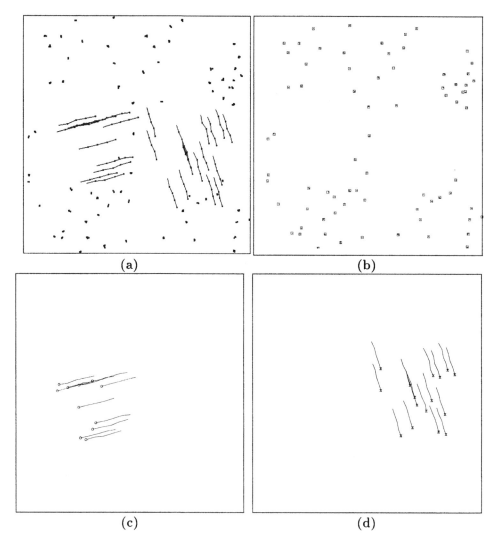

(a)   (b)

(c)   (d)

Figure 4.20: *Clustering with pure image translation: (a) Input trajectories (objects undergoing fronto–parallel translation* $\mathbf{d}_1(k) = (4, 1)$ *and* $\mathbf{d}_2(k) = (-1, 3)$ *); (b)(c)(d) Final clusters (after Stage 1).*

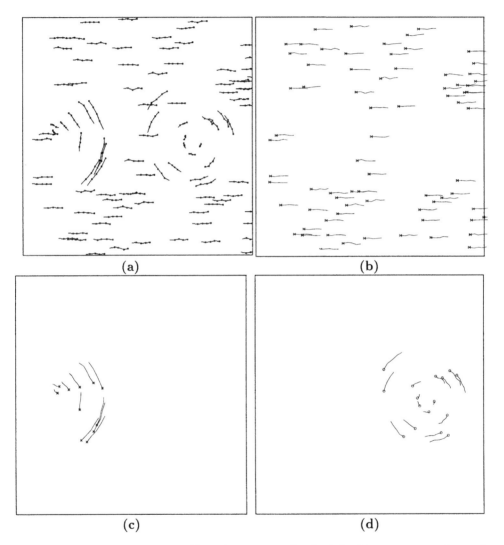

Figure 4.21: *Image plane motion (Beverley sequence): the left object rotates and translates* ($\mathbf{d} = (0,2), \theta = 8°$), *the right object rotates* ($\theta = -7°$) *and the background translates* ($\mathbf{d} = (2,0)$): *(a) Input trajectories; (b)(c)(d) Final clusters (after Stage 2).*

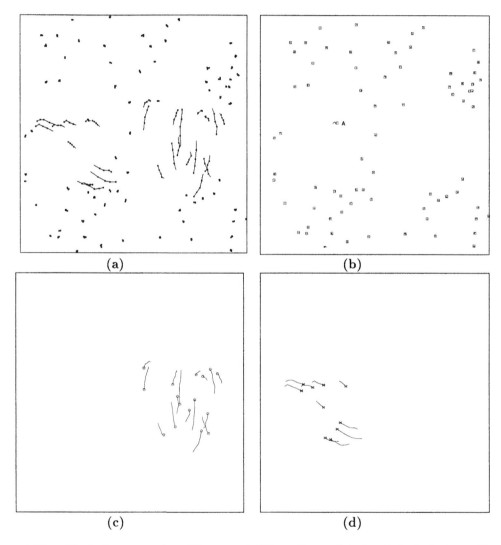

Figure 4.22: *Clustering example with general 3D motion: (a) Input trajectories with*
$(\theta_1, \phi_1, \rho_1) = (4°, 45°, 10°)$ *and* $(\theta_2, \phi_2, \rho_2) = (-3°, 0°, 9°)$ *(see Appendix D.3 for notation);*
(b) Final clusters (after Stage 3).

4.7.2   Real data

Figure 4.23 shows a moving motor vehicle filmed from a stationary camera. The image trajectories over several frames are given, along with the final clusters. The individual clusters are shown in more detail in Figure 4.24, illustrating that the algorithm simultaneously groups point and rejects outliers (electing not to incorporate a point when it exceeds the tolerable statistical variation in the point–set). Clearly, the scheme has coped with sparse, noisy and partially incorrect data. (Image noise was assumed to be $\sigma = 0.7$ pixels throughout.)

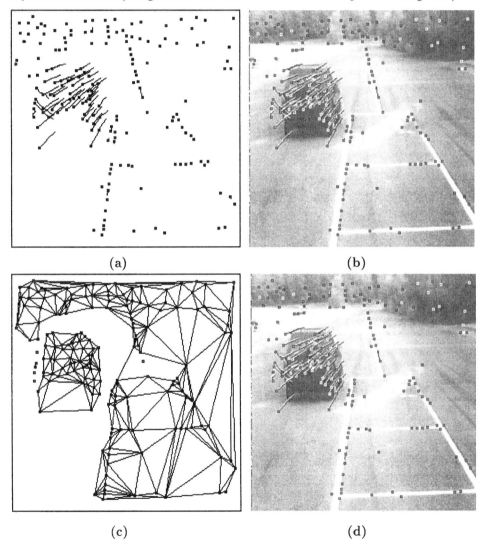

(a)   (b)

(c)   (d)

Figure 4.23: *Segmenting a moving car from a static background (squares indicate corner positions in the first image): (a) Initial trajectories (taken over 4 frames); (b) Trajectories superimposed on final image; (c)(d) Valid Delaunay edges, demarcating the segmented regions. Inconsistent matches are excluded automatically from the clusters (see Figure 4.24).*

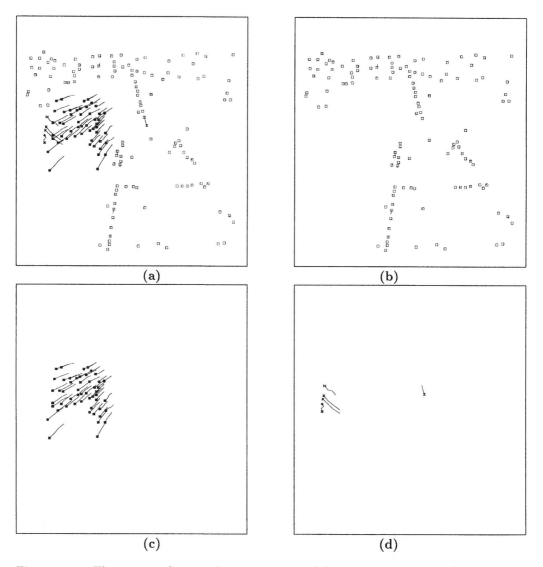

Figure 4.24: *The groups of points for Figure 4.23: (a) Input trajectories; (b) Background cluster; (c) Car cluster; (d) Leftover points.*

Figure 4.25 shows a moving object (a mannequin head) seen from a translating camera and the subsequent segmentation. The excluded corner is a "false corner" caused by the conjunction of the top of the head and the vertical pillar. Finally, Figure 4.26 shows two rotating heads, one nodding and one shaking. A moving 5–frame window is used to form the clusters, and the size of the groups change due to points disappearing and new points coming into view. The trajectory of the centroid of each cluster is also shown.

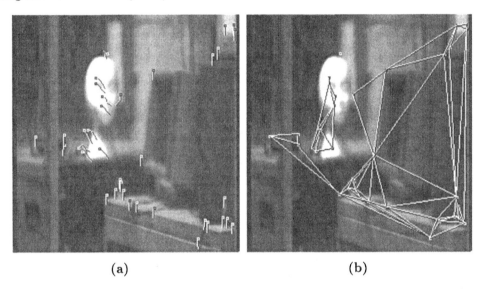

(a)   (b)

Figure 4.25: *Segmenting a moving head from a moving background: (a) The flow vectors; (b) The groups of points.*

4.7.3   Discussion

The above algorithm could be improved in several ways. First, cluster growth is currently monotonic; there is no facility to "split" a group once formed. While overzealous acquisition can be prevented by conservative limits on the termination confidence levels, this can also result in many small clusters that refuse to merge (e.g. the left head in Figure 4.26(h)). A solution to this problem would be to relax the limits and then allow a redistribution of points between clusters, e.g. start with the motion parameters of the existing clusters and find all the points most consistent with them. This solves the problem illustrated in Figure 4.22(b) (where the background incorrectly acquires point A) by returning wrongly acquired points to their correct clusters.

Second, although bootstrapping the affine structure groupings by means of locally similar image trajectories generally works well when the points are dense and the motions are small, the procedure can fail if initial seeds cannot be established. For instance, the trajectories in Figure 4.22 vary significantly, and if the background moved in such a way that its trajectories were similar to those of the moving objects, the clustering would fail. In such a case, however, the algorithm simply fails to form clusters; it doesn't form *incorrect* clusters (the termination

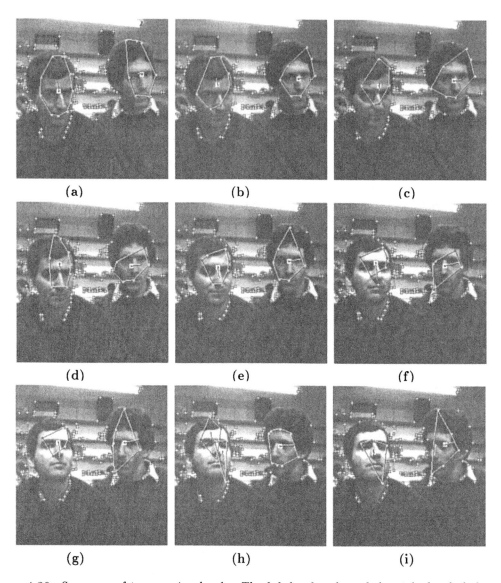

(a)   (b)   (c)

(d)   (e)   (f)

(g)   (h)   (i)

Figure 4.26: *Sequence of two moving heads. The left head nods and the right head shakes. Crosses indicate background points, and a convex hull is drawn around the moving points. The centroid of these points (along with its trajectory) is also shown, with the marker indicating the current centroid position.*

criterion prevents this). This conservatism ensures graceful degradation, leaving scope for more sophisticated/expensive pre–grouping techniques (e.g. exhaustive enumeration) to be used instead.   No single technique can work in every situation, so it is important that algorithms recognise when they are failing.

Finally, the algorithm only operates on a single graph $\mathcal{G}$; for instance, the clusters for the sequence in Figure 4.26 were recomputed anew for each set of frames. It would obviously aid efficiency to simply *update* the previous segmentation when a new graph $\mathcal{G}'$ is presented.

4.8   Conclusions

This chapter has presented a local, parallel clustering scheme anchored in a graph theory framework. The clusters are formed by applying a novel cluster definition to simultaneously evolving MAST's. The resulting partitions have provable properties – in short, the clusters are identical to those of a sequential, hierarchical, agglomerative, single–link clustering algorithm. Efficiency has been considerably enhanced by our "trust thy neighbour" philosophy, whereby adjacent processors cooperate to form the final partition.

This framework has been applied to the problem of segmenting moving 3D objects under affine viewing conditions, using multiple frames. The solution employs a displacement–based approach with a hierarchy of models that group points on the basis of their structural integrity over time. Termination criteria with a sound statistical basis have been developed, and the network has been implemented and run successfully on real image sequences.

Chapter 5

Affine epipolar geometry

5.1 Introduction

Chapter 3 introduced the affine camera and this chapter derives its epipolar geometry. The concept of an epipolar line is familiar in the stereo and motion literature [9, 13, 43, 57, 87, 112], and Figure 5.1 shows the classical construction for a perspective stereo–pair. Epipolar geometry provides a useful relationship between two different images of a scene point: given $\mathbf{x}_i$ in I_1, the corresponding point $\mathbf{x}'_i$ in I_2 is constrained to lie on a line in I_2 (the epipolar line), namely the intersection between the epipolar plane and I_2.

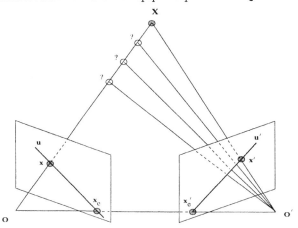

Figure 5.1: *Perspective epipolar geometry. The baseline connecting optic centres* $\mathbf{O}$ *and* $\mathbf{O}'$ *intersects the image planes at the epipoles* $\mathbf{x}_e$ *and* $\mathbf{x}'_e$. *A point* $\mathbf{X}$, *together with the baseline, defines an epipolar plane, which cuts the image planes in the epipolar lines* $\mathbf{u}$ *and* $\mathbf{u}'$. *The point* $\mathbf{x}'$ *corresponding to* $\mathbf{x}$ *must lie on the epipolar line* $\mathbf{u}'$. *All epipolar lines pass through the epipole.*

The epipolar constraint is widely used in structure and motion applications for assisting the correspondence process [16], generating new views of objects [35], segmenting moving objects [147, 168], calibrating cameras [42], and computing motion parameters [168]. This chapter makes the following contributions:

- The epipolar geometry of the *affine camera* is defined (Section 5.2) and its special fundamental matrix is derived (Section 5.3). No camera calibration is needed at this juncture.

- A reliable solution is provided for the epipolar geometry parameters (Section 5.4), which underpin subsequent motion computations (cf. Chapter 7). Three least squares algorithms based on image distances are evaluated, and a 4D linear method is shown to be optimal. Experiments on real images are described (Section 5.5).

- Affine epipolar geometry is interpreted in terms of CI space (Section 5.6).

5.2   The affine epipolar line

Figure 5.2 shows the epipolar geometry for two *affine* cameras. All projection rays are parallel (the optic centre lies at infinity), and because the affine camera preserves parallelism, the epipolar lines are also parallel, i.e. the epipoles are situated at infinity in the image planes. To derive the equation of an affine epipolar line, recall Equation (3.21),

$$\boxed{\mathbf{x}'_i = \boldsymbol{\Gamma}\,\mathbf{x}_i + Z_i\,\mathbf{d} + \boldsymbol{\varepsilon}} \tag{5.1}$$

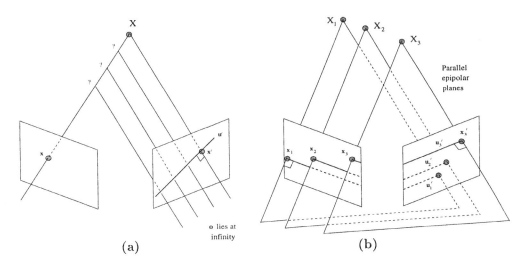

Figure 5.2: *Affine epipolar geometry: (a) All projection rays are parallel to one another (the optic centre lies at infinity) and perpendicular to the image plane.* **X** *lies along the ray from the optic centre through* **x**, *and the projection of this ray into* I_2 *gives the epipolar line* **u**′, *along which* **x**′ *must lie; (b) All epipolar planes (and hence lines) are parallel, and their normal is parallel to the line of intersection of the two image planes.*

where $\boldsymbol{\Gamma}$, $\mathbf{d}$ and $\boldsymbol{\varepsilon}$ depend only on the camera parameters $\{\mathbf{M}, \mathbf{t}, \mathbf{M}', \mathbf{t}'\}$. Equation (5.1) shows that the point $\mathbf{x}'_i$ associated with $\mathbf{x}_i$ lies on a line in the second image with offset $\boldsymbol{\Gamma}\,\mathbf{x}_i + \boldsymbol{\varepsilon}$ and direction $\hat{\mathbf{d}} = \mathbf{d}/\,|\,\mathbf{d}\,|$ (Figure 5.3). The unknown depth Z_i determines how far along this line $\mathbf{x}'_i$ lies. The epipolar lines are clearly parallel ($\hat{\mathbf{d}}$ is constant) and have different offsets (depending on $\mathbf{x}_i$). Inverting Equation (5.1) yields the epipolar line for $\mathbf{x}_i$ in the first image, with offset $\boldsymbol{\Gamma}^{-1}(\mathbf{x}'_i - \boldsymbol{\varepsilon})$ and direction parallel to $\boldsymbol{\Gamma}^{-1}\mathbf{d}$ (cf. Equation (3.22)):

$$\boxed{\mathbf{x}_i = \boldsymbol{\Gamma}^{-1}(\mathbf{x}'_i - \boldsymbol{\varepsilon}) - Z_i\,\boldsymbol{\Gamma}^{-1}\mathbf{d}} \tag{5.2}$$

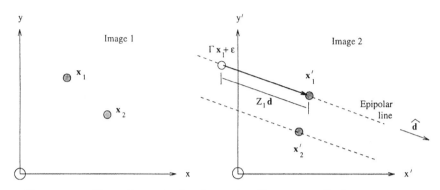

Figure 5.3: *The affine epipolar line:* $\mathbf{x}'_i = \boldsymbol{\Gamma}\,\mathbf{x}_i + \boldsymbol{\varepsilon} + Z_i\,\mathbf{d}$.

Finally, taking difference vectors $\boldsymbol{\Delta}\mathbf{x}_i = \mathbf{x}_i - \mathbf{x}_0$ and $\boldsymbol{\Delta}\mathbf{x}'_i = \mathbf{x}'_i - \mathbf{x}'_0$ gives translation–invariant versions of these formulae[1], eliminating $\boldsymbol{\varepsilon}$ (and hence $\mathbf{D}$, $\mathbf{t}$ and $\mathbf{t}'$):

$$\boldsymbol{\Delta}\mathbf{x}'_i = \mathbf{B}' \begin{bmatrix} \Delta X_i \\ \Delta Y_i \end{bmatrix} + \Delta Z_i\,\mathbf{b}' = \boldsymbol{\Gamma}\,\boldsymbol{\Delta}\mathbf{x}_i + \Delta Z_i\,\mathbf{d} \tag{5.3}$$

$$\boldsymbol{\Delta}\mathbf{x}_i = \mathbf{B} \begin{bmatrix} \Delta X_i \\ \Delta Y_i \end{bmatrix} + \Delta Z_i\,\mathbf{b} = \boldsymbol{\Gamma}^{-1}\boldsymbol{\Delta}\mathbf{x}'_i - \Delta Z_i\,\boldsymbol{\Gamma}^{-1}\mathbf{d} \tag{5.4}$$

An alternative expression of the affine epipolar line can be derived in terms of a local coordinate frame, based on the analysis in [35]. Equation (3.25) provides two linear equations in the three unknowns $\{\alpha_i, \beta_i, \gamma_i\}$, and $\{\alpha_i, \beta_i\}$ are eliminated by expressing them in terms of γ_i,

$$\alpha_i = \frac{(\boldsymbol{\Delta}\mathbf{x}_i \cdot \mathbf{e}_2^{\perp}) - \gamma_i\,(\mathbf{e}_3 \cdot \mathbf{e}_2^{\perp})}{\mathbf{e}_1 \cdot \mathbf{e}_2^{\perp}} \quad \text{and} \quad \beta_i = -\frac{(\boldsymbol{\Delta}\mathbf{x}_i \cdot \mathbf{e}_1^{\perp}) - \gamma_i\,(\mathbf{e}_3 \cdot \mathbf{e}_1^{\perp})}{\mathbf{e}_1 \cdot \mathbf{e}_2^{\perp}},$$

where $(a, b)^{\perp} = (b, -a)$ and $\mathbf{e}_1 \cdot \mathbf{e}_2^{\perp} = -\mathbf{e}_2 \cdot \mathbf{e}_1^{\perp}$. In the second view, then, $\mathbf{x}'_i$ lies on the line

$$\mathbf{x}'_i = \mathbf{x}'_0 + \alpha_i\,\mathbf{e}'_1 + \beta_i\,\mathbf{e}'_2 + \gamma_i\,\mathbf{e}'_3,$$

that is,

$$\boldsymbol{\Delta}\mathbf{x}'_i = \frac{(\boldsymbol{\Delta}\mathbf{x}_i \cdot \mathbf{e}_2^{\perp})\,\mathbf{e}'_1 - (\boldsymbol{\Delta}\mathbf{x}_i \cdot \mathbf{e}_1^{\perp})\,\mathbf{e}'_2}{\mathbf{e}_1 \cdot \mathbf{e}_2^{\perp}} + \gamma_i \left(\mathbf{e}'_3 - \frac{(\mathbf{e}_3 \cdot \mathbf{e}_2^{\perp})\,\mathbf{e}'_1 - (\mathbf{e}_3 \cdot \mathbf{e}_1^{\perp})\,\mathbf{e}'_2}{\mathbf{e}_1 \cdot \mathbf{e}_2^{\perp}} \right). \tag{5.5}$$

This is an epipolar line parameterised by γ_i, and has the same form as Equation (5.3), e.g. $\boldsymbol{\Gamma} \equiv (\mathbf{e}'_1\,\mathbf{e}_2^{\perp\mathsf{T}} - \mathbf{e}'_2\,\mathbf{e}_1^{\perp\mathsf{T}})/(\mathbf{e}_1 \cdot \mathbf{e}_2^{\perp})$, $\Delta Z_i \equiv \gamma_i$, and so on.

---

[1]This formulation ties in neatly with the scheme of Koenderink and van Doorn [79] (see Section 3.4.4). Three world points $\{\mathbf{X}_0, \mathbf{X}_1, \mathbf{X}_2\}$ define the reference plane π_r, establishing the X–Y axes of the affine world frame (with $\mathbf{X}_0$ the reference point). Since these points lie on π_r, $\Delta Z_1 = \Delta Z_2 = 0$. From Equation (5.3), a 2D affine transform then maps the image I_1 of π_r to its image I_2, that is, $\boldsymbol{\Delta}\mathbf{x}'_i = \boldsymbol{\Gamma}\,\boldsymbol{\Delta}\mathbf{x}_i$ with $\boldsymbol{\Gamma} = [\boldsymbol{\Delta}\mathbf{x}'_1\ \boldsymbol{\Delta}\mathbf{x}'_2][\boldsymbol{\Delta}\mathbf{x}_1\ \boldsymbol{\Delta}\mathbf{x}_2]^{-1}$. A point $\mathbf{X}_3$ lying *off* π then satisfies $\boldsymbol{\Delta}\mathbf{x}'_3 = \boldsymbol{\Gamma}\,\boldsymbol{\Delta}\mathbf{x}_3 + \Delta Z_3\,\mathbf{d}$, where $\boldsymbol{\Gamma}\,\boldsymbol{\Delta}\mathbf{x}_3$ is the "piercing point" of $\mathbf{X}_3$, that is, the position it would project to in I_2 if it *did* lie on π. The difference vector $\Delta Z_3\,\mathbf{d}$ (known since both $\boldsymbol{\Delta}\mathbf{x}_3$ and $\boldsymbol{\Delta}\mathbf{x}'_3$ are known) yields the direction of $\mathbf{d}$, $\hat{\mathbf{d}}$, and the scaled depth coordinate $\Delta Z_3\,|\mathbf{d}|$. A second point lying off π ($\mathbf{X}_4$) gives a second scaled depth $\Delta Z_4\,|\mathbf{d}|$, and the third affine coordinate is then formed from the ratio $\Delta Z_4/\Delta Z_3$.

5.3   The affine fundamental matrix

Equation (5.1) defined the epipolar line in parametric form; an *explicit* form is obtained by eliminating the depths Z_i, giving a single equation in the *image measurables*,

$$(\mathbf{x}'_i - \mathbf{\Gamma}\mathbf{x}_i - \boldsymbol{\varepsilon}) \cdot \mathbf{d}^{\perp} = 0, \qquad (5.6)$$

where $\mathbf{d}^{\perp}$ is the perpendicular[2] to $\mathbf{d}$. Equation (5.6) can also be written

$$\boxed{a\,x'_i + b\,y'_i + c\,x_i + d\,y_i + e = 0} \qquad (5.7)$$

with $(a, b)^{\mathsf{T}} = \mathbf{d}^{\perp}$, $(c, d)^{\mathsf{T}} = -\mathbf{\Gamma}^{\mathsf{T}}\mathbf{d}^{\perp}$ and $e = -\boldsymbol{\varepsilon}^{\mathsf{T}}\mathbf{d}^{\perp}$. This *affine epipolar constraint equation* [173] is a linear equation in the unknown constants $a \ldots e$, which depend only on the camera parameters and the relative motion. Only the *ratios* of the five parameters $a \ldots e$ can be computed, so Equation (5.7) has only *four* independent degrees of freedom. The difference vector form is

$$a\,\Delta x'_i + b\,\Delta y'_i + c\,\Delta x_i + d\,\Delta y_i = 0. \qquad (5.8)$$

Equation (5.7) may also be expressed in the form of a *fundamental matrix* $\mathbf{F}_A$,

$$\mathbf{p}'^{\mathsf{T}} \mathbf{F}_A \, \mathbf{p} = \begin{bmatrix} x'_i & y'_i & 1 \end{bmatrix} \begin{bmatrix} 0 & 0 & a \\ 0 & 0 & b \\ c & d & e \end{bmatrix} \begin{bmatrix} x_i \\ y_i \\ 1 \end{bmatrix} = 0, \qquad (5.9)$$

where $\mathbf{p}' = (x', y', 1)^{\mathsf{T}}$ and $\mathbf{p} = (x, y, 1)^{\mathsf{T}}$ are homogeneous 3–vectors representing points in the image plane. The matrix $\mathbf{F}_A$ has maximum rank two, and generalises the form given in [173] (which had $e = 1$). The epipolar lines corresponding to $\mathbf{p}$ and $\mathbf{p}'$ are $\mathbf{u}' = \mathbf{F}_A\mathbf{p}$ and $\mathbf{u} = \mathbf{F}_A^{\mathsf{T}}\mathbf{p}'$ respectively, where $\mathbf{u} = (u_1, u_2, u_3)^{\mathsf{T}}$ represents the line $u_1 x + u_2 y + u_3 = 0$ (and similarly for $\mathbf{u}'$). The *normal* to $\mathbf{u}$ thus lies in the direction $(u_1, u_2) = (c, d)$, while for $\mathbf{u}'$, the normal is $(u'_1, u'_2) = (a, b)$. The form of $\mathbf{F}_A$ in Equation (5.9) is a special case of the general 3×3 fundamental matrix $\mathbf{F}$ used in stereo and motion algorithms (e.g. [42, 89]). A synthetic example is shown in Figure 5.4. The solution of Equation (5.7) does not require a calibrated camera, since an affine model has been used throughout.

5.4   Solving the affine epipolar equation

Equation (5.7) is defined up to a scale factor, so only four point correspondences are needed to solve for the four independent degrees of freedom (conditions for *existence* of a solution are discussed later). When n correspondences are available ($n > 4$), it is advantageous to use *all* the points, since this improves the accuracy of the solution, allows detection of (and hence provides immunity to) outliers, and obviates the need to select a minimal point set.

However, the presence of "noise" in the overdetermined system means that points won't lie exactly on their epipolar lines (Figure 5.5), and an appropriate minimisation is required.

---

[2] Orthogonality is not defined in an affine plane, but we could equally well have resolved *parallel* to $\mathbf{d}^{\perp}$.

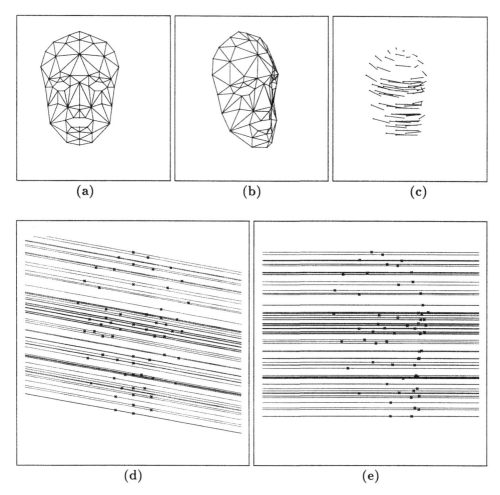

Figure 5.4: *Epipolar lines for noise–free synthetic data with* $\mathbf{n} = (0.00, 0.70, -0.13, -0.71)$*:* *(a)(b) Images* I_1 *and* I_2 *of a wire–frame face; (c) Motion vectors; (d)(e) Epipolar lines for (a) and (b). Note that the epipolar lines are parallel whereas the motion vectors are not.*

Optimal estimation requires knowledge of the image noise distribution, which depends on the specific camera, its lens and the image processing performed. It may also depend on the camera aspect ratio, though with suitable scaling, on no other calibration parameter. When necessary, we assume image noise to be Gaussian and isotropic[3] and return to the validity of this assumption later.

The following sections discuss three minimum variance cost functions involving the epipolar parameters, and differing in the image distances minimised. These functions are assessed in terms of accuracy and complexity.

---

[3]Kanatani [74] discusses the case of anisotropic image noise.

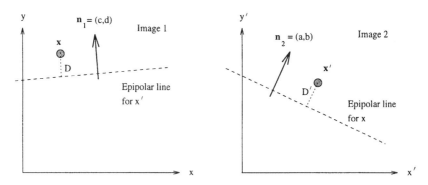

Figure 5.5: *The normals to the epipolar lines are n_1 and n_2. Noise displaces a point x' in I_2 from the epipolar line associated with its counterpart x by perpendicular distance D'. A similar displacement by D occurs in I_1.*

5.4.1   Notation

The two image coordinates of a corresponding point are combined into a vector $\mathbf{r}_i = (x'_i, y'_i, x_i, y_i)^\top$. The centroid of these 4–vectors is $\bar{\mathbf{r}}$ and the centred points are denoted $\mathbf{v}_i = \mathbf{r}_i - \bar{\mathbf{r}}$. The 4D normal vector is defined as $\mathbf{n} = (a, b, c, d)^\top$, with $\mathbf{n}_1 = (c, d)^\top$ and $\mathbf{n}_2 = (a, b)^\top$ being the 2D normal vectors to the epipolars in I_1 and I_2 respectively. The perpendicular distance D'_i between x'_i and its associated epipolar line in I_2 is

$$D'_i = \frac{ax'_i + by'_i + cx_i + dy_i + e}{\sqrt{a^2 + b^2}},$$

and the counterpart distance D_i in I_1 is

$$D_i = \frac{ax'_i + by'_i + cx_i + dy_i + e}{\sqrt{c^2 + d^2}},$$

as in Figure 5.5. The real, symmetric scatter matrix $\mathbf{W}$ is partitioned into four 2×2 matrices as follows:

$$\mathbf{W} = \sum_{i=0}^{n-1} \mathbf{v}_i \mathbf{v}_i^\top = \begin{bmatrix} \mathbf{K}_1 & \mathbf{K}_2 \\ \mathbf{K}_2^\top & \mathbf{K}_3 \end{bmatrix} = \begin{bmatrix} \sum_i (x'_i - \bar{x}')\,(x'_i - \bar{x}')^\top & \sum_i (x'_i - \bar{x}')\,(x_i - \bar{x})^\top \\ \sum_i (x_i - \bar{x})\,(x'_i - \bar{x}')^\top & \sum_i (x_i - \bar{x})\,(x_i - \bar{x})^\top \end{bmatrix}.$$

5.4.2   Cost functions

We consider the following three cost functions:

$$E_1(\mathbf{n}, e) = \left(\frac{1}{a^2 + b^2} + \frac{1}{c^2 + d^2} \right) \sum_{i=0}^{n-1} (ax'_i + by'_i + cx_i + dy_i + e)^2 \qquad (5.10)$$

$$E_2(\mathbf{n}, e) = \frac{1}{a^2 + b^2} \sum_{i=0}^{n-1} (ax'_i + by'_i + cx_i + dy_i + e)^2 \qquad (5.11)$$

$$E_3(\mathbf{n}, e) = \frac{1}{a^2 + b^2 + c^2 + d^2} \sum_{i=0}^{n-1} (ax'_i + by'_i + cx_i + dy_i + e)^2 \qquad (5.12)$$

All three functions minimise the sum of squares of a perpendicular distance measure (see below), all are *scale–invariant* (i.e. if $\{\mathbf{n}, e\}$ is a solution, then so is $\{k\mathbf{n}, ke\}$ where k is a non–zero scalar), and all can be minimised over e directly, giving $e = -\mathbf{n}^\top \bar{\mathbf{r}}$ (see Appendix B).

1. Cost function E_1

   E_1 sums the squared perpendicular image distances over I_1 and I_2: $E_1 = \sum_{i=0}^{n-1} D_i^2 + (D_i')^2$. The solution satisfies a system of non–linear simultaneous equations (Appendix B.1)

$$\left(1 + \frac{1}{s^2}\right) \begin{bmatrix} \mathbf{K}_1 & \mathbf{K}_2 \\ s^4\, \mathbf{K}_2^\top & s^4\, \mathbf{K}_3 \end{bmatrix} \begin{bmatrix} \mathbf{n}_2 \\ \mathbf{n}_1 \end{bmatrix} = \lambda \begin{bmatrix} \mathbf{n}_2 \\ \mathbf{n}_1 \end{bmatrix}, \quad |\mathbf{n}_2|^2 = 1,$$

   where $s = |\mathbf{n}_1| / |\mathbf{n}_2|$ is a scale factor[4] and λ is a Lagrange multiplier. The solution requires non–linear minimisation, the minimum cost being $E_{1,min} = \lambda(1 + 1/s^2)$.

2. Cost function E_2

   E_2 sums the squared perpendicular distances in a single image (I_2): $E_2 = \sum_i (D_i')^2$. The normal $\mathbf{n}_2$ satisfies a 2D eigenvector equation (Appendix B.2)

$$(\mathbf{K}_1 - \mathbf{K}_2\, \mathbf{K}_3^{-1}\, \mathbf{K}_2^\top)\, \mathbf{n}_2 = \lambda_1\, \mathbf{n}_2, \quad |\mathbf{n}_2|^2 = 1,$$

   and is the eigenvector associated with the minimum eigenvalue λ_1. Then $\mathbf{n}_1$ is given by $\mathbf{n}_1 = -\mathbf{K}_3^{-1}\, \mathbf{K}_2^\top \mathbf{n}_2$, giving minimum cost $E_{2,min} = \lambda_1$. A similar algorithm can be obtained by minimising the distances in I_1, namely $\sum_i D_i^2$.

3. Cost function E_3

   Equation (5.7) can be written as $\mathbf{r}_i \cdot \mathbf{n} + e = 0$, where $\mathbf{n}$ is the normal to a hyperplane in 4D and $(\mathbf{r}_i \cdot \mathbf{n} + e)/|\mathbf{n}|$ is the 4D perpendicular distance from $\mathbf{r}_i$ to this hyperplane. E_3 sums these squared 4D perpendicular distances,

$$E_3 = \sum_{i=0}^{n-1} \frac{(\mathbf{r}_i \cdot \mathbf{n} + e)^2}{|\mathbf{n}|^2} = \sum_{i=0}^{n-1} \frac{(\mathbf{v}_i \cdot \mathbf{n})^2}{|\mathbf{n}|^2} = \frac{\mathbf{n}^\top \mathbf{W}\, \mathbf{n}}{|\mathbf{n}|^2}. \tag{5.13}$$

   This is the classic linear least squares problem. The solution employs *orthogonal regression* (see Appendix B.3) and satisfies the eigenvector equation

$$\mathbf{W}\, \mathbf{n} = \lambda_1\, \mathbf{n}, \quad |\mathbf{n}|^2 = 1$$

   where $\mathbf{n}$ is the unit eigenvector corresponding to the minimum eigenvalue λ_1. The minimum cost is $E_{3,min} = \lambda_1$. We show later that minimising E_3 is equivalent to minimising ϵ_{tk} (see Section 3.5), the point–to–point image distance between the observed points and the locations obtained by projecting the computed affine structure using the computed affine cameras.

---

[4]Section 7.3 provides an alternative definition for s, namely the ratio of the average depth planes Z_{ave}/Z'_{ave}. Thus s effectively measures divergence ($s > 1$ when the object approaches the camera).

5.4.3   Discussion and previous work

The three above–mentioned functions all involve image distances (a fact not immediately apparent for E_3 but which we show to be true); this is important since the observations are made in the image and the system noise originates there [55]. Various arguments can then be advanced in favour of the different cost functions; we show that E_3 is superior to E_1 and E_2 in several respects.

Faugeras et al. [42, 89] evaluated candidate cost functions for computing the fundamental matrix $\mathbf{F}$ of a *projective* camera; E_1 is the affine analogue of their favoured non–linear criterion (using distances to epipolar lines[5]) and E_3 is the analogue of their linear criterion (using the eigenvector method). They criticised the latter approach for failing to impose the rank constraint[6] on $\mathbf{F}$ and for introducing bias into the computation by shifting the epipole towards the image centre. In the *affine* case, however, $\mathbf{F}_A$ is *guaranteed* to have a maximum rank of two (cf. Equation (5.9)) and the epipole lies at infinity, removing these two objections against the linear method.

Furthermore, although E_3 may be interpreted as a 4D algebraic distance measure, it is actually an *image* distance measure based on point–to–point (rather than point–to–line) distances. It is derived directly from the ϵ_{tk} cost function of Section 3.5, i.e.

$$E_3 \equiv \epsilon_{tk} = \sum_{i=0}^{n-1} |\mathbf{x}_i - \mathbf{M}\mathbf{X}_i - \mathbf{t}|^2 + \sum_{i=0}^{n-1} |\mathbf{x}'_i - \mathbf{M}'\mathbf{X}_i - \mathbf{t}'|^2,$$

as proven in Appendix B.4. Thus, E_3 has all the advantages of ϵ_{tk} discussed in Section 3.5.1, and the relationship will be further explored in Section 5.6.

Finally, when $s = 1$ (so $|\mathbf{n}_1| = |\mathbf{n}_2|$), the solutions returned by *all three methods* coincide[7]. Thus, when the scale change is small, the stationary point $\mathbf{n} = (a, b, c, d)^\top$ of E_3 is an excellent approximation to that of E_1. The unity scale condition occurs frequently with an affine camera, which itself is only valid over small scale changes (otherwise perspective effects become significant). When the scale change is large, E_3 provides a good initial estimate for E_1. In short, for an affine camera, the linear method (E_3) not only minimises a meaningful quantity, but also generally performs as well as its non–linear counterpart (E_1).

Like E_3, E_2 also arises from a point–based minimisation (cf. Equation (5.1)), i.e.

$$E_2 \equiv \epsilon_h = \sum_{i=0}^{n-1} |\mathbf{x}'_i - \Gamma \mathbf{x}_i - Z_i \mathbf{d} - \boldsymbol{\varepsilon}|^2,$$

which minimises the distance in I_2 between the observed location and the location predicted by the computed motion parameters $\{\Gamma, \mathbf{d}\}$ and affine coordinates Z_i. (See Appendix B.4 for proof.) This approach has several drawbacks. First, Appendix B.2 shows that an obscure constraint is imposed implicitly on the other image, namely $\sum_i D_i \Delta \mathbf{x}_i = \mathbf{0}$ (the distribution

---

[5]They also weighted each point by its inverse distance to the epipole; in the affine case, the epipole lies at infinity so all points are weighted equally.

[6]The constraint rank($\mathbf{F}$) = 2 (or det($\mathbf{F}$) = 0) ensures that all epipolar lines pass through the epipole.

[7]When $s = 1$, $E_1 = 2 \sum (\mathbf{n} \cdot \mathbf{r}_i + e)^2 / |\mathbf{n}_1|^2$, $E_2 = E_1/2$ and $E_3 = E_1/4$, so the solutions for $\mathbf{n}$ are identical (up to an arbitrary scale factor).

of points about the centroid, weighted by the distances from their epipolar lines, must sum to zero). Second, as mentioned earlier with regard to ϵ_h (Section 3.5.5), minimising the noise in only *one* image leaves the errors unevenly distributed between I_1 and I_2: a set of epipolars which fits one image well may not do likewise in the other image, causing discrepancies in the epipolar geometry [42, 89]. The E_2 method is therefore unattractive.

5.4.4   Cost function results

The cost functions are compared using simulated data. A set of 63 scene points (wire frame triangle vertices) are projected into two images of size 256×256 pixels, and the images are then perturbed by Gaussian noise with variance σ^2. Two forms of E_2 are examined (E_{2a} uses I_1 distances and E_{2b} uses I_2 distances), and a Newton–Raphson method is employed to minimise E_1, starting from the E_3 solution.

First consider the example in Figure 5.4, which has an approximately unity scale change between views ($s = 1.036$). The epipolar geometry parameters are computed using each of the four cost functions, and Table 5.1 shows the values of the cost functions for these four solutions[8] (with $\sigma = 1$ and $\sigma = 2$ pixels). Evidently, the costs are very similar with the four different solutions (within 1% of one another). The distances in I_2 (E_{2b}) are slightly larger than in I_1 (E_{2a}) since $s > 1$ (the theoretical ratio is s^2).

Cost fn	E_1	E_{2a}	E_{2b}	E_3	E_1	E_{2a}	E_{2b}	E_3
E_1	429.963	206.958	223.005	107.341	1719.423	826.195	893.228	429.202
E_{2a}	430.145	206.870	223.275	107.380	1722.391	824.770	897.622	429.827
E_{2b}	430.121	207.197	222.923	107.387	1722.022	830.128	891.894	429.952
E_3	429.964	206.946	223.018	107.341	1719.440	825.987	893.452	429.198
		(a)					(b)	

Table 5.1: *A comparison of the cost functions for Figure 5.4. Each row shows the four functions evaluated with the solution obtained from minimising the function listed for that row: (a) $\sigma = 1$ pixel; (b) $\sigma = 2$ pixels.*

A more useful way to compare the results is to examine the actual solutions (Table 5.2), i.e. the epipolar parameters (a, b, c, d). To aid understanding, we interpret these parameters in terms of rigid motion parameters, namely s (the scale factor), ϕ (the projection of the axis of rotation) and θ (the cyclotorsion angle between views). These parameters will be explained in more detail in Section 7.3.2. The solutions are clearly very similar, as expected from the similarity of the cost function values above. However, the difficulty with E_{2a} and E_{2b} becomes apparent, since by minimising the noise in only a single image, they describe the extreme values of the parameter range. E_1 and E_3 give more balanced solutions, and are in fact very similar over a wide range of noise values ($\sigma = 1$ and $\sigma = 2$ are shown).

A second example, with a larger scale change ($s = 3.015$), is given in Figure 5.6 and Table 5.3. The minimum values of the cost functions are shown to illustrate the range of

---

[8]The cost function value that is smallest in a given column is obviously the one that was actually minimised.

Function	Computed $\mathbf{n} = (a, b, c, d)$	ϕ	θ	s
Fiducial	(0.000, 0.695, -0.125, -0.709)	90.00	10.00	1.036
E_1	(0.004, 0.694, -0.126, -0.709)	89.68	9.75	1.038
E_{2a}	(0.003, 0.693, -0.125, -0.709)	89.61	9.72	1.037
E_{2b}	(0.005, 0.694, -0.126, -0.709)	89.76	9.77	1.039
E_3	(0.004, 0.694, -0.126, -0.709)	89.69	9.75	1.038

(a)

E_1	(0.009, 0.693, -0.127, -0.709)	89.27	9.46	1.040
E_{2a}	(0.005, 0.692, -0.125, -0.711)	89.61	9.57	1.043
E_{2b}	(0.013, 0.694, -0.130, -0.708)	88.94	9.35	1.037
E_3	(0.008, 0.693, -0.127, -0.710)	89.30	9.47	1.040

(b)

Table 5.2: *A comparison of the cost functions for Figure 5.4. The columns give the computed solution $\mathbf{n}$ for each cost function and their rigid motion interpretations in terms of s, θ and ϕ: (a) $\sigma = 1$ pixel; (b) $\sigma = 2$ pixels.*

values (e.g. there are much larger errors in I_2 than I_1 due to the large scale). Importantly, the E_3 solution is still similar to that obtained with E_1, despite the large value of s.

In summary, the four cost functions give similar solutions for the affine epipolar geometry. Deeper probing reveals that E_1 and E_3 are most alike, and that E_2 is unsuitable. We adopt E_3 since it is both easier to compute than E_1 and has a sounder theoretical justification.

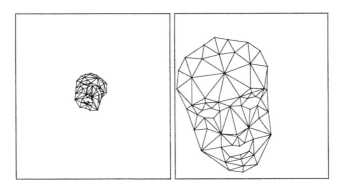

Figure 5.6: *Images I_1 and I_2 for a large scale change ($s = 3.015$).*

5.4.5   Existence of solutions and noise models

First, consider the conditions for existence of a solution $\{\mathbf{n}, e\}$. Let $\mathbf{V}$ be the $4 \times n$ matrix $[\mathbf{v}_0 \mid \mathbf{v}_1 \mid \ldots \mid \mathbf{v}_{n-1}]$. The equations $\mathbf{v}_i^\mathsf{T} \mathbf{n} = 0$ (from Equation (5.8)) then require $\mathbf{n}^\mathsf{T} \mathbf{V} = \mathbf{0}^\mathsf{T}$:

$$\mathbf{n}^\mathsf{T} \left[\begin{array}{c|c|c|c} \mathbf{x}'_0 - \bar{\mathbf{x}}' & \mathbf{x}'_1 - \bar{\mathbf{x}}' & \cdots & \mathbf{x}'_{n-1} - \bar{\mathbf{x}}' \\ \hline \mathbf{x}_0 - \bar{\mathbf{x}} & \mathbf{x}_1 - \bar{\mathbf{x}} & \cdots & \mathbf{x}_{n-1} - \bar{\mathbf{x}} \end{array} \right] = \mathbf{0}^\mathsf{T}$$

Function	Value	Computed $\mathbf{n} = (a, b, c, d)$	ϕ	θ	s
Fiducial	—	(0.310, 0.055, -0.892, 0.325)	10.00	30.00	3.015
E_1	794.342	(0.311, 0.044, -0.882, 0.352)	8.04	29.80	3.023
E_{2a}	77.890	(0.309, 0.044, -0.883, 0.350)	8.12	29.77	3.042
E_{2b}	715.963	(0.311, 0.044, -0.882, 0.352)	8.04	29.81	3.021
E_3	70.291	(0.309, 0.044, -0.883, 0.351)	8.11	29.77	3.040

(a)

E_1	3169.137	(0.315, 0.033, -0.868, 0.382)	5.97	29.71	2.997
E_{2a}	310.419	(0.308, 0.033, -0.873, 0.378)	6.17	29.56	3.073
E_{2b}	2850.863	(0.316, 0.033, -0.868, 0.382)	5.95	29.73	2.989
E_3	280.622	(0.308, 0.033, -0.872, 0.378)	6.15	29.58	3.065

(b)

Table 5.3: *The example from Figure 5.6: (a) $\sigma = 1$ pixel; (b) $\sigma = 2$ pixels.*

Task

Given two sets of n image points, $\mathbf{x}_i$ and $\mathbf{x}'_i$ ($i = 0 \ldots n-1$), compute the parameters of the affine epipolar geometry $\{\mathbf{n}, e\}$, if possible.

Algorithm

1. Compute the data centroid $\bar{\mathbf{r}}$ and centre the points, giving $\mathbf{v}_i = \mathbf{r}_i - \bar{\mathbf{r}}$.

2. Define $\mathbf{V} = [\mathbf{v}_0 \mid \mathbf{v}_1 \mid \ldots \mid \mathbf{v}_{n-1}]$ and compute its rank. Stop unless rank $(\mathbf{V}) = 3$ (within the bounds of noise).

3. Construct the real, symmetric scatter matrix $\mathbf{W} = \sum_{i=0}^{n-1} \mathbf{v}_i \mathbf{v}_i^\top$.

4. Solve for $\mathbf{n}$ by minimising E_3 (linear eigenvector computation).

5. Calculate $e = -\mathbf{n} \cdot \bar{\mathbf{r}}$.

6. Calculate the covariance matrix $\mathbf{\Lambda_n}$ for $\mathbf{n}$ (Equation (6.21)).

Figure 5.7: Affine epipolar geometry algorithm.

To obtain a unique, non–trivial solution for $\mathbf{n}$, $\mathbf{V}$ must have rank three; no unique solution can be found when the rank of $\mathbf{V}$ is *less than* 3. The causes of such rank–deficiencies were discussed in Section 3.4.3.

The noise present in $\mathbf{r}_i$ propagates through to the solution vector $\mathbf{n}$, whose covariance matrix ($\mathbf{\Lambda_n}$) provides a confidence measure in the parameters of the epipolar fit. This covariance matrix will be formally derived in Chapter 6 and used in Chapter 7 to estimate the confidence in the motion parameters computed from the epipolar geometry. The final algorithm is summarised in Figure 5.7.

5.5   Experimental results

Figure 5.8 shows a sequence taken at frame rate (25 Hz) from a robot head rotating in a static environment. Corner features were extracted (Figure 5.8(c)) and tracked, and motion vectors inconsistent with the main statistical distribution (i.e. outliers) were removed (using the scheme in Chapter 6). Figure 5.8(d) shows the motion vectors that remain; in general, these need not be parallel (cf. Figure 5.4(c)). Finally, Figures 5.8(e) and (f) show the epipolar lines computed using the algorithm in Figure 5.7. The sum of squared perpendicular distances in I_1 and I_2 is 141.55, giving a mean perpendicular distance of 0.55 pixels between each corner and its epipolar line. This error value depends on the noise in the system, which is a function of the particular camera, the feature detection and tracking algorithm, and the presence of outliers.

Figure 5.9 shows two other sequences, with a camera moving in a static world and with an object moving relative to a stationary camera. The mean perpendicular distances are 0.76 and 0.49 pixels respectively. The epipolar lines are thus typically within a pixel accuracy (on 256×256 images), despite the lack of subpixel accuracy in the corner detection stage. These epipolar lines therefore provide effective constraints for correspondence.

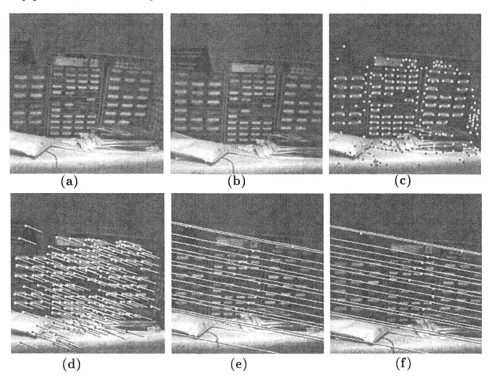

Figure 5.8: *Computing epipolar geometry for a real sequence:* (a)(b) *frames 0 and 5 (I_1 and I_2); (c) corner features; (d) 231 motion vectors remain after outlier rejection; (e)(f) epipolar lines for I_1 and I_2 (every 15th line shown).*

Finally, we illustrate the advantage of using *all* available points when computing the

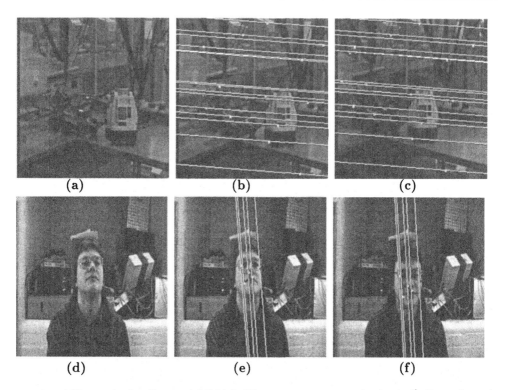

Figure 5.9: *Affine epipolar lines:* (a)(b)(c) *The camera moves (every 10th line shown);* (d)(e)(f) *The object moves (every 2nd line shown).*

epipolar geometry. A synthetic scene with 63 points had its images corrupted by independent, isotropic, Gaussian noise ($\sigma = 0.6$ pixels). Subsets of the data comprising p points (where p varied from 4 to 63) were randomly selected and a fit $\{\mathbf{n}, e\}$ computed using this subset. The E_1 distance was then computed for the whole point set, summing the squared perpendicular image distances from each point to its computed epipolar line. For each value of p, 500 experiments were run. Figure 5.10 shows the median distance and the standard deviation of the distances for each value of p. Both decrease as p increases, showing that the use of more points leads not only to better fits but also to more consistent ones.

5.6 Epipolar geometry and CI space

A key motivation for computing epipolar geometry is to isolate the motion parameters from the structure. At first sight, our cost function ϵ_{tk} (Equation (3.33)) does not permit this: structure and motion ($\mathbf{S}$ and $\mathbf{L}$) appear inextricably intertwined, and the SVD solution seems to compute them "simultaneously". However, ϵ_{tk} *does* decompose naturally into its constituent parts, and this revolves around epipolar geometry.

The intuition is easiest explained in CI space ($m = 2$). Section 3.5.3 showed that the *orientation* of the hyperplane π depends solely on motion, while the *distribution of points within π* depends solely on scene structure. One way to describe π is to specify its basis

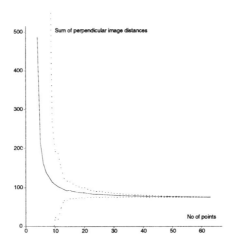

Figure 5.10: *Improvement in the epipolar geometry as the number of points increases. The solid line shows the median distance (from 500 experiments) and the dotted line shows the standard deviation (1σ level).*

$\mathbf{L}$; however, $\mathbf{L}$ is coupled to $\mathbf{S}$. An alternative approach is to specify $\mathbf{L}^{\perp}$, the *orthogonal subspace*; this is *independent* of $\mathbf{S}$, and so isolates the motion solution. In the two–view case, $\mathbf{L}^{\perp}$ is a single 4D unit vector $\boldsymbol{\ell}_4$ (see Section 3.5.1), making $\boldsymbol{\ell}_4$ the key parameter to compute. Now Section 3.5.2 showed that SVD determines π by orthogonal regression in CI space, i.e. by minimising the perpendicular distances between π and $\mathbf{v}_i$. These residual vectors encode the component of $\mathbf{v}_i$ in the orthogonal subspace, and have lengths $(\mathbf{v}_i \cdot \boldsymbol{\ell}_4)$. Thus, minimising $\sum_i |\mathbf{v}_i - \mathbf{L}\mathbf{s}_i|^2$ is equivalent to minimising $\sum_i (\mathbf{v}_i \cdot \boldsymbol{\ell}_4)^2$, and it follows from Equation (5.13) that $\boldsymbol{\ell}_4 = \mathbf{n}/|\mathbf{n}|$. Thus, $\boldsymbol{\ell}_4$ encodes the affine epipolar geometry parameters.

   To prove this mathematically, recall from Section 3.5.2 that SVD decomposes $\mathbf{V}$ into $\mathbf{V} = \mathbf{L}^{\star}\,\mathbf{S}^{\star}$, with $\mathbf{L}^{\star}$ a 4×4 orthogonal matrix and $\mathbf{S}^{\star}$ a $4 \times n$ matrix with mutually orthogonal rows. It follows that

$$\mathbf{V}^{\mathsf{T}}\,\mathbf{V} = \mathbf{S}^{\star\mathsf{T}}\,\mathbf{S}^{\star} \quad \text{and} \quad \mathbf{V}\,\mathbf{V}^{\mathsf{T}} = \mathbf{L}^{\star}\,\boldsymbol{\Theta}\,\mathbf{L}^{\star\mathsf{T}},$$

where $\boldsymbol{\Theta}$ is a 4×4 diagonal matrix containing the four eigenvalues of $\mathbf{V}\,\mathbf{V}^{\mathsf{T}}$. These equations clearly separate out the structure and the motion; in particular, $\mathbf{V}\,\mathbf{V}^{\mathsf{T}}$ is independent of structure and is the logical matrix to use first (since our interest here lies in motion). This corresponds exactly to the solution method for minimising E_3 given in Appendix B.3, where the global minimum for $\sum_i (\mathbf{v}_i \cdot \boldsymbol{\ell}_4)^2$ is determined from the eigenvector corresponding to the minimum eigenvalue of $\mathbf{W} = \mathbf{V}\,\mathbf{V}^{\mathsf{T}}$. (The remaining three eigenvectors of $\mathbf{W}$ then form the spanning set $\mathbf{L}$.)

   Thus, ϵ_{tk} is minimised in progressive stages, each of which retains the overall optimality: first the epipolar geometry is computed using E_3 (giving the normal to the hyperplane π, namely $\boldsymbol{\ell}_4 \equiv \mathbf{n}$), then the three vectors spanning π are determined (giving $\mathbf{L} = \{\boldsymbol{\ell}_1, \boldsymbol{\ell}_2, \boldsymbol{\ell}_3\}$), and finally the structure is determined by projecting $\mathbf{v}_i$ onto π and expressing the location in terms of $\mathbf{L}$ (giving $\mathbf{S}$).

5.7   Conclusions

This chapter has introduced affine epipolar geometry and defined the special form of its fundamental matrix. Three different least–squares solutions have been examined to allow the use of all available points. The 4D linear method has been shown to be superior to other popular methods, not least because it is directly related to the favoured image distance cost function ϵ_{tk}.

The two chapters that follow both utilise affine epipolar geometry. Chapter 6 identifies outliers to a fit by detecting when a point is inconsistent with the epipolar geometry of its group, and Chapter 7 computes the rigid motion parameters of a set of points directly from their epipolar geometry (without requiring a local coordinate frame).

Chapter 6

Outlier rejection in an orthogonal regression framework

6.1 Introduction

Although much–used in computer vision applications, least squares (LS) minimisation is by nature global, and hence vulnerable to distortion by outliers. This aspect of data fitting is frequently either ignored or treated heuristically, adding further to the already considerable difficulty of devising vision algorithms that work reliably on real imagery. The outlier problem is well–known in the statistics literature [14, 17, 32, 53, 58, 67, 124, 160], and arises when a given set of data actually comprises two subsets (Figure 6.1): a large, dominant subset (the main body of valid data) and a relatively small subset of "outliers" (the contaminants). The task of removing the contaminants is further complicated when, as is normally the case, the data in the dominant subset have also been perturbed by *noise*. The outlier problem is important since an analysis based both on the real data and the outliers distorts conclusions about the underlying process (Figure 6.1). It is therefore of interest to seek a means of effectively rejecting such "maverick" points, thereby restoring the propriety of the data and improving parameter estimation.

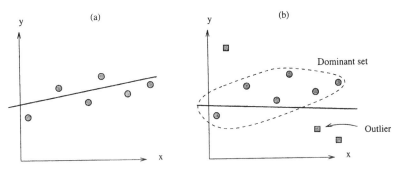

Figure 6.1: *Noise and outliers: (a) A least squares fit minimises the distances of the noise–perturbed data (circles) from the fitted line; (b) Outliers (squares) distort the correct fit.*

We encounter this outlier problem when trying to solve for affine epipolar geometry using the algorithm in the previous chapter (Figure 5.7). Since this algorithm involves hyperplane fitting, we tackle outlier rejection in this context. Let the points $\{\mathbf{r}_i, i = 0 \ldots n-1\}$ be given in $\mathbb{R}^m$ and let $\bar{\mathbf{r}}$ be their centroid. Then the points lie on an $(m-1)$–dimensional linear hyperplane π of $\mathbb{R}^m$ if and only if there exists a non–zero vector $\mathbf{n} \in \mathbb{R}^m$ such that

$$\mathbf{n}^\top (\mathbf{r}_i - \bar{\mathbf{r}}) = 0, \quad i = 0 \dots n-1. \tag{6.1}$$

This chapter addresses the case where the measurements $\mathbf{r}_i$ are contaminated by Gaussian noise and there is, in addition, a relatively small set of outliers. The aim is to identify and eliminate the outliers, in order to estimate the hyperplane by least squares fitting to the remaining data. Although much neglected, outliers are an unavoidable factor in complex vision systems, and certainly so in the field of motion estimation. Much of the early work on structure from motion (SFM) [87, 148, 151] completely ignored both noise perturbations and outliers. There has subsequently been a trend towards consideration of noise (e.g. [41, 73, 163]), but the problem of outliers remains largely unexplored (a notable exception being [146, 147]).

One means of rejecting outliers is to employ *regression diagnostics*. This involves calculating an initial fit to the data, and then assessing the validity of each point based on a computed residual or influence measure. Such schemes are well–suited to our problem domain (see Section 6.6). Unfortunately, the vast majority of existing diagnostics apply to *ordinary least squares* (OLS), which is inappropriate for our purposes; we require *orthogonal regression* (OR). The regression diagnostic devised in this chapter applies to general problems involving hyper–plane fitting, and relaxes some of the statistical assumptions imposed by existing OR schemes.

Section 6.2 introduces OLS and OR, Section 6.3 reviews existing outlier rejection schemes, and Section 6.4 presents our new approach. Once the outliers have been rejected, it is important to know the remaining uncertainty in the fit (caused by the inevitable noise), so Section 6.5 derives the appropriate variances and covariances. Finally, Section 6.6 applies the technique to the computation of affine epipolar geometry.

6.2 Linear regression

Regression is used to study relationships between measurable variables; *linear regression* deals with the particular class of relationships that can be described by straight lines, or by their generalisations to many dimensions (called "hyperplanes"). The objective is to fit a hyperplane to a set of m-dimensional points, e.g. a line in 2D or a plane in 3D. Consider n data vectors in $\mathbb{R}^m$, denoted $\hat{\mathbf{r}}_i = (\hat{x}_{i1}, \hat{x}_{i2}, \dots, \hat{x}_{im})^\top$, which satisfy the linear relation

$$\mathbf{n}^\top \hat{\mathbf{r}}_i + e = n_1 \hat{x}_{i1} + n_2 \hat{x}_{i2} + \dots + n_m \hat{x}_{im} + e = 0, \qquad i = 0 \dots n-1. \tag{6.2}$$

The "hat" indicates noise–free quantities, and the vector $\mathbf{n} = (n_1, n_2, \dots, n_m) \in \mathbb{R}^m$ contains the parameters (or *regression coefficients*) to be estimated. Equation (6.2) has the following geometric interpretation:

- $\mathbf{n}$ is the normal to the $(m-1)$–dimensional hyperplane, with magnitude $|\mathbf{n}|$;

- $-e/|\mathbf{n}|$ is the perpendicular distance from the hyperplane to the origin.

Equation (6.2) has m unknowns since only the *ratios* of $n_1 : n_2 : \ldots : n_m : e$ can be recovered; thus, m data points are sufficient to determine $\mathbf{n}$ and e (up to an arbitrary scale factor). When more points are available $(n > m)$, the system is overdetermined, and because noise makes it unlikely that all n points will lie precisely on the same hyperplane, an optimisation problem arises. We initially ignore outliers, and assume that each data point is perturbed by a noise vector $\delta \mathbf{r}_i \in \mathbb{R}^m$ to give the measurement $\mathbf{r}_i$, where

$$\mathbf{r}_i = \hat{\mathbf{r}}_i + \delta \mathbf{r}_i. \qquad (6.3)$$

The perpendicular distance from $\mathbf{r}_i$ to the hyperplane π is then $h_i = (\mathbf{n} \cdot \mathbf{r}_i + e)/ \mid \mathbf{n} \mid$. Section 6.2.1 justifies the use of orthogonal regression to determine π, and Section 6.2.2 describes the solution method.

6.2.1 Choice of objective function

Least squares fitting yields maximum likelihood estimates of the parameters if the measurement errors $\delta \mathbf{r}_i$ are independent and follow a normal distribution with zero mean and common variance. It is popular since it offers straightforward, unique, closed–form solutions. Indeed, Weisberg [160] remarks that LS estimation has been used for almost 200 years precisely because it is computationally simple, geometrically elegant and optimal in several important respects (given some assumptions).

Harter [56] traces the method of ordinary least squares (OLS) to Legendre and Gauss in the early nineteenth century (1805–1809). OLS computes the hyperplane π such that the sum of squared distances from the points to π is minimised in a particular direction. Figure 6.2(a) shows the familiar 2D case where a line is fitted to minimise the distances in the vertical direction (i.e. along the y axis). The method of *orthogonal regression* (OR), also termed *total least squares* or *principal component regression,* was proposed almost a century later by Adcock [1, 2], Kummel [83] and Pearson [109]. OR minimises the sum of squared distances *perpendicular* to the fitted hyperplane, i.e. along the direction of its normal $\mathbf{n}$ (Figure 6.2(b)).

These approaches differ in two important ways. First, OLS requires the explicit definition of axes and a minimisation direction, i.e. an external coordinate system is imposed on the data. In contrast, OR automatically computes an intrinsic coordinate system (Figure 6.2(b)), with the new axis variables being linear combinations of the original ones. The OLS approach is more appropriate in a range of applications, not least in the social and behavioural sciences, where combinations of dissimilar variables (e.g. height and weight) yield meaningless quantities. However, when (as in our case) the variables are spatial coordinates, one coordinate system is as meaningful as any other, and the facility to select a natural reference frame independent of the external coordinate system is a distinct advantage of the OR method.

Second, the two methods make different assumptions about the error distribution of the variables. OLS only accommodates errors along the minimisation axis (the *dependent* variable), and assumes that all remaining variables are independent and known accurately. Thus, in Figure 6.2(a), all x components are treated as noise–free, and all errors are ascribed to the y components. The choice of dependent variable affects the fit, as noted by Pearson [109]: "we get one straight line or plane if we treat some one variable as independent, and a quite different one if we treat another variable as the independent variable" (page 559). In contrast, OR caters for errors in *all* coordinate directions, and simply seeks a functional relationship between the variables.

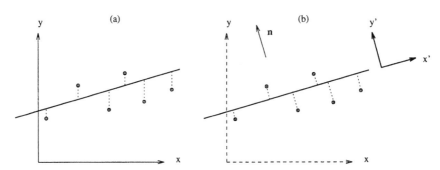

Figure 6.2: *Ordinary least squares versus orthogonal regression: (a) The minimisation direction is specified to be the y axis; (b) An intrinsic coordinate system (x', y') is computed and the minimisation direction is automatically set to be the normal direction n.*

Thus, although the OLS formulae are simpler (and easier to solve), OR is generally better suited to the problem of hyperplane fitting, and the objective function we minimise is the sum of the squared perpendicular distances

$$\varepsilon(\mathbf{n}, e) = \sum_{i=0}^{n-1} h_i^2 = \sum_{i=0}^{n-1} (\mathbf{n} \cdot \mathbf{r}_i + e)^2 / |\mathbf{n}|^2 . \tag{6.4}$$

6.2.2   Orthogonal regression

We solve Equation (6.4) for $\mathbf{n}$ and e by minimising

$$\varepsilon(\mathbf{n}, e) = \sum_{i=0}^{n-1} (\mathbf{n}^\top \mathbf{r}_i + e)^2 \quad \text{subject to} \quad |\mathbf{n}|^2 = 1. \tag{6.5}$$

The resulting hyperplane passes through the centroid $\bar{\mathbf{r}}$ (see Appendix B.3), so $e = -\mathbf{n} \cdot \bar{\mathbf{r}}$. We therefore eliminate e by first centering the data points, writing $\mathbf{v}_i = \mathbf{r}_i - \bar{\mathbf{r}}$:

$$\varepsilon(\mathbf{n}) = \sum_{i=0}^{n-1} (\mathbf{n} \cdot \mathbf{v}_i)^2 = \mathbf{n}^\top \left(\sum_{i=0}^{n-1} \mathbf{v}_i \mathbf{v}_i^\top \right) \mathbf{n} = \mathbf{n}^\top \mathbf{W} \mathbf{n}. \tag{6.6}$$

The solution $\mathbf{n}$ is well known to be the unit eigenvector of $\mathbf{W}$ corresponding to the smallest eigenvalue (Appendix B.3). The eigenvalues of $\mathbf{W}$ are the m roots of its characteristic polynomial $p(\lambda) = \det(\mathbf{W} - \lambda \mathbf{I}_m)$, where $\mathbf{I}_m$ is the $m \times m$ identity matrix. These eigenvalues are denoted $\lambda(\mathbf{W}) = \{\lambda_1, \ldots, \lambda_m\}$ and arranged in non–decreasing order. If the corresponding eigenvectors are $\mathbf{u}_1, \ldots, \mathbf{u}_m$ (all non–zero), then $\mathbf{n} = \mathbf{u}_1$. Since $\mathbf{W}$ is real and symmetric, its eigenvectors form an orthonormal basis; furthermore, since $\mathbf{W}$ is also positive semi–definite ($\mathbf{v}_i^\top \mathbf{W} \mathbf{v}_i \geq 0$), the eigenvalues are all non–negative, i.e. $0 \leq \lambda_1 \leq \cdots \leq \lambda_m$.

The matrix $\mathbf{W}$, termed a scatter matrix, measures the dispersion of the data about the means in each of the m variables $(x_1, x_2, \ldots, x_m)$. In statistics parlance, we are performing *principal component regression* on the *covariance* matrix[1] The algorithm is summarised in Figure 6.4.

Geometry provides useful insight into how orthogonal regression works. As mentioned earlier, OR finds an optimal set of axes (an "intrinsic coordinate system") to describe the data, where "optimal" refers to the best summarisation of the data. The "best" axis is the line which the cloud of points is closest to in Euclidean space, i.e. the line onto which the projections of the points have maximum variance (Figure 6.3). For instance, if all the points lie on a single line, that line is the most descriptive axis and no further axes are needed. The second best–fitting axis (perpendicular to the first) defines the best–fitting plane, the third best–fitting axis (perpendicular to the first two) defines the best–fitting 3D linear subspace, and so on until all m dimensions have been explained. The new axes are the *eigenvectors* and the variances of the projections onto these axes are the *eigenvalues,* specifying the relative order of importance (or "explaining power") of the various axes.

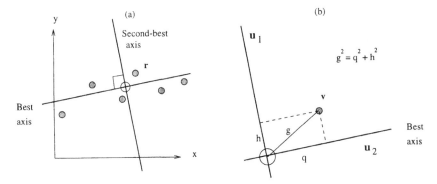

Figure 6.3: *Orthogonal regression: (a) The best axis passes closest to the points in terms of perpendicular distance, i.e. the projections onto this axis have maximum variance; (b) Maximising the projection of* $\mathbf{v}$ *onto* $\mathbf{u}_2$ *(length q) is equivalent to minimising the projection onto* $\mathbf{u}_1$ *(length h), since the distance g from* $\mathbf{v}$ *to the centroid O is fixed, and* $g^2 = h^2 + q^2$.

In fitting the best hyperplane, our interest lies in the axis with smallest eigenvalue, i.e. the axis onto which the projections of the data points have *minimum* variance. These projections are the *residuals* of the fit, i.e. the residual for the ith point is the projection of $\mathbf{v}_i$ onto the unit axis $\mathbf{u}_1$,

$$h_i = \mathbf{u}_1^\top \mathbf{v}_i, \tag{6.7}$$

giving the perpendicular distance from $\mathbf{v}_i$ to π. The residuals would be zero in the absence

---

[1]The population covariance matrix, or variance–covariance matrix, is actually $\frac{1}{n}\mathbf{W}$ and the sample version is $\frac{1}{n-1}\mathbf{W}$. These scale factors only change the eigenvalues, having no effect on the eigenvectors. One might also use a *correlation* matrix, where the data points are additionally normalised in terms of variance; this is unnecessary when, as in our case, the variables are comparable in magnitude of variance and units of measurement [81].

Task

Given $\mathbf{r}_i \in \mathbb{R}^m$ ($i = 0 \ldots n-1$) where $n \geq m$, compute $\mathbf{n}$ and e to minimise

$$\varepsilon(\mathbf{n}, e) = \sum_{i=0}^{n-1} (\mathbf{n}^\top \mathbf{r}_i + e)^2 \quad \text{where} \quad |\mathbf{n}| = 1.$$

Algorithm

1. Compute the data centroid $\bar{\mathbf{r}}$ and centre the points, writing $\mathbf{v}_i = \mathbf{r}_i - \bar{\mathbf{r}}$.

2. Construct the scatter matrix $\mathbf{W} = \sum_{i=0}^{n-1} \mathbf{v}_i \mathbf{v}_i^\top$.

3. Find the unit eigenvector $\mathbf{n}$ corresponding to the minimum eigenvalue of $\mathbf{W}$ ($\mathbf{W}\mathbf{n} = \lambda_1 \mathbf{n}$).

4. Calculate $e = -\mathbf{n} \cdot \bar{\mathbf{r}}$.

Figure 6.4: Orthogonal regression algorithm.

of noise, since the actual data set only has $m - 1$ independent dimensions. The *residual vector* $\mathbf{h} = (h_0, h_1, \ldots, h_{n-1})^\top$ is defined as

$$\mathbf{h}^\top = \mathbf{u}_1^\top \mathbf{V}, \tag{6.8}$$

where $\mathbf{V} = [\mathbf{v}_0 \mid \mathbf{v}_1 \mid \cdots \mid \mathbf{v}_{n-1}]$.

Although the algorithm in Figure 6.4 caters for Gaussian noise in an optimal way, the problem of *outliers* remains; least squares estimation is *global* and outliers distort the solution. We address this problem in the sections that follow.

6.3 Previous work on outlier rejection

Two main approaches to the outlier problem have evolved in the form of *regression diagnostics* [14, 17, 32, 58] and *robust statistics* [53, 67, 124]. The diagnostics method computes an initial fit to the data, pinpoints outliers, rejects them and then re-analyses the remaining data (possibly in an iterative process). Thus, it simultaneously "builds and criticises" the model [104]. In contrast, the robust statistics method first finds a fit to explain the majority of the data without removing the contaminants. The outliers are then identified (if necessary) as those points which are inconsistent with the dominant fit. The robust approach is therefore said to "accommodate" the outliers. In some applications, the two schemes yield identical results; in others, they differ significantly, and several papers have debated their relative merits and shortcomings (see [124]).

6.3.1 Regression diagnostics

The classical least squares approach to outlier rejection computes the initial fit, determines the residual for each data point, and rejects all points whose residuals exceed a predetermined threshold (based, say, on a chosen confidence level and a prior statistical noise model). The procedure is then repeated with the reduced set of points until all outliers have been removed. This approach works well when the percentage of outliers is small, and their deviations from the valid data are not too large; unfortunately, a single outlier far removed from the data centroid can strongly distort the fit, yet still have a very small residual.

A refinement of the above scheme uses *influence measures* to pinpoint potential outliers. These measures assess the extent to which a particular point influences the fit by determining the change in the solution when that point is omitted. Examples include Cook's D distance [32, 160] and the DFFITS/DFBETAS statistics [17], which measure the effect of point deletion on various regression parameters. Several such measures were evaluated by Torr and Murray [146]; unfortunately, all were designed for the ordinary least squares formulation.

We therefore formulate our diagnostic directly in terms of the *eigensolution*. Much of the previous work in this area revolves around principal component regression, and the proposed solutions generally have an ad hoc, intuitively–justified basis, with little sound statistical foundation [14]. In general, a p–dimensional data point is transformed into a different p–dimensional point (its principal component vector) by projecting the original data point onto each of the p new principal component axes. Gnanadesikan and Kettenring [46] surveyed the field and suggested highlighting different types of outlier by using the first few and last few principal component vectors of the data, the former being sensitive to outliers inflating variances/covariances, and the latter to outliers adding spurious dimensions to the data. They proposed no formal tests; instead, they recommended graphical methods (such as bivariate plotting of the different components) to elicit putative contaminants.

Hawkins [58] employed two formal test statistics; however, his tests (like many others) require the strong assumption that the data points are a random sample from a *multivariate normal distribution*. When the underlying data distribution is unknown (as in most cases, including our own), his theory only holds asymptotically as the number of points $n \to \infty$, so that the Central Limit Theorem can be invoked (yielding an approximately normal distribution of principal components). He pointed out that in practice, this requirement on n can be prohibitively large. He concluded that despite the appealing properties of tests involving principal component residuals, they are not generally valid for formal testing with controlled probability of Type I error[2] since the underlying (null) data distribution is unknown for n of small to moderate size. Chatfield and Collins [28] concurred that the available sampling theory for principal components regression (PCR) is of limited use (even under the assumption of multivariate normality), and went so far as to suggest that PCR be viewed solely as a mathematical technique with no underlying statistical model.

We address these concerns in Section 6.4.6 and illustrate how our particular formulation (which uses only the minimum variance principal component) overcomes them for our class of problem.

---

[2]Type I errors occur when one incorrectly rejects a valid point as an outlier.

6.3.2 Robust statistics

Other estimators besides least squares estimators can be found, and concern for sensitivity to outliers spawned a search for "robust" estimators that would better tolerate the perturbations [67, 124]. In this context, "robust" means "insensitive to small departures from the ideal assumptions for which the estimator was optimised", often implying large departures for a small number of points. One class of robust estimators is the "maximum likelihood type" or M–estimators [67], which include the least − absolute deviation estimator.

Torr and Murray [147] suggested that robust estimators are appropriate when the number of outliers is large or when the outliers possess structure. Their least median squares solution repeatedly sampled the universal set of data, computing a statistic from each subset and averaging the results of many such "trials" (via robust statistical methods) to compute the dominant fit. The robustness of this method stems from the fact that it only considers a subset of the universal data set at any one time. Although this approach is reliable and could be adapted easily from the OLS framework to the OR one, it has a significant computational overhead. Moreover, since in many cases (including our own) the outliers constitute a small percentage of the data and their maximum deviation is bounded, the least squares methods suffice.

6.4 Outlier rejection techniques

We examine two methods of identifying outliers. The first, a novel approach, computes the improvement in the minimum eigenvalue of the scatter matrix $\mathbf{W}$ when a data point is deleted. The second, the traditional residuals method, serves as a benchmark to evaluate the performance of the first method. We show that the residuals method is in fact *subsumed* by the minimum eigenvalue method, and that the results coincide when a first order perturbation model is used in the minimum eigenvalue scheme.

6.4.1 Minimum eigenvalue method: basic algorithm

The intuition behind this approach is as follows. The minimum eigenvalue λ_1 of the scatter matrix $\mathbf{W}$ measures the total error in the fit; if this error is statistically significant (i.e. partly due to outliers rather than pure random noise), then the point whose removal most decreases the error is identified as an outlier, and deleted. The parameters are then recomputed for the reduced set of points, and the process continues until the termination criteria are satisfied. This section outlines the basic algorithm, and Section 6.4.2 discusses ways to improve its efficiency.

Consider the effect of deleting the ith data point. The data centroid changes from $\bar{\mathbf{r}}$ to $\bar{\mathbf{r}}^\star$, and the points $\mathbf{v}_j$ ($j = 0 \ldots n - 1, j \neq i$) acquire new coordinates $\mathbf{v}_j^\star$. The scatter matrix is modified from $\mathbf{W} = \sum_{j=0}^{n-1}(\mathbf{r}_j - \bar{\mathbf{r}})(\mathbf{r}_j - \bar{\mathbf{r}})^\top$ (summed over n points) to $\mathbf{W}^\star = \sum_{j=0, j \neq i}^{n-1}(\mathbf{r}_j - \bar{\mathbf{r}}^\star)(\mathbf{r}_j - \bar{\mathbf{r}}^\star)^\top$ (summed over $n-1$ points). It is straightforward to show that the new quantities are

$$\mathbf{W}^\star = \mathbf{W} - \frac{n}{n-1}(\mathbf{r}_i - \bar{\mathbf{r}})(\mathbf{r}_i - \bar{\mathbf{r}})^\top = \mathbf{W} - \frac{n}{n-1}\mathbf{v}_i\,\mathbf{v}_i^\top \tag{6.9}$$

$$\bar{\mathbf{r}}^{\star} = \bar{\mathbf{r}} - \frac{1}{n-1}(\mathbf{r}_i - \bar{\mathbf{r}}) = \bar{\mathbf{r}} - \frac{1}{n-1}\mathbf{v}_i \tag{6.10}$$

$$\mathbf{v}_j^{\star} = \mathbf{v}_j + \frac{1}{n-1}\mathbf{v}_i \tag{6.11}$$

Naturally, the eigensolution also changes when $\mathbf{W}$ is perturbed to $\mathbf{W}^{\star}$. We now identify λ_1 as an appropriate statistical variable for assessing the improvement in the fit when a point is deleted. By definition, $\mathbf{W}\mathbf{u}_1 = \lambda_1\mathbf{u}_1$, so

$$\lambda_1 = \mathbf{u}_1^{\mathsf{T}}\mathbf{W}\mathbf{u}_1 = \sum_{i=0}^{n-1}(\mathbf{u}_1 \cdot \mathbf{v}_i)^2 = \sum_{i=0}^{n-1}h_i^2.$$

Thus, λ_1 sums the squared distances h_i^2 between the data points and the fitted hyper-plane π. If the residuals h_i are independent random variables drawn from a zero–mean, Gaussian distribution with variance σ_h^2, then λ_1/σ_h^2 is distributed as χ^2 with $(n-m)$ degrees of freedom (see, for instance, [115]). Expressions for the variances and covariances of h_i are derived in Section 6.5.2, where it is shown that the assumption of a univariate distribution on h is not strictly true; the residual variances differ slightly from point to point, and are also correlated. However, we show these effects to be minor, and approximate σ_h^2 by $(n-1)\sigma^2/n$ (of which more later), where σ^2 is the variance of the zero–mean, independent, isotropic, Gaussian noise in the original points $\mathbf{r}_i$.

A one–tailed significance test can therefore be performed on λ_1/σ_h^2, corresponding to the (null) hypothesis that π explains the data to a predetermined confidence level. If, for instance, $\lambda_1/\sigma_h^2 < \chi_{0.95}^2$ (95% confidence level), there are deemed to be no outliers to the fit; otherwise, we delete that point whose removal maximally reduces λ_1, and decrement by one the degrees of freedom on the χ^2 variable. A new fit is then computed using the remaining data, and the data centroid and scatter matrix are updated for the next iteration. This process continues until λ_1 falls within the specified confidence interval (indicating that no outliers remain), or until a specified number of iterations/outliers has been reached (m is a lower bound on the number of retained points).

The algorithm is summarised in Figure 6.5. The full eigensolution is recomputed to determine the change in λ_1 when point i is removed, so to remove k outliers, $k(2n-k+1)/2$ eigendecompositions (of an $m \times m$ matrix) are required. Ways of reducing this computational cost are discussed in Section 6.4.2. We do not delete more than one outlier at a time since the new fit may yield substantially different influence values for the remaining data. While this might appear cautious, this caution is justified by the example in Section 6.4.5.

6.4.2 Minimum eigenvalue method: efficiency considerations

To determine the point with maximum influence, the algorithm in Figure 6.5 recomputes the full eigensolution for every point at each iteration. This is inefficient, and we present two techniques to redress this problem. The first uses an exact eigenvalue identity and the second uses matrix perturbation theory. Both express Equation (6.9) as $\mathbf{W}^{\star} = \mathbf{W} + \Delta\mathbf{W}_i$, where $\Delta\mathbf{W}_i = -n\mathbf{v}_i\mathbf{v}_i^{\mathsf{T}}/(n-1)$ corresponds to removal of point i. Note that $\Delta\mathbf{W}$ is a dyadic product and hence a real–symmetric matrix of rank one.

Task

Given $\mathbf{r}_i \in \mathbb{R}^m$ ($i = 0 \ldots n-1$, $n \geq m$) perturbed by zero–mean, independent, isotropic, Gaussian noise with variance σ^2, reject outliers from the set $\{\mathbf{r}_i\}$ to a $\zeta\%$ confidence level.

Algorithm

1. Compute the data centroid $\bar{\mathbf{r}}$ and centre the points, writing $\mathbf{v}_i = \mathbf{r}_i - \bar{\mathbf{r}}$. Construct the scatter matrix $\mathbf{W} = \sum_{i=0}^{n-1} \mathbf{v}_i \mathbf{v}_i^\top$.

2. Find the eigenvector $\mathbf{u}_1$ corresponding to the minimum eigenvalue λ_1 of $\mathbf{W}$.

3. Perform a one–tailed χ^2 significance test on λ_1 / σ_h^2, with $\sigma_h^2 = (n-1)\sigma^2/n$; if the test falls within the $\zeta\%$ confidence bound, set $\mathbf{n} = \mathbf{u}_1$ and goto step 6.

4. For each point i, delete it from the data set and compute the new minimum eigenvalue, $\lambda_1^\star(i)$. Hence determine the change in λ_1 when point i is deleted, namely $\Delta\lambda_1(i) = \lambda_1 - \lambda_1^\star(i)$.

5. Delete the point i for which $\Delta\lambda_1(i)$ is greatest. Update the scatter matrix and centroid using Equations (6.9) and (6.10), and return to step 2.

6. Calculate $e = -\mathbf{n} \cdot \bar{\mathbf{r}}$. The final hyperplane parameters are $\{\mathbf{n}, e\}$.

Figure 6.5: Outlier rejection algorithm: minimum eigenvalue method.

Eigenvalue identity

Let $\mathbf{D}$ be an $m \times m$ non–singular matrix and let $\mathbf{D} - c\mathbf{v}\mathbf{v}^\top$ be singular, where c is a non–zero scalar and $\mathbf{v}$ a non–zero m–vector. Then the vector $\mathbf{D}^{-1}\mathbf{v}$ lies in the nullspace of the singular matrix[3]. Thus, if $\lambda^\star$ is an eigenvalue of $\mathbf{D} - c\mathbf{v}\mathbf{v}^\top$ with associated eigenvector $\mathbf{u}^\star$, then $(\mathbf{D} - \lambda^\star \mathbf{I}_m - c\mathbf{v}\mathbf{v}^\top)\mathbf{u}^\star = \mathbf{0}$ and the eigenvector has direction $(\mathbf{D} - \lambda^\star \mathbf{I}_m)^{-1}\mathbf{v}$. The eigenvalue therefore satisfies the relation

$$(\mathbf{D} - \lambda^\star \mathbf{I}_m - c\mathbf{v}\mathbf{v}^\top)(\mathbf{D} - \lambda^\star \mathbf{I}_m)^{-1}\mathbf{v} = \mathbf{v} - c\mathbf{v}\mathbf{v}^\top(\mathbf{D} - \lambda^\star \mathbf{I}_m)^{-1}\mathbf{v} = \mathbf{0},$$

yielding the identity [47]

$$c\mathbf{v}^\top(\mathbf{D} - \lambda^\star \mathbf{I}_m)^{-1}\mathbf{v} = 1.$$

In the notation of Equation (6.9), we have $\mathbf{D} = \mathbf{W}$, $\mathbf{v} = \mathbf{v}_i$ and $c = n/(n-1)$, so $\lambda^\star$ is an eigenvalue of $\mathbf{W}^\star$ if

$$\mathbf{v}_i^\top (\mathbf{W} - \lambda^\star \mathbf{I}_m)^{-1} \mathbf{v}_i = \frac{n-1}{n} \tag{6.12}$$

---

[3]The proof is simple: a non–zero vector e lying in this nullspace satisfies $(\mathbf{D} - c\mathbf{v}\mathbf{v}^\top)e = \mathbf{0}$, giving $e = c(e^\top\mathbf{v})\mathbf{D}^{-1}\mathbf{v}$, which is parallel to $\mathbf{D}^{-1}\mathbf{v}$.

Now the eigensolution for $\mathbf{W}$ is known to be $\mathbf{W}\mathbf{u}_k = \lambda_k\,\mathbf{u}_k$, whence

$$\mathbf{W} = \sum_{k=1}^{m} \lambda_k\,\mathbf{u}_k\,\mathbf{u}_k^\mathsf{T} \quad\text{and}\quad \mathbf{I}_m = \sum_{k=1}^{m} \mathbf{u}_k\,\mathbf{u}_k^\mathsf{T}.$$

Thus,

$$\mathbf{W} - \lambda^\star\,\mathbf{I}_m = \sum_{k=1}^{m}(\lambda_k - \lambda^\star)\,\mathbf{u}_k\,\mathbf{u}_k^\mathsf{T} \quad\text{and}\quad (\mathbf{W} - \lambda^\star\,\mathbf{I}_m)^{-1} = \sum_{k=1}^{m}\frac{\mathbf{u}_k\,\mathbf{u}_k^\mathsf{T}}{\lambda_k - \lambda^\star}.$$

Equation (6.12) therefore reduces to

$$\sum_{k=1}^{m}\frac{(\mathbf{u}_k \cdot \mathbf{v}_i)^2}{\lambda_k - \lambda^\star} = \frac{n-1}{n}. \tag{6.13}$$

This equation has one root $\lambda^\star$ such that $\lambda^\star < \lambda_1$ if $\mathbf{u}_1^\mathsf{T}\mathbf{v}_i$ is non–zero[4]. This suggests an efficient way to check whether deleting point i causes a bigger change in λ_1 than deleting one of the other points that have already been examined. Let $\lambda_1^{\,\star}$ be the smallest of the minimum eigenvalues calculated so far, that is $\underline{\lambda_1^{\,\star}} = \min\{\lambda_1^\star(0),\,\lambda_1^\star(1),\,\ldots,\,\lambda_1^\star(i-1)\}$. Then the minimum eigenvalue for point i, $\lambda_1^\star(i)$, will be smaller than $\lambda_1^{\,\star}$ if

$$\sum_{k=1}^{m}\frac{(\mathbf{u}_k \cdot \mathbf{v}_i)^2}{\lambda_k - \underline{\lambda_1^{\,\star}}} > \frac{n-1}{n},$$

in which case point i becomes the one favoured for deletion. The *true* value of $\lambda_1^\star(i)$ can then be computed to high accuracy by doing the eigendecomposition, because on average this will only be done on relatively few occasions. The modification to step 4 of the algorithm is given below.

---

4. Delete point 0 from the data set, compute the new minimum eigenvalue $\lambda_1^\star(0)$, and set $\underline{\lambda_1^{\,\star}} = \lambda_1^\star(0)$. For each remaining point i, where $i = 1\ldots n-1$:

   If $\displaystyle\sum_{k=1}^{m}\frac{(\mathbf{u}_k \cdot \mathbf{v}_i)^2}{\lambda_k - \underline{\lambda_1^{\,\star}}} > \frac{n-1}{n}$,

   (a) delete point i from the data set and compute the new minimum eigenvalue $\lambda_1^\star(i)$
   (b) set $\underline{\lambda_1^{\,\star}} = \lambda_1^\star(i)$ and $\Delta\lambda_1(i) = \lambda_1 - \lambda_1^\star(i)$.

Perturbation model

An alternative approach is to use *matrix perturbation theory* [48, 165] to evaluate the change in λ_1 induced by deleting point i. Various worst case bounds for eigenvalue perturbation

---

[4]If $\mathbf{u}_1^\mathsf{T}\mathbf{v}_i = 0$, then $\{\lambda_1, \mathbf{u}_1\}$ is an eigensolution of both $\mathbf{W}$ and $\mathbf{W}^\star$.

exist in the literature (e.g. Weyl theorem, Wielandt–Hoffman theorem), derived mainly
from Gerschgorin disk theory [137, 165]. These bounds impose restrictions on the maximum
variation of the eigenvalues; however, while useful for devising numerical algorithms, their
worth is limited by their conservatism [163]. We employ instead a Taylor series expansion to
compute the first and second order eigenvalue variations. Consider a perturbation ϵ in the
eigenvalue λ_1, where $\lambda_1 = \lambda_1(0)$:

$$\lambda_1(\epsilon) = \lambda_1(0) + \dot{\lambda}_1(0)\epsilon + \frac{1}{2}\ddot{\lambda}_1(0)\epsilon^2 + O(\epsilon^3)$$

The quantity ϵ is the 2–norm of $\Delta\mathbf{W}$, defined formally in Appendix C.1, where it is also
shown that the first and second order perturbations in λ_1 due to deleting point i are

$$\dot{\lambda}_1(0)\epsilon = -\frac{n}{n-1}(\mathbf{u}_1 \cdot \mathbf{v}_i)^2 \tag{6.14}$$

$$\frac{1}{2}\ddot{\lambda}_1(0)\epsilon^2 = -\frac{n^2}{(n-1)^2}(\mathbf{u}_1 \cdot \mathbf{v}_i)^2 \sum_{k=2}^{4}\frac{(\mathbf{u}_k \cdot \mathbf{v}_i)^2}{\lambda_k - \lambda_1}. \tag{6.15}$$

This scheme is incorporated into the algorithm by replacing step 4 as follows:

---

4. For every point i, compute the second order perturbation in λ_1 when that
   point is deleted, namely

$$\Delta\lambda_1(i) = \frac{n^2}{(n-1)^2}(\mathbf{u}_1 \cdot \mathbf{v}_i)^2 \left[\frac{n-1}{n} + \sum_{k=2}^{4}\frac{(\mathbf{u}_k \cdot \mathbf{v}_i)^2}{\lambda_k - \lambda_1}\right]$$

Once it has been decided which point to remove, the accurate eigensolution is computed to
prevent errors accumulating over time. Thus, while perturbation theory is used to speed up
the search for the outlier, the true solution is calculated when the point is actually removed.
The removal of k outliers therefore involves only k eigendecompositions, substantially reducing the previous computational cost.

The use of this approximation may sometimes identify an outlier incorrectly, and improvements can be made to the above algorithm to reduce the chance of this occurring.
For instance, one can compute the accurate solutions for several of the points with large
perturbations, ensuring that the worst offender is pinpointed correctly. One could also use
higher order perturbations. In any case, the main value of the perturbation analysis is the
insight it provides into the operation of the outlier rejection method (elegantly demonstrat-
ing in Section 6.4.4 how the minimum eigenvalue and residual methods are related) and the
tractability of the noise analysis in Section 6.5.

6.4.3   Method of residuals

We now turn to the second outlier rejection method, the method of residuals. Recall Equa-
tion (6.8), $\mathbf{h}^{\top} = \mathbf{u}_1^{\top}\mathbf{V}$, where $\mathbf{h} = (h_0, h_1, \ldots, h_{n-1})^{\top}$. Clearly, h_i is a linear combination
of random Gaussian variables and is thus itself a Gaussian variable, with $E\{h_i\} = 0$ and

---

Task

Given $\mathbf{r}_i \in \mathbb{R}^m$ ($i = 0 \ldots n - 1$, $n \geq m$), with $\mathbf{r}_i$ perturbed by zero–mean, independent, isotropic, Gaussian noise having variance σ^2, reject outliers from the set $\{\mathbf{r}_i\}$ to a $\zeta\%$ confidence level.

Algorithm

1. Compute the data centroid $\bar{\mathbf{r}}$ and centre the points, writing $\mathbf{v}_i = \mathbf{r}_i - \bar{\mathbf{r}}$. Construct the scatter matrix $\mathbf{W} = \sum_{i=0}^{n-1} \mathbf{v}_i \mathbf{v}_i^\mathsf{T}$.

2. Find the eigenvector $\mathbf{u}_1$ corresponding to the minimum eigenvalue λ_1 of $\mathbf{W}$, and compute the residual vector $\mathbf{h} = \mathbf{u}_1^\mathsf{T} \mathbf{V}$.

3. Find the maximum residual $h_{max} = \max |h_i|$ (for $0 \leq i \leq n - 1$), and perform a two–tailed Gaussian significance test on h_{max}/σ_h. If this is within acceptable limits, set $\mathbf{n} = \mathbf{u}_1$ and goto step 5.

4. Delete the point with maximum residual. Update the scatter matrix and centroid according to Equations (6.9) and (6.10), and return to step 2.

5. Calculate $e = -\mathbf{n} \cdot \bar{\mathbf{r}}$. The final hyperplane parameters are $\{\mathbf{n}, e\}$.

Figure 6.6: Outlier rejection algorithm: residuals method.

$\mathrm{Var}\{h_i\} = \sigma_h^2$ (σ_h is derived in Section 6.5.2). The elements of $\mathbf{h}$ thus form a Gaussian distribution, and standard statistical tests can be performed on them to identify outliers. Since the residuals can be positive or negative ("behind" or "in front of" the hyperplane), a two–tailed test is needed, such as $-1.96 \leq h_i/\sigma_h \leq 1.96$ for a 95% confidence level. The algorithm is summarised in Figure 6.6.

6.4.4   Comparison between methods

The two outlier rejection schemes in Section 6.4.1 and Section 6.4.3 share many similarities, and the following analogy can be made. Consider n samples $\{t_1, t_2, \ldots, t_n\}$ drawn from a univariate population with mean $\bar{t}$ and variance σ_t^2. The statistic

$$T^2 = \frac{(t_1 - \bar{t})^2 + (t_2 - \bar{t})^2 + \cdots + (t_n - \bar{t})^2}{\sigma_t^2}$$

has a χ^2 distribution if the underlying population is Gaussian. Then $(t_i - \bar{t})/\sigma_t$ is the "residual" (individual distance), and T^2 is the "eigenvalue" (sum of the squared distances). A large residual causes a corresponding increase in the eigenvalue, and the reliability of both schemes hinges on the validity of the Gaussian distribution assumption and the assumed value of σ_t. The difference is that whereas the residual scheme simply rejects the point that deviates most from the current fit, the influence function rejects the point whose exclusion will result in the best fit on the *next* iteration. Put differently, the residual scheme looks only at the *existing* fit to identify the "villain", while the influence fit "looks ahead" to the *next* fit to see what improvements will actually materialise.

The two schemes often agree on which point to discard, though this is not true in general. To see why, recall from Equations (6.14) and (6.15) that the first and second order approximations to $\Delta\lambda_1$ following removal of point i are

$$\dot{\lambda}_1(0)\epsilon = -\frac{n}{n-1}(\mathbf{u}_1 \cdot \mathbf{v}_i)^2 \quad \text{and} \quad \frac{1}{2}\ddot{\lambda}_1(0)\epsilon^2 = -\frac{n^2}{(n-1)^2}(\mathbf{u}_1 \cdot \mathbf{v}_i)^2 \sum_{k=2}^{4} \frac{(\mathbf{u}_k \cdot \mathbf{v}_i)^2}{\lambda_k - \lambda_1},$$

while the residual for point i is (Equation (6.7))

$$h_i = \mathbf{u}_1 \cdot \mathbf{v}_i.$$

Evidently, *there is agreement at the first order approximation*, since $\Delta\lambda_1$ is then simply proportional to h_i^2. In other words, the point with largest residual will also be that point inducing maximum change in λ_1 at a first order expansion! The residual method is therefore subsumed by the influence function method; the results are identical if a first order eigenvalue perturbation model is used. The second (and higher) order terms start to account for the change in eigenvector structure (the "look–ahead effect"), so a different point might then have a larger overall influence.

We demonstrate this by means of a simple 2D example. Consider the set of points in Figure 6.7(a). The dominant data (7 points) are noise–free and lie on the straight line $3.8x + 12.2y + 9.6 = 0$. There is a single contaminant (point 3), and the OR fit to the full data set is shown in Figure 6.7(b). The outlier has a significant detrimental effect, "pulling" the line over towards point 3. The residuals h_i are listed in Table 6.1, and it is clearly impossible to identify the outlier on the basis of these perpendicular distances. In fact, point 4 has a larger residual than point 3! The minimum eigenvalue scheme offers a much clearer distinction, discriminating between point 3 and point 4 by a factor greater than 2. This discrimination power is illustrated graphically in Figure 6.8, where the relative values of h_i^2 are shown in (a) and those of $\Delta\lambda_1$ in (b). We therefore only consider the minimum eigenvalue method in the sections that follow. Table 6.1 also lists the 2nd order eigenvalue perturbations to show that they provide a fairly good approximation to the true changes in λ_1. The approximations are worse for points further from the centroid (e.g. points 3 and 6), but still identify the most influential point correctly.

6.4.5   Experiments

Although our theory generalises to any number of dimensions, the data used in this section are two–dimensional, since higher dimensional spaces are harder to visualise (examples with 4D data are given in Section 6.6). Our first example illustrates the facility to cope with multiple outliers, while the second illustrates "masking".

Figure 6.9 shows the OR fit for 16 data points perturbed from the line $-6.5x + 2.1y + 3.2 = 0$ by Gaussian noise ($\sigma = 1$). There are 7 contaminants (points 1, 3, 4, 5, 9, 17 and 21), and a 95% significance level is specified for the χ^2 test, i.e. λ_1 must fall within the limit set by $\chi^2_{0.95}$. Table 6.2 gives the second–order eigenvalue perturbations at each iteration,

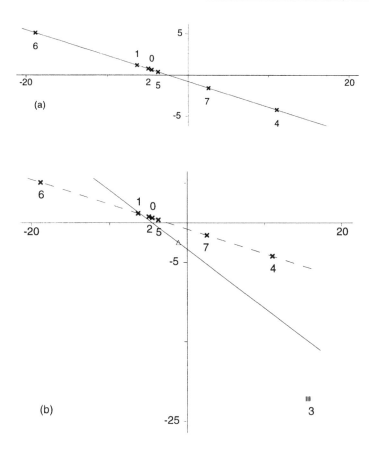

Figure 6.7: *Data lying on the line* $3.8x + 12.2y + 9.6 = 0$ *(crosses) with a single outlier (square): (a) The correct fit; (b) The orthogonal regression fit affected by the outlier (point 3). The triangle shows the centroid and the dashed line shows the correct fit.*

with the largest perturbation identifying the point to be deleted. The 6 iterations eliminate contaminants 5, 21, 1, 3, 17 and 4 in order.

We make several observations. First, the procedure terminates automatically, with the algorithm itself deciding (based on a statistical decision) when to stop removing outliers. Errors still remain after the final iteration, but they fall within acceptable levels, i.e. they are consistent with the assumed levels of noise. Second, as predicted by theory, λ_1 decreases with the deletion of each point. Third, a contaminant is sometimes sufficiently consistent with the underlying fit to be indistinguishable from a valid noisy point; point 9 is not recognised as an outlier since it lies in the centre of the data. This is not serious since the error introduced by the outlier falls within the tolerable bound, so isn't severely disruptive. Indeed, a principal dilemma in outlier detection lies in deciding whether a potential outlier is an extreme (but valid) perturbation of the dominant set, or a contaminant from another population. Such a decision is necessarily a statistical one and guidance must be obtained

Point	Residual (h_i, h_i^2)		$\Delta\lambda_1$ (true, approx)	
0	0.5337	0.2849	0.2911	0.2910
1	-0.1285	0.0165	0.0172	0.0172
2	0.3753	0.1409	0.1446	0.1445
3	-6.2510	39.0751	97.8422	64.6086
4	6.2607	39.1961	44.2979	43.8900
5	0.8231	0.6775	0.6877	0.6875
6	-4.7517	22.5791	34.7413	30.7303
7	3.1384	9.8497	9.9089	9.9090

Table 6.1: *Data for the example in Figure 6.7. The eigenvalue scheme provides better discrimination between the outlier (point 3) and the valid data than the residual scheme. The important comparison is between h_i^2 and the true change in λ_1 (columns 3 and 4). The last column gives the 2nd order approximation to $\Delta\lambda_1$.*

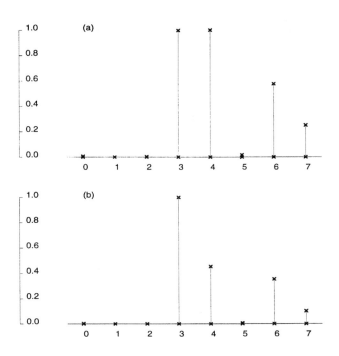

Figure 6.8: *Superior discrimination power of eigenvalue method versus residual method. Point 3 is the outlier: (a) Residual h_i^2 for each data point relative to the largest; (b) True change in minimum eigenvalue, $\Delta\lambda_1$, for each data point relative to the largest.*

from the application (e.g. in the form of prior knowledge of σ). Finally, we note that the outliers are confidently detected, despite comprising a third of the data set.

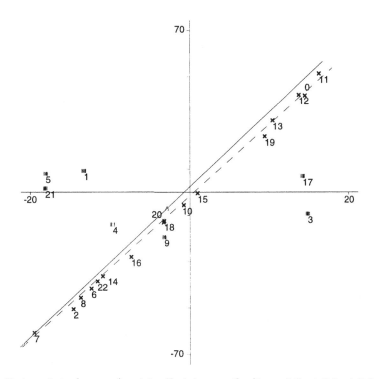

Figure 6.9: *Data points (crosses) originally lying on the line* $-6.5x + 2.1y + 3.2 = 0$ *(dashed) are perturbed by Gaussian noise ($\sigma = 1$) and contaminants are added (squares). The orthogonal regression fit (solid) is affected by both the contaminants and the noise. The centroid of the entire data set is also shown (triangle).*

Our second example illustrates why only one point is deleted at a time. Figure 6.10 shows points displaced from their line $-2.5x + 8y + 7.1 = 0$ by Gaussian noise ($\sigma = 1$). Four outliers are added (points 5, 8, 17 and 19) and Table 6.3 summarises the iterations for selected points. We observe that a poor initial fit can incorrectly attribute influence to points which are actually correct; for instance, point 18 has a large influence in iteration 1 even though it isn't an outlier. This influence decreases as the fit improves. It is also important to recompute fits after removing points since outliers are sometimes "masked" by other outliers. For instance, the fact that point 19 is an outlier only becomes apparent in iteration 3, once outliers 17 and 8 have been removed.

6.4.6   Discussion

Section 6.3.1 mentioned some drawbacks of existing outlier tests for orthogonal regression, and chief among them was the often unrealistic requirement for a Gaussian null distribution. This requires the data points r_i to occupy a Gaussian-like hyper-ellipsoid about the centroid

Point	1	2	3	4	5	6
0	5.7709	0.9641	0.0189	2.5845	0.3214	0.3719
1	228.4474	260.0890	291.4183	–	–	–
2	2.8790	1.4140	0.1834	0.0007	0.4857	0.7606
3	324.4107	293.1365	264.0619	236.4255	–	–
4	21.4058	29.5759	39.6449	50.1245	39.7098	33.5104
5	375.4156	–	–	–	–	–
6	1.3879	0.3553	0.0340	0.4923	0.0003	0.0777
7	0.0057	0.2396	1.5087	2.3972	0.7615	0.6540
8	1.0954	0.2477	0.0749	0.5652	0.0019	0.0326
9	11.5638	6.8778	3.1767	1.0760	3.3018	5.3344
10	2.6872	0.5479	0.0214	1.0614	0.0443	0.1708
11	1.4071	0.1299	2.3753	9.9370	4.2309	0.5780
12	2.2814	0.0078	1.0651	6.2725	2.1465	0.0856
13	2.5045	0.0895	0.5705	4.2978	1.1999	0.0042
14	0.9153	0.1088	0.2150	1.0677	0.0923	0.0001
15	3.1933	0.7043	0.0044	1.0119	0.0280	0.2600
16	3.7735	1.5443	0.1828	0.0515	0.2760	0.8571
17	159.4018	134.3370	113.5211	92.4945	110.5386	–
18	1.6782	0.2114	0.1622	1.4740	0.1745	0.0182
19	7.3900	2.2923	0.2468	0.5360	0.0457	1.3662
20	1.9686	0.3277	0.0830	1.1962	0.0894	0.0617
21	306.2009	339.7749	–	–	–	–
22	0.9459	0.1328	0.1795	0.9438	0.0611	0.0022
Delete	5	21	1	3	17	4
λ_1	1019.4191	679.6477	388.2411	151.8177	41.2524	7.7420

Table 6.2: *Table of data for the example in Figure 6.9. Each column refers to an iteration and gives the 2nd order eigenvalue perturbation caused by deleting each point. The largest perturbation determines which point is deleted, and the eigensolution is then recomputed to determine λ_1 accurately.*

$\bar{r}$. In many applications, there is no justification for such an assumption, since the data r_i are often *not* random variables in the sense that they estimate a stationary mean. Instead, they may simply represent an arbitrary structure perturbed by noise, where the *noise errors* are the fundamental random variables. In our case, for instance, fixed points are displaced from their hyperplane π by small noise vectors. The "small signal" therefore introduces randomness into the "large signal", and the statistical assumptions should therefore only be imposed on the noise, not on the distribution of features within the hyperplane.

Since we have m–dimensional data with a single constraint, the first $m-1$ eigenvectors explain the structure of the hyperplane (irrelevant from a noise viewpoint), and the last eigenvector explains the noise; if there was no noise in the system, λ_1 would be zero. By

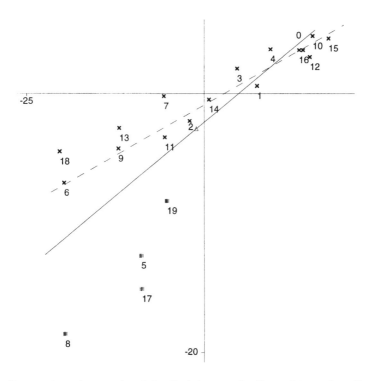

Figure 6.10: *Data points (crosses) originally lying on the line* $-2.5x + 8y + 7.1 = 0$ *(dashed) are perturbed by Gaussian noise* $(\sigma = 1)$ *and contaminants are added (squares). The orthogonal regression fit (solid) and data centroid (triangle) are shown.*

Point	1	2	3	4
5	35.3175	46.2081	68.8767	−
8	56.0784	78.4477	−	−
11	1.6243	0.4591	0.0631	1.0286
17	71.5647	−	−	−
18	47.4049	33.8555	14.4025	5.6792
19	12.0295	17.0913	27.0447	36.3764
Delete	17	8	5	19
λ_1	201.4694	120.7046	51.6937	15.3057

Table 6.3: *Subset of the data table for Figure 6.10. Each column refers to an iteration and gives the* 2nd *order eigenvalue perturbation caused by deleting each point.*

only focussing on this last dimension, we avoid imposing conditions on the distribution of the data itself. This contrasts with other schemes (e.g. [46, 58]) that analyse the full set of principal components, and thus require knowledge of how the data are distributed along all other axes.

6.5   Error analysis

Once the outliers have been removed, it is useful to relate the noise in the input to the orthogonal regression solution. Several researchers have recently stressed the advantages of systematically studying the statistical error behaviour of an algorithm [73, 163]. We additionally emphasise the importance of having first removed the outliers, since their presence can severely distort such calculations, leading to serious bias or reduction in precision [14]. Qualitatively, outliers tend to deflate correlations and inflate variances. Indeed, Barnett and Lewis [14] mention in this regard that "even one or two outliers in a large set can wreak havoc!" (page 249).

In Section 6.5.1, we perform a similar error analysis to that of Weng, Huang and Ahuja [163], and in Section 6.5.2 we derive the variance and covariance expressions for the residuals. We discover that this variance differs from point to point, and modify our previous algorithm accordingly.

6.5.1   Hyperplane covariance matrix

Let the data point $\hat{\mathbf{r}}$ be perturbed by *independent, isotropic, additive, Gaussian noise* $\delta\mathbf{r}$, giving the measurement $\mathbf{r} = \hat{\mathbf{r}} + \delta\mathbf{r}$. It is assumed that each noise perturbation has zero mean ($E\{\delta\mathbf{r}_i\} = \mathbf{0}$) with variance σ^2, i.e. $E\{\mathbf{r}_i\} = E\{\hat{\mathbf{r}}_i + \delta\mathbf{r}_i\} = \hat{\mathbf{r}}_i$, Var $\{\mathbf{r}_i\}$ = Var $\{\delta\mathbf{r}_i\}$ and

$$\Lambda_\mathbf{r} = E\{\delta\mathbf{r}_i \, \delta\mathbf{r}_i^\top\} = \sigma^2 \, \mathbf{I}_m. \tag{6.16}$$

We further assume (as in [163]) that the data points have independent errors, i.e. $E\{\delta\mathbf{r}_i\delta\mathbf{r}_j^\top\} = \delta_{ij}\,\Lambda_\mathbf{r}$, where δ_{ij} is the Kronecker delta product. Our objective is to assess the effects of these errors on $\mathbf{u}_1$, and hence obtain a confidence estimate in the computed normal $\mathbf{n}$.

Consider the centred data points $\mathbf{v}_i$. The noise in $\mathbf{r}_i$ induces an error $\delta\mathbf{v}_i$ in $\mathbf{v}_i$:

$$\mathbf{v}_i = \mathbf{r}_i - \bar{\mathbf{r}} = (\hat{\mathbf{r}}_i - \hat{\bar{\mathbf{r}}}) + (\delta\mathbf{r}_i - \delta\bar{\mathbf{r}}) = \hat{\mathbf{v}}_i + \delta\mathbf{v}_i$$

Noting that $\delta\bar{\mathbf{r}} = \sum_{i=0}^{n-1} \delta\mathbf{r}_i/n$, we have

$$\begin{aligned}
E\{\delta\mathbf{v}_i \, \delta\mathbf{v}_i^\top\} &= E\{(\delta\mathbf{r}_i - \delta\bar{\mathbf{r}})(\delta\mathbf{r}_i - \delta\bar{\mathbf{r}})^\top\} \\
&= E\{\delta\mathbf{r}_i \, \delta\mathbf{r}_i^\top\} - E\{\delta\bar{\mathbf{r}} \, \delta\mathbf{r}_i^\top\} - E\{\delta\mathbf{r}_i \, \delta\bar{\mathbf{r}}^\top\} + E\{\delta\bar{\mathbf{r}} \, \delta\bar{\mathbf{r}}^\top\} \\
&= \sigma^2\mathbf{I}_m - \frac{1}{n}\sigma^2\mathbf{I}_m - \frac{1}{n}\sigma^2\mathbf{I}_m + \frac{1}{n^2}(n\,\sigma^2\mathbf{I}_m) \quad = \quad \frac{n-1}{n}\sigma^2\mathbf{I}_m,
\end{aligned}$$

and for $i \neq j$,

$$E\{\delta\mathbf{v}_i \, \delta\mathbf{v}_j^\top\} = E\{(\delta\mathbf{r}_i - \delta\bar{\mathbf{r}})(\delta\mathbf{r}_j - \delta\bar{\mathbf{r}})^\top\}$$

$$\begin{aligned} &= E\{\delta\mathbf{r}_i\,\delta\mathbf{r}_j^\mathsf{T}\} - E\{\delta\bar{\mathbf{r}}\,\delta\mathbf{r}_j^\mathsf{T}\} - E\{\delta\mathbf{r}_i\,\delta\bar{\mathbf{r}}^\mathsf{T}\} + E\{\delta\bar{\mathbf{r}}\,\delta\bar{\mathbf{r}}^\mathsf{T}\}\\ &= \mathbf{0} - \frac{1}{n}\sigma^2\mathbf{I}_m - \frac{1}{n}\sigma^2\mathbf{I}_m + \frac{1}{n^2}(n\,\sigma^2\mathbf{I}_m) \quad = \quad -\frac{1}{n}\sigma^2\mathbf{I}_m \end{aligned}$$

The covariance matrix for $\mathbf{v}_i$ is thus

$$\mathbf{\Lambda}_\mathbf{v} = E\{\delta\mathbf{v}_i\,\delta\mathbf{v}_i^\mathsf{T}\} = \frac{\sigma^2}{n}(n-1)\mathbf{I}_m = \frac{n-1}{n}\mathbf{\Lambda}_\mathbf{r}, \tag{6.17}$$

and that for $\mathbf{v}_i$ and $\mathbf{v}_j$ $(i \neq j)$ is

$$\mathbf{\Upsilon}_\mathbf{v} = E\{\delta\mathbf{v}_i\,\delta\mathbf{v}_j^\mathsf{T}\} = -\frac{\sigma^2}{n}\mathbf{I}_m = -\frac{1}{n}\mathbf{\Lambda}_\mathbf{r} \tag{6.18}$$

When n is large, the covariance matrices for the centred data $\mathbf{v}_i$ tend towards those for the uncentred data $\mathbf{r}_i$, since $(n-1)/n \rightarrow 1$ and $-1/n \rightarrow 0$.

In matrix form, $\mathbf{V} = [\mathbf{v}_0 \mid \mathbf{v}_1 \mid \cdots \mid \mathbf{v}_{n-1}]$ and $\delta\mathbf{V} = [\delta\mathbf{v}_0 \mid \delta\mathbf{v}_1 \mid \cdots \mid \delta\mathbf{v}_{n-1}]$. The perturbation caused in the scatter matrix $\mathbf{W} = \mathbf{V}\mathbf{V}^\mathsf{T}$ due to the noise in $\mathbf{V}$ is:

$$\mathbf{W} = (\hat{\mathbf{V}} + \delta\mathbf{V})\,(\hat{\mathbf{V}} + \delta\mathbf{V})^\mathsf{T} = \hat{\mathbf{V}}\,\hat{\mathbf{V}}^\mathsf{T} + \hat{\mathbf{V}}\,\delta\mathbf{V}^\mathsf{T} + \delta\mathbf{V}\,\hat{\mathbf{V}}^\mathsf{T} + \delta\mathbf{V}\,\delta\mathbf{V}^\mathsf{T}.$$

We write $\mathbf{W} = \hat{\mathbf{W}} + \delta\mathbf{W}$ and note that $\hat{\mathbf{W}} = \hat{\mathbf{V}}\,\hat{\mathbf{V}}^\mathsf{T}$. Then, using a first order approximation [163],

$$\delta\mathbf{W} \approx \hat{\mathbf{V}}\,\delta\mathbf{V}^\mathsf{T} + \delta\mathbf{V}\,\hat{\mathbf{V}}^\mathsf{T}. \tag{6.19}$$

Finally we can consider the eigenvector $\hat{\mathbf{u}}_1$. Since $\hat{\mathbf{W}}\hat{\mathbf{u}}_j = \hat{\lambda}_j\hat{\mathbf{u}}_j$ gives the noise–free solution, it follows that $\hat{\lambda}_1 = 0$. Moreover, the noise–free residuals $\hat{h}_i = \hat{\mathbf{u}}_1 \cdot \hat{\mathbf{v}}_i$ are zero, because all points then lie *on* the hyperplane. Since $\delta\mathbf{W}$ is a real symmetric matrix, the first order change in $\hat{\mathbf{u}}_1$ is (Appendix C.1):

$$\delta\mathbf{u}_1 = -\sum_{k=2}^{4} \frac{(\hat{\mathbf{u}}_k^\mathsf{T}\,\delta\mathbf{W}\,\hat{\mathbf{u}}_1)\hat{\mathbf{u}}_k}{\hat{\lambda}_k} = -\left(\sum_{k=2}^{4}\frac{\hat{\mathbf{u}}_k\hat{\mathbf{u}}_k^\mathsf{T}}{\hat{\lambda}_k}\right)\delta\mathbf{W}\,\hat{\mathbf{u}}_1.$$

Now $\delta\mathbf{W}\,\hat{\mathbf{u}}_1 = (\hat{\mathbf{V}}\,\delta\mathbf{V}^\mathsf{T} + \delta\mathbf{V}\,\hat{\mathbf{V}}^\mathsf{T})\,\hat{\mathbf{u}}_1 = \hat{\mathbf{V}}\,\delta\mathbf{V}^\mathsf{T}\,\hat{\mathbf{u}}_1$ since $\hat{\mathbf{V}}^\mathsf{T}\,\hat{\mathbf{u}}_1 = \mathbf{0}$ (the noise–free residuals $\hat{\mathbf{u}}_1 \cdot \hat{\mathbf{v}}_i$ equal 0), so $\delta\mathbf{u}_1$ can be written

$$\delta\mathbf{u}_1 = \hat{\mathbf{J}}\,\hat{\mathbf{V}}\,\delta\mathbf{V}^\mathsf{T}\,\hat{\mathbf{u}}_1 = \hat{\mathbf{J}}\sum_{i=0}^{n-1}\hat{\mathbf{v}}_i\,(\delta\mathbf{v}_i \cdot \hat{\mathbf{u}}_1), \quad \text{where} \quad \hat{\mathbf{J}} = -\sum_{k=2}^{4}\frac{\hat{\mathbf{u}}_k\,\hat{\mathbf{u}}_k^\mathsf{T}}{\hat{\lambda}_k} \tag{6.20}$$

Finally, the covariance matrix for $\mathbf{u}_1$ can be computed, giving a measure of confidence in the eigenvector solution (Appendix C.2.1):

$$\mathbf{\Lambda}_{\mathbf{u}_1} = E\{\delta\mathbf{u}_1\,\delta\mathbf{u}_1^\mathsf{T}\} = -\sigma^2\hat{\mathbf{J}}. \tag{6.21}$$

Many of the above equations require the true noise–free quantities (e.g. $\hat{\mathbf{V}}, \hat{\mathbf{u}}_1, \hat{\mathbf{J}}$), which are not available in general. Weng *et al.* [163] pointed out that if one writes, for instance, $\hat{\mathbf{V}} = \mathbf{V} - \delta\mathbf{V}$ and substitutes this in the relevant equations, the terms in $\delta\mathbf{V}$ disappear in the first order expressions, allowing $\mathbf{V}$ to be simply interchanged with $\hat{\mathbf{V}}$, and so on. The covariance matrix for $\mathbf{u}_1$ can thus be expressed in terms of directly measurable quantities:

$$\mathbf{\Lambda}_{\mathbf{u}_1} = -\sigma^2\sum_{k=2}^{4}\frac{\mathbf{u}_k\,\mathbf{u}_k^\mathsf{T}}{\lambda_k}. \tag{6.22}$$

6.5.2   Residual variance and covariance

The residual is

$$h_i = \hat{h}_i + \delta h_i = (\hat{\mathbf{u}}_1 + \delta\mathbf{u}_1) \cdot (\hat{\mathbf{v}}_i + \delta\mathbf{v}_i) = \hat{\mathbf{u}}_1 \cdot \hat{\mathbf{v}}_i + \hat{\mathbf{u}}_1 \cdot \delta\mathbf{v}_i + \hat{\mathbf{v}}_i \cdot \delta\mathbf{u}_1 + \delta\mathbf{u}_1 \cdot \delta\mathbf{v}_i,$$

where $\hat{h}_i = 0$. We neglect second–order terms and obtain an expression for the perturbation,

$$\delta h_i \approx \hat{\mathbf{u}}_1 \cdot \delta\mathbf{v}_i + \hat{\mathbf{v}}_i \cdot \delta\mathbf{u}_1.$$

Thus $E\{\delta h_i\} = 0$ and its variance σ_{hi}^2 is

$$
\begin{aligned}
\text{Var}\{\delta h_i\} &= E\left\{(\hat{\mathbf{u}}_1 \cdot \delta\mathbf{v}_i + \hat{\mathbf{v}}_i \cdot \delta\mathbf{u}_1)^2\right\} \\
&= E\left\{(\hat{\mathbf{u}}_1 \cdot \delta\mathbf{v}_i)^2 + (\hat{\mathbf{v}}_i \cdot \delta\mathbf{u}_1)^2 + 2\,(\hat{\mathbf{v}}_i \cdot \delta\mathbf{u}_1)\,(\hat{\mathbf{u}}_1 \cdot \delta\mathbf{v}_i)\right\} \\
&= \hat{\mathbf{u}}_1^\top \mathbf{\Lambda}_v \hat{\mathbf{u}}_1 + \hat{\mathbf{v}}_i^\top \mathbf{\Lambda}_{\mathbf{u}_1} \hat{\mathbf{v}}_i + 2\,\hat{\mathbf{v}}_i^\top\, E\{\delta\mathbf{u}_1 \delta\mathbf{v}_i^\top\}\hat{\mathbf{u}}_1 \qquad (6.23)
\end{aligned}
$$

Appendix C.2.2 shows that this reduces to

$$\sigma_{hi}^2 = \sigma^2\left[\frac{n-1}{n} - \sum_{k=2}^{4}\frac{(\mathbf{v}_i \cdot \mathbf{u}_k)^2}{\lambda_k}\right] \qquad (6.24)$$

The residual variance for point i therefore consists of a *constant* term $\sigma_h^2 = (n-1)\sigma^2/n$, dependent on the variance of the raw data, and a *variable* term, dependent on the specific location of $\mathbf{v}_i$. Evidently, no single variance applies to all the residuals; *the residual error distribution is different for every point*. As a rough guide, points further away from the data centroid have smaller residuals. This is because the further a point is from the centre along a given axis, the greater its potential influence in altering that axis. This is analogous to a lever, where the moment caused by a constant force varies with the distance between the pivot and the point of application. Further details are given in [129].

To illustrate this effect, we return the example in Figure 6.10, where points 5, 8, 17 and 19 were identified as outliers using the algorithm in Figure 6.5. Figure 6.11(a) graphs the residual variances σ_{hi}^2 for the valid points at each iteration, illustrating that the presence of outliers tends to *inflate* the computed variances. Figure 6.11(b) plots the final variances against the projected distances $d_i = (\mathbf{u}_2 \cdot \mathbf{v}_i)$, showing that points further from the centroid (measured along the axis $\mathbf{u}_2$) have smaller variances. Equation (6.24) reduces to a simple quadratic in the 2D case:

$$\sigma_{hi}^2 = \sigma^2\left[\frac{n-1}{n} - \frac{d_i^2}{\lambda_2}\right]$$

This phenomenon of inhomogeneous residual variances (heteroscedasticity) is termed "ballooning" [14, 32]. It is a common effect, arising even with a simple linear regression model (i.e. 2D case with a single regressor variable). It is inconvenient because if the residuals all have different Gaussian distributions, there is no way to compare them sensibly; a single χ^2 test is invalid. This problem was ignored in the algorithms of Section 6.4.1 and 6.4.3, which assumed the residuals h_i to be from a *univariate* distribution. One solution is to *compute* the variance for each point and scale the residual appropriately [14], thus ensuring that all

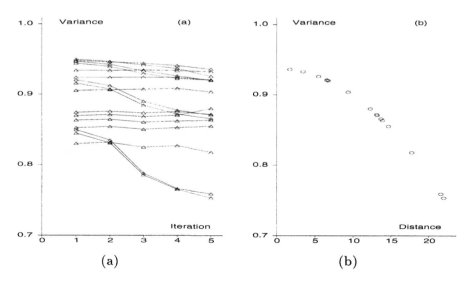

Figure 6.11: *Computed residual variances σ_{hi}^2 for the valid data points in Figure 6.10: (a) The presence of outliers tends to* inflate *the variance estimates, which reduce to the correct theoretical value as more outliers are removed; (b) The variance falls off with increasing distance from the centroid $d_i = \mathbf{u}_2 \cdot \mathbf{v}_i$ (measured along the fitted axis).*

residuals have unit standard deviation. The difficulty here is that the formula for computing σ_{hi} assumes that there are no outliers! When there *are* outliers, the computed variances are distorted, rendering them useless.

We solve this problem by proceeding in two stages. First we note that $\sigma_h^2 = (n-1)\sigma^2/n$ is the *upper bound* for σ_{hi}^2; as points move further away from the centroid, the variance *decreases,* and for these points the upper bound exceeds the correct value. We therefore initially use σ_h^2 as the common variance for *all* points. By overestimating the variance for some points, we err on the side of conservatism, since all *valid* points will then fall *well* inside the allowed probability region – indeed, further inside this region than the specified confidence level merits. Consequently, any points falling *outside* the limit are certainly contaminants.

Once the worst outliers have been removed, we refine the dividing line by introducing the computed variances, assured that σ_{hi} will not be too inaccurate. Each residual is then scaled by its individual σ_{hi} value, giving the new χ^2 test statistic

$$\tau^2 = \sum_{i \in \mathcal{V}} \frac{h_i^2}{\sigma_{hi}^2}, \tag{6.25}$$

where $\mathcal{V}$ is the current set of valid points, a subset of the initial data set with some outliers removed. As before, the modified algorithm proceeds until the scaled variances fall within specified probability limits, indicating that no further outliers can be detected. Details of these algorithms, along with experimental results, are given in [129].

Finally, we note that the residuals are not mutually independent; the covariance between any two residuals h_i and h_j is given by (Appendix C.2.3):

$$\text{Cov}\left\{\delta h_i, \delta h_j\right\} = E\{\delta h_i\,\delta h_j\} = -\sigma^2 \left[\frac{1}{n} + \sum_{k=2}^{4} \frac{(\mathbf{v}_i \cdot \mathbf{u}_k)\,(\mathbf{v}_j \cdot \mathbf{u}_k)}{\lambda_k}\right] \tag{6.26}$$

We have found empirically that this is a minor effect.

6.6   Affine epipolar geometry revisited

The outlier rejection scheme is now applied to the computation of affine epipolar geometry, whose algorithm was given in Figure 5.7. This involves minimising E_3 (cf. Equation (5.12)), namely

$$\sum_{i=0}^{n-1}(ax_i' + by_i' + cx_i + dy_i + e)^2 \quad \text{subject to} \quad a^2 + b^2 + c^2 + d^2 = 1.$$

This expression is simply Equation (6.5) with $m = 4$, i.e. a 4D hyperplane is being fitted. Figure 6.12 shows an example with synthetic data, satisfying $11x' - 3y' - 9x + 1.5y + 7 = 0$. The correct solution is thus $\mathbf{n} = (0.7533, -0.2054, -0.6163, 0.1027)^\top$. The initial 27 points were chosen randomly to fit a 256×256 image and were perturbed by Gaussian noise ($\sigma = 1$). Eight outliers were then introduced (points 0, 3, 4, 6, 9, 10, 11 and 19). The correct epipolar lines are also shown, illustrating that the noise has displaced the valid data slightly from their epipolars, and that the outliers generally lie off their predicted lines. Table 6.4 gives the computed solution at each iteration (a 95% confidence test is used). The improvement in the normal after removing the outliers can also be assessed by comparing the computed slope of the epipolar lines against their true slopes. Figure 6.13 illustrates this marked improvement.

Iteration:	1	2	3	4	5	6
a	0.7624	0.7616	0.7612	0.7544	0.7533	0.7526
b	-0.2976	-0.3012	-0.2842	-0.2309	-0.2140	-0.2023
c	-0.5562	-0.5548	-0.5669	-0.6037	-0.6129	-0.6190
d	0.1443	0.1465	0.1360	0.1145	0.1052	0.0977
λ_1	171.1771	132.3706	99.0762	62.0155	47.6647	33.0349
Delete	3	6	11	4	10	END

Table 6.4:   *The solution for* $\mathbf{n}$ *at each iteration.   The correct solution is* $\mathbf{n} = (0.7533, -0.2054, -0.6163, 0.1027)^\top$).

The scheme is now illustrated on real images. System noise arises from quantisation error, corner localisation error and camera model assumptions. This noise can be estimated [91, 143], and we find $\sigma = 0.7$ pixels. Outliers arise mainly from mismatches in the correspondence algorithm, failures in the segmentation algorithm (e.g. inclusion of a feature which doesn't belong to the object of interest) and false corners (see Section 2.3.2). A 95% confidence level is used throughout.

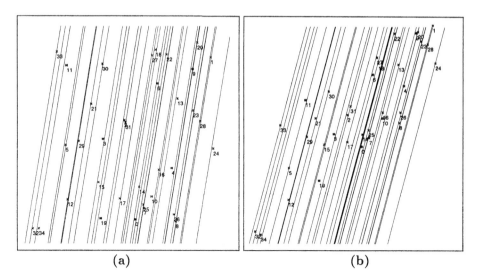

Figure 6.12: *Synthetic correspondences (stars) satisfying* $11x' - 3y' - 9x + 1.5y + 7 = 0$ *along with outliers (squares). The correct epipolar lines are shown: (a) l_1; (b) l_2.*

	Image	True	Before	After
(a)	1	9.46°	14.54°	8.97°
	2	15.26°	21.33°	15.05°

(b)   (c)

Figure 6.13: *Outlier rejection improves parameter estimation: (a) Angles of epipolar lines before and after outlier rejection; (b)(c) True angle (solid), angle computed before outlier rejection (dashed) and angle computed after outlier rejection (dotted). The dotted line is almost identical to the solid one.*

Figure 6.14(a) shows the first frame in a sequence taken from a camera moving to the right in a static scene. The computed flow vectors (for 219 corners) are shown in Figure 6.14(b), and while they certainly convey the motion with good qualitative accuracy, outliers arise from the error sources discussed earlier. The black left edge of the image also provides an interesting performance test. Figure 6.14(c) shows the 22 outliers identified by our method, all of which were confirmed as incorrect matches (by manual inspection). Figure 6.14(d) shows the final data set. Not all outliers have been removed, but those that remain have negligible effect on the fit. The minimum eigenvalue λ_1 decreased from 370.13 to 42.94. A more intuitive error measure is E_1 (cf. Equation (5.10)), the sum of squared perpendicular image distances from the points to their respective epipolar lines[5]:

$$E_1 = \sum_{i=0}^{n-1} \frac{(ax'_i + by'_i + cx_i + dy_i + e)^2}{a^2 + b^2} + \sum_{i=0}^{n-1} \frac{(ax'_i + by'_i + cx_i + dy_i + e)^2}{c^2 + d^2}$$

In the above example, E_1 is reduced from 1933.36 to 171.83, giving the final fit an average perpendicular distance of 0.66 pixels between each corner and its epipolar line (a reasonable result given $\sigma = 0.7$). Figure 6.15 shows two additional examples, with a stationary camera and a moving object. This introduces an additional source of error, namely the segmentation of background points from moving points (e.g. some motion of the shirt is included with the head motion in Figure 6.15(a)). The majority of outliers are successfully rejected.

Although the technique evidently performs well when the outliers are "randomly" distributed, it is not designed to cope with "structured noise". It is therefore unsuitable for segmenting independent motions in a scene, such as multiple moving objects (as in Figure 4.26). This is because least squares estimation is severely distorted by multiple populations. Larger scale segmentation techniques must therefore be used first (e.g. our MAST algorithm or [147]), and each object can then be handled in turn.

Finally, although the noise model in Section 6.5.1 implicitly assumes that x, y, x' and y' are all subject to the *same* image noise (a zero–mean Gaussian with variance σ^2), $\mathbf{x}$ and $\mathbf{x}'$ may well have different σ values (e.g. if two different cameras are used). Moreover, x may have a different σ from y (e.g. if aspect ratio hasn't been corrected for). The changes to the theory are straightforward (if tedious); one modifies the variances in Equation (6.16) and propagates the changes through the subsequent derivations.

6.7   Conclusions

This chapter has proposed a novel scheme for rejecting contaminants from a set of data lying on an $(m$–$1)$–dimensional hyperplane. The method operates in the orthogonal regression framework and is based on the simple (yet powerful) principle of an influence function. By assessing the change in the minimum eigenvalue of the scatter matrix when a point is deleted, the total error in the fit can be represented without modelling how the data points themselves are distributed. Algorithm termination is based on a statistical decision rather than prior knowledge of the number of outliers present. This minimum eigenvalue scheme has also been

---

[5]The value of E_1 exceeds E_3 since the 4D distances are projected into 2D and renormalised.

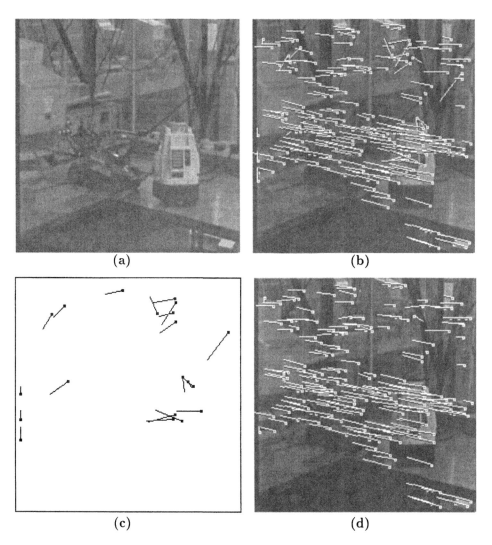

Figure 6.14: *Outlier rejection with a moving camera and static scene (camera moves right).
Motion vectors are shown double length for clarity: (a) First frame; (b) Initial motion vectors; (c) Rejected motion vectors; (d) Final motion vectors (outliers removed).*

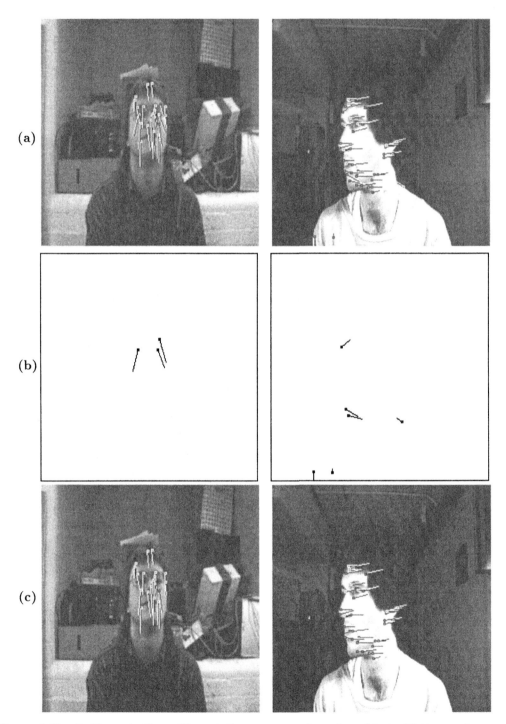

Figure 6.15: *Outlier rejection with a static camera and moving object. Motion vectors are shown double length for clarity: (a) Initial motion vectors; (b) Rejected motion vectors; (c) Final motion vectors with outliers removed.*

shown to subsume the more familiar method of residuals, and its error characteristics have been investigated. Its successful operation has been demonstrated both on synthetic data and images from a real application.

Two interesting research directions deserve further study. First, the contributions of various data points could be weighted on the basis of their influence, downgrading "alleged contaminants" rather than rejecting them outright. Second, the proposed technique applies to an $(m-1)$–dimensional hyperplane in $\mathbb{R}^m$, and requires modification to cope with lower dimensional surfaces; for an $(m{-}r)$–dimensional surface $(r \geq 2)$, λ_1 isn't well separated from $\{\lambda_2 \ldots \lambda_r\}$, and the eigensolution perturbation analysis would have to be rederived.

Chapter 7

Rigid motion from
affine epipolar geometry

7.1 Introduction

This chapter tackles the *motion estimation* problem, using affine epipolar geometry as the tool. Given m distinct views of n points located on a rigid object, the task is to compute its 3D motion without any prior 3D knowledge. There are several reasons why many existing point–based motion algorithms are of limited practical use: the inevitable presence of noise is often ignored; unreasonable demands are often made on prior processing (e.g. a suitable perceptual frame must first be selected, the features must appear in every frame, etc.); algorithms often only work in special cases (e.g. rotation about a fixed axis); and some algorithms require batch processing, rather than more natural sequential processing.

Although the epipolar constraint has been widely used in perspective and projective motion applications [43, 57, 87] (e.g. to aid correspondence, recover the translation direction and compute rigid motion parameters), it has seldom been used under *affine* viewing conditions (though see [66, 79]). This chapter therefore makes the following contributions:

- Affine epipolar geometry is related to the rigid motion parameters, and Koenderink and van Doorn's novel motion representation is formalised [79]. The scale, cyclotorsion angle and projected axis of rotation are then computed *directly* from the epipolar geometry (i.e. using two views). The only camera calibration parameter needed here is aspect ratio. A suitable error model is also derived.

- Images are processed in successive pairs of frames, facilitating extension to the m–view case in a sequential (rather than batch) processing mode.

- A linear Kalman filter is defined to determine optimal estimates over long sequences. Unlike some previous point–based structure and motion schemes (e.g. [26]), we do not assign an individual Kalman filter to each 3D feature. This liberates us from having to track individual 3D points through multiple views.

- Least squares formulations are employed to utilise *all* available points, not just a minimum set. This improves the accuracy of the motion solution (by providing immunity to noise and enabling detection of outliers) and also obviates the need to *select* a LCF. Our n–point framework subsumes the results for minimum configurations.

- Computation of the remaining turn angle about the 3D axis (using three distinct views) is discussed.

This research was inspired by the work of Koenderink and van Doorn [79], who recovered the 3D motion of an object simply by observing the local coordinate frame they attached to it. Their entire computation relied on this LCF and was thus extremely sensitive to errors. Furthermore, their motion algorithm used only four points and was not extendable when additional points were available. This chapter builds on their work in an attempt to redress these shortcomings. Section 7.2 briefly summarises the motion ambiguities that arise under parallel projection, and Sections 7.3 and 7.4 then discuss the two–view and three–view cases.

7.2   Motion ambiguities

Ambiguous interpretations of object motion (and structure) arise when two or more unknown parameters are confounded and there are insufficient data to identify their individual contributions to the imaged effect. Two well–known ambiguities specific to parallel projection are Necker reversal and the bas–relief ambiguity.

Necker reversal occurs because an object rotating by ρ and its mirror image rotating by $(-\rho)$ generate the same image under parallel projection (Figure 7.1(a)). Thus, structure is only recovered up to a reflection about the frontal plane.

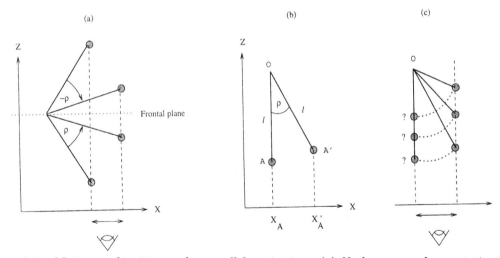

Figure 7.1: *Motion ambiguities under parallel projection: (a) Necker reversal: a rotating object generates the same image as its mirror object rotating in the opposite sense; (b) The bas–relief ambiguity: a rigid rod OA rotates through ρ in the X–Z plane; (c) We observe $X'_A - X_A = \ell \sin \rho$ and cannot deduce both ℓ and ρ.*

The bas–relief ambiguity is illustrated in Figures 7.1(b) and (c). Consider a rigid rod of length ℓ, which starts in position OA and rotates about O in the X–Z plane through angle ρ (Figure 7.1(b)). That is, $X'_A - X_A = \ell \sin \rho$. If $X'_A - X_A$ is observed without any prior knowledge of the rod or its motion, then it is impossible to deduce both ℓ and ρ, because an infinite family of (ℓ, ρ) solutions could generate the same image (Figure 7.1(c)). This *bas–relief* (or *depth–turn*) ambiguity is so–named because a shallow object experiencing a large turn (i.e. small ℓ and big ρ) generates the same image as a deep object experiencing a small turn (i.e. big ℓ and small ρ). Extra points cannot resolve this ambiguity since each new point adds one new piece of information (X) and one new unknown (its depth). Fixing any *one* depth (or the angle ρ) determines the structure and the motion uniquely, i.e. there is a *one–parameter* family of solutions. This ambiguity can only be resolved from two views when perspective effects are significant; otherwise, three views are needed.

Finally, there remains a "depth–scale" ambiguity (as in the perspective case). The algorithm can recover scaled depth $\Delta Z_i^c / Z_{ave}^c$, but the true depth ΔZ_i^c cannot be determined unless Z_{ave}^c is known. For instance, an object twice as big and twice as far away as the real one generates the identical image. The true depth of at least one point on the object is needed to resolve this ambiguity.

7.3 Rigid motion: two views

It is well–known that two distinct views of four non–coplanar, rigid points generate a one–parameter family of structure and motion solutions under parallel projection [18, 66, 79]. Koenderink and van Doorn [79] showed further that from two views, the change in scale, the cyclorotation angle and the projections of the axes of rotation can be recovered. Their algorithm used the minimum set of points, required a perceptual frame and involved a succession of stages. These shortcomings are overcome by deriving this partial motion solution *directly from the affine epipolar geometry*. The resulting algorithm uses the full set of points and requires no LCF.

7.3.1 Weak perspective epipolar geometry

Rigidity is imposed on the world motion parameters $\{\mathbf{A}_m, \mathbf{D}_m\}$ by requiring $\mathbf{A}_m$ to be a rotation matrix[1], denoted $\mathbf{A}_m = \mathbf{R}_m$. Equation (3.16) then becomes

$$\mathbf{X'} = \mathbf{R}_m \mathbf{X} + \mathbf{D}_m. \tag{7.1}$$

Rigidity reduces the degrees of freedom in the motion parameters from 12 to 6 (see Appendix D), and the use of difference vectors eliminates $\mathbf{D}_m$,

$$\Delta \mathbf{X'} = \mathbf{X'} - \mathbf{X}_0' = \mathbf{R}_m \, \Delta \mathbf{X},$$

leaving the three rotational degrees of freedom. There are various ways to parameterise these rotation angles (see Appendix D), the most popular being Euler angles and the angle–axis form. Solving for $\mathbf{R}$ requires the measurement of angles, which are not affine invariants; it

---

[1]There are four rotation matrices here: the pose of the two cameras ($\mathbf{R}_p$ and $\mathbf{R}_p'$), the motion of the object within the world coordinate system ($\mathbf{R}_m$), and the composite relative rotation between scene and camera ($\mathbf{R}$). The latter is the matrix of interest to us.

is therefore necessary to use *weak perspective* cameras here, namely $\mathbf{M}$ and $\mathbf{M}'$ (see Equation (3.7)):

$$\mathbf{M} = \frac{f}{Z^c_{ave}} \left[\begin{array}{c} \xi\,\mathbf{R}^{\mathsf{T}}_{p1} \\ \mathbf{R}^{\mathsf{T}}_{p2} \end{array} \right] \quad \text{and} \quad \mathbf{M}' = \frac{f'}{Z^{c'}_{ave}} \left[\begin{array}{c} \xi'\,\mathbf{R}'^{\mathsf{T}}_{p1} \\ \mathbf{R}'^{\mathsf{T}}_{p2} \end{array} \right].$$

Here $\mathbf{R}_p$ and $\mathbf{R}'_p$ are rotation matrices representing the camera positions relative to the world coordinate frame. The aspect ratios ξ and ξ' must be known in order to compute angles, and the focal lengths (f, f') must be equal (though they may be unknown) in order to determine scale. No other calibration parameters are needed. Without loss of generality, we set $\mathbf{R}_p = \mathbf{I}_3$ (the identity matrix) and $\mathbf{R}'_p = \mathbf{R}$, incorporating the composite camera poses and object motion into $\mathbf{R}$. The scale factor $s = Z^c_{ave}/Z^{c'}_{ave}$ is introduced ($s > 1$ for a "looming" object and $s < 1$ for one that is "receding"), and scaled depth is defined as $\Delta z_i = f\Delta Z^c_i/Z^c_{ave} = f(Z^c_i - Z^c_{ave})/Z^c_{ave}$. Equation (5.3) then becomes

$$\boxed{\Delta\mathbf{x}' = s \left[\begin{array}{cc} R_{11} & R_{12} \\ R_{21} & R_{22} \end{array} \right] \Delta\mathbf{x} + s\,\Delta z \left[\begin{array}{c} R_{13} \\ R_{23} \end{array} \right]} \tag{7.2}$$

This is the rigid motion form of the epipolar line, with direction $(R_{13}, R_{23})^{\mathsf{T}}$. Taking the component of $\Delta\mathbf{x}'$ perpendicular to this direction and using standard cross product equalities for a rotation matrix gives the rigid motion form of the affine epipolar constraint equation (Equation (5.8)):

$$\boxed{R_{23}\Delta x' - R_{13}\Delta y' + sR_{32}\Delta x - sR_{31}\Delta y = 0} \tag{7.3}$$

Equations (7.2) and (7.3) generalise the pure orthographic forms ($s = 1$) derived by Huang and Lee [66] and used in [29, 64]. Note that there are only three independent degrees of freedom in Equation (7.3), since only the ratios of the coefficients may be computed; we will show these to be the scale factor s and two rotation angles.

7.3.2   The KvD rotation representation

Koenderink and van Doorn [79] introduced a novel rotation representation (which we term *KvD* and show in Appendix D to be a variant of Euler angles), and presented a geometric analysis of it. We formalise their representation algebraically to illustrate its advantages. In *KvD*, a rotation matrix $\mathbf{R}$ is decomposed into two parts (Figure 7.2),

$$\mathbf{R} = \mathbf{R}_\rho\,\mathbf{R}_\theta. \tag{7.4}$$

First, there is a rotation $\mathbf{R}_\theta$ in the image plane through angle θ (i.e. about the line of sight). This is followed by a rotation $\mathbf{R}_\rho$ through an angle ρ about a unit axis $\boldsymbol{\Phi}$ lying in a plane parallel to the image plane, with $\boldsymbol{\Phi}$ angled at ϕ to the positive X axis, i.e. a pure rotation *out of* the image plane. We define $\boldsymbol{\Phi}$ and its perpendicular as $\boldsymbol{\Phi}^\perp$ as

$$\boldsymbol{\Phi} = \left[\begin{array}{c} \cos\phi \\ \sin\phi \end{array} \right] \quad \text{and} \quad \boldsymbol{\Phi}^\perp = \left[\begin{array}{c} \sin\phi \\ -\cos\phi \end{array} \right]$$

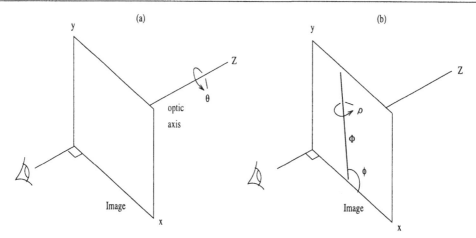

Figure 7.2: *The KvD rotation representation: (a) rotation by θ about the Z axis; (b) subsequent rotation by ρ about a fronto–parallel axis $\mathbf{\Phi}$ angled at ϕ to the X axis.*

The *KvD* representation has three main advantages. First, rotation about the optic axis provides no new information about structure, so it makes sense to first remove this "useless" component. Second, *KvD* exposes the bas–relief ambiguity in a way that the more popular angle–axis form doesn't – an advantage of Euler forms in general [55]. Third, *KvD* is elegant in that two views enable us to completely solve for two rotation angles (ϕ and θ), with the third (ρ) parameterising the remaining family of solutions. This contrasts with, say, the angle–axis form (Appendix D.1), for which only one angle can be solved from two views, the two remaining angles satisfying a non–linear constraint equation [18]. The disadvantage of *KvD* is that the physical interpretation of rotation occurring about a single 3D axis is lost.

7.3.3   Solving for s, ϕ and θ

It is now shown how to solve for the scale factor (s), the projection of the axis of rotation (ϕ) and the cyclotorsion angle (θ) directly from the affine epipolar geometry. The formal derivations are preceded by a geometric explanation of how the epipolar lines relate to the unknown motion parameters.

Geometry

Consider a camera rotating about an axis $\mathbf{\Phi}$ lying parallel to the image plane (Figure 7.3(a)). The epipolar plane π is perpendicular to both this axis and the two images, and intersects the images in the epipolar lines $\mathbf{u}$ and $\mathbf{u}'$. This is because a world point A defines the epipolar plane π and will be projected into the images along these lines of intersection (cf. Figure 5.2). Consequently:

The projection of the axis of rotation $\mathbf{\Phi}$ is perpendicular to the epipolar lines.

This relation still holds if there is additionally a cyclotorsion θ in the image plane (Figure 7.3(b)); the axis $\mathbf{\Phi}$ and intersection $\mathbf{u}'$ remain fixed in space, and are simply observed at a new angle in the image, maintaining the orthogonality between the epipolar lines and the projected axis. The orientations of the epipolars in the two images therefore differ by θ. Importantly, changing the magnitude of the turn angle ρ doesn't alter the epipolar geometry in any way (Figure 7.4). This angle is therefore indeterminate from two views, a consequence of the bas–relief ambiguity.

Figure 7.4 illustrates the effect of scale. Consider a 3D object to be sliced into parallel epipolar planes, with each plane constraining how a particular slice of the object moves. Altering the effective size of the object (e.g. by moving closer to it) simply changes the relative spacing between successive epipolar planes.

In summary, cyclotorsion simply rotates the epipolars, rotation out of the plane causes foreshortening along the epipolar lines (orthogonal to $\mathbf{\Phi}$), and a scale change uniformly alters the epipolar line spacing (Figure 7.5).

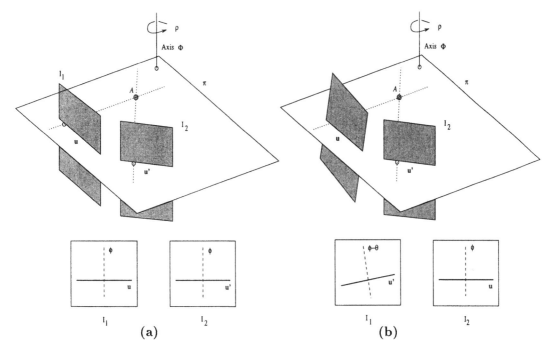

Figure 7.3: *The camera rotates about the axis $\mathbf{\Phi}$ which is parallel to the image plane. The intersection of the epipolar plane π with the image planes gives epipolar lines $\mathbf{u}$ and $\mathbf{u'}$, and the projections of $\mathbf{\Phi}$ in the images are orthogonal to these epipolars: (a) no cyclotorsion occurs ($\theta = 0°$); (b) the camera counter–rotates by θ in I_1, so the orientations of the epipolars change by θ.*

Theory

A detailed analysis of the KvD forms of Equations (7.2) and (7.3) is provided in Appendix E; only equations relevant to the epipolar geometry are given below. Substituting the KvD

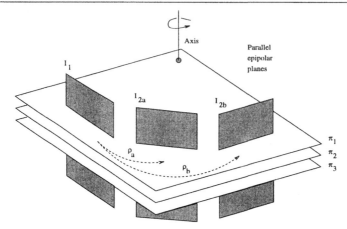

Figure 7.4: *The scene can be sliced into parallel epipolar planes. The magnitude of ρ has no effect on the epipolar geometry (provided ρ ≠ 0), so it is indeterminate from two views.*

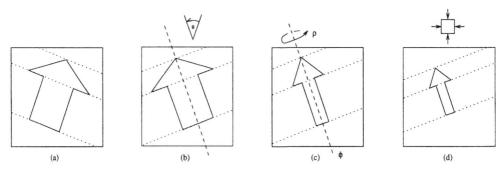

Figure 7.5: *The effect of scale and KvD rotation angles on the epipolar lines for an object moving relative to a stationary camera. This also illustrates the assumed sequence of events accounting for the transition from I_1 to I_2: (a) I_1; (b) cyclotorsion (θ); (c) rotation out of the plane (φ and ρ); (d) scaling, giving I_2.*

expressions for R_{ij} into Equation (7.2) gives the direction of the epipolar line in I_2,

$$\begin{bmatrix} R_{13} \\ R_{23} \end{bmatrix} = \sin \rho \, \mathbf{\Phi}^{\perp},$$

proving that the epipolar is perpendicular to the axis of rotation $\mathbf{\Phi}$. Similarly, the epipolar constraint (Equation (7.3)) becomes

$$\boxed{\sin \rho \, [\cos \phi \, \Delta x'_i + \sin \phi \, \Delta y'_i - s \cos(\phi - \theta) \, \Delta x_i - s \sin(\phi - \theta) \, \Delta y_i] = 0} \quad (7.5)$$

It is evident from Equation (7.5) that s, θ and ϕ can be computed directly from the affine epipolar geometry, because the algorithm in Figure 5.7 solves

$$a\Delta x'_i + b\Delta y'_i + c\Delta x_i + d\Delta y_i = 0$$

for the ratios of a, b, c and d. A direct comparison with Equation (7.5) yields the central result,

$$\tan \phi = \frac{b}{a}, \quad \tan(\phi - \theta) = \frac{d}{c} \quad \text{and} \quad s^2 = \frac{c^2 + d^2}{a^2 + b^2}, \quad (7.6)$$

with $s > 0$ (by definition). Note that ϕ is the angle of projection in I_2 of the axis of rotation out of the plane, while $(\phi - \theta)$ is its angle of projection in I_1. Equation (7.5) shows immediately that Equation (7.3) has only *two* independent rotation parameters, θ and ϕ, because the angle ρ cancels out (provided it is non–zero). If $\rho = 0°$, then there is no rotation out of the image plane and Φ is obviously undefined, so this technique cannot be used. Equation (7.5) is therefore more informative than Equation (7.3) since it identifies explicitly what quantities can be computed, and under what circumstances.

7.3.4   Error model

We now compute a noise model for s, ϕ and θ, each of which is a non–linear function of $\mathbf{n} = (a, b, c, d)^{\mathsf{T}}$, itself a random variable due to image noise. Given the covariance matrix $\Lambda_{\mathbf{n}} = [\Lambda_{ij}]$ for $\mathbf{n}$ from Equation (6.21), our objective is to compute the means and variances of s, ϕ and θ.

Let the true (i.e. noise–free) value of $\mathbf{n}$ be $\tilde{\mathbf{n}}$, and write $\mathbf{n} = (n_1, n_2, n_3, n_4)^{\mathsf{T}}$ for convenience. The noise perturbation of $\tilde{\mathbf{n}}$ is $\delta\mathbf{n} = (\delta n_1, \delta n_2, \delta n_3, \delta n_4)^{\mathsf{T}}$, so that $\mathbf{n} = \tilde{\mathbf{n}} + \delta\mathbf{n}$. The diagonal elements of $\Lambda_{\mathbf{n}}$ define the variance of $\delta\mathbf{n}$ ($\Lambda_{ii} = E\{\delta n_i^2\}$) while the off–diagonal elements give the covariances ($\Lambda_{ij} = \Lambda_{ji} = E\{\delta n_i \, \delta n_j\}$). The Taylor series for a function $q(\tilde{\mathbf{n}})$ expanded about $\mathbf{n}$ is[2]

$$q(\tilde{\mathbf{n}}) = q(\mathbf{n} - \delta\mathbf{n}) = q(\mathbf{n}) - \sum_{i=1}^{4} \frac{\partial q(\mathbf{n})}{\partial \tilde{n}_i} \delta n_i + \frac{1}{2} \sum_{i=1}^{4} \sum_{j=1}^{4} \frac{\partial^2 q(\mathbf{n})}{\partial \tilde{n}_i \, \partial \tilde{n}_j} \delta n_i \, \delta n_j - \cdots$$

We ignore terms above second order, assume that $\partial^2 q / \partial n_i \, \partial n_j = \partial^2 q / \partial n_j \, \partial n_i$, and note that $E\{\delta\mathbf{n}\} = \mathbf{0}$ and $E\{\tilde{\mathbf{n}}\} = \tilde{\mathbf{n}}$. Then,

$$E\{q(\tilde{\mathbf{n}})\} \approx E\{q(\mathbf{n})\} + \frac{1}{2} \sum_{i=1}^{4} \sum_{j=1}^{4} \frac{\partial^2 q(\mathbf{n})}{\partial \tilde{n}_i \, \partial \tilde{n}_j} E\{\delta n_i \, \delta n_j\}$$

$$\text{i.e.} \quad q(\tilde{\mathbf{n}}) \approx E\{q(\mathbf{n})\} + \frac{1}{2} \sum_{i=1}^{4} \sum_{j=1}^{4} \frac{\partial^2 q(\mathbf{n})}{\partial \tilde{n}_i \, \partial \tilde{n}_j} \Lambda_{ij}.$$

This is a *biased* estimate, since the expected value of $q(\mathbf{n})$ does not equal the true value $q(\tilde{\mathbf{n}})$. The systematic error (or *bias*) is

$$B = \frac{1}{2} \sum_{i=1}^{4} \sum_{j=1}^{4} \frac{\partial^2 q(\mathbf{n})}{\partial \tilde{n}_i \, \partial \tilde{n}_j} \Lambda_{ij} \tag{7.7}$$

where $E\{q(\mathbf{n})\} = q(\tilde{\mathbf{n}}) - B$. Since $\mathbf{n}$ and $\Lambda_{\mathbf{n}}$ are known, B is fully determined and is added to the computed value $q(\mathbf{n})$. The variance of q is $E\{\,[\,q(\mathbf{n}) - E\{q(\mathbf{n})\}\,]^2$, i.e.

$$\text{Var}\,\{q(\mathbf{n})\} \approx E\left\{ \sum_{i=1}^{4} \frac{\partial q(\mathbf{n})}{\partial \tilde{n}_i} \delta n_i - \frac{1}{2} \sum_{i=1}^{4} \sum_{j=1}^{4} \frac{\partial^2 q(\mathbf{n})}{\partial \tilde{n}_i \, \partial \tilde{n}_j} \delta n_i \, \delta n_j + B \right\}^2 = \sum_{i=1}^{4} \sum_{j=1}^{4} \frac{\partial q(\mathbf{n})}{\partial \tilde{n}_i} \frac{\partial q(\mathbf{n})}{\partial \tilde{n}_j} \Lambda_{ij}$$

$$\tag{7.8}$$

---

[2]We use this form, rather than $q(\mathbf{n}) = q(\tilde{\mathbf{n}} + \delta\mathbf{n})$, in order that the expressions will be functions of the known vector $\mathbf{n}$, rather than the unknown $\tilde{\mathbf{n}}$.

Similarly, the covariance between two different expressions $q_1(\mathbf{n})$ and $q_2(\mathbf{n})$ is given by $E\{\,[\,q_1(\mathbf{n}) - E\{q_1(\mathbf{n})\}\,]\,[\,q_2(\mathbf{n}) - E\{q_2(\mathbf{n})\}\,]\,\}$, i.e.

$$\text{Cov }\{q_1(\mathbf{n}), q_2(\mathbf{n})\} \approx \left(\sum_{i=1}^{4} \sum_{j=1}^{4} \frac{\partial q_1(\mathbf{n})}{\partial \tilde{n}_i} \frac{\partial q_2(\mathbf{n})}{\partial \tilde{n}_j} \Lambda_{ij} \right). \tag{7.9}$$

The three functions of interest are

$$s(\mathbf{n}) = \frac{\sqrt{n_3^2 + n_4^2}}{\sqrt{n_1^2 + n_2^2}}, \quad \phi(\mathbf{n}) = \frac{n_1}{\sqrt{n_1^2 + n_2^2}} \quad \text{and} \quad \theta(\mathbf{n}) = \frac{n_1}{\sqrt{n_1^2 + n_2^2}} - \frac{n_3}{\sqrt{n_3^2 + n_4^2}},$$

and it is straightforward to derive the relevant bias, variance and covariance expressions. These provide confidence regions for the solution, and are used later in the Kalman filter.

7.3.5   Algorithm

The final algorithm is given in Figure 7.6. The *centroid* serves as the reference point rather than some designated feature point (e.g. $\mathbf{x}_0$) since this relates better to the minimisation theory of Section 5.4. The solution for θ in Equation (7.6) has a 180° ambiguity since only the *directions* of the projected axes are known, not their positive or negative senses. In other words, it remains to determine "which way" the axis cyclo–rotated between I_1 and I_2. Equation (7.5) is therefore used to check whether $(\phi - \theta)$ is correct.

The algorithm fails in two cases: (i) the object is planar; and (ii) the object is non–planar but doesn't rotate out of the image plane[3]. The rank test of Section 5.4.5 alerts us to these problems because in both cases, a 2D matrix $\boldsymbol{\Gamma}$ explains the image motion ($\Delta \mathbf{x}' = \boldsymbol{\Gamma} \, \Delta \mathbf{x}$), so the system has rank two (within the bounds of noise).

Figure 7.7(a) graphs successive two–frame estimates of s, θ and ϕ in a synthetic 30–frame sequence with additive Gaussian image noise. The object undergoes two different, constant motions separated by a step change: s is initially unity (no translation in depth) and then increases as the object approaches the camera at constant speed; θ changes from 4° to −2°; and ϕ changes from 82° to 50°. The true parameter values clearly lie within the computed 95% error bounds.

7.3.6   Kalman filter

Physical objects have inertia and it is sensible to exploit this temporal continuity to improve the motion estimates. This is achieved by means of a linear discrete–time Kalman filter [11, 38], a popular framework for weighting observations and predictions [26, 41, 101, 113, 172]. The state–transition equation (*plant* model) describes the evolution of the state $\mathbf{y}$,

$$\mathbf{y}(k+1) = \mathbf{F}\,\mathbf{y}(k) + \mathbf{g}(k) \tag{7.10}$$

---

[3]Lee and Huang [85] termed this "degenerate motion", and noted that it also arises when the rotation angle about *any* axis is a multiple of 360° (equivalent to no motion) and when $\rho = 180°$. In all such cases, the projection plane remains the same, so the observer doesn't get a new viewing direction.

Task
Given $\{a, b, c, d\}$ (computed from the affine epipolar geometry algorithm using two distinct views of at least four non–coplanar points), determine the scale s, cyclotorsion θ and axis projection ϕ.

Algorithm

1. Set $s = \sqrt{c^2 + d^2}/\sqrt{a^2 + b^2}$.

2. Set $\phi = \arctan(b/a)$ and $\theta = \phi - \arctan(d/c)$.

3. Calculate the sums of square residuals

$$r^- = \sum_{i=0}^{n-1}[\Delta\mathbf{x}'_i \cdot \boldsymbol{\Phi} - s\Delta\mathbf{x}_i \cdot \mathbf{R}(-\theta)\,\boldsymbol{\Phi}]^2, \quad r^+ = \sum_{i=0}^{n-1}[\Delta\mathbf{x}'_i \cdot \boldsymbol{\Phi} + s\Delta\mathbf{x}_i \cdot \mathbf{R}(-\theta)\,\boldsymbol{\Phi}]^2.$$

If $r^+ < r^-$, set $\theta \leftarrow \theta + 180°$.

Figure 7.6: Weak perspective epipolar motion algorithm.

where $\mathbf{y}(k)$ is the state at time k, $\mathbf{g}(k)$ is the constant additive process noise, $\mathbf{F}$ is the state–transition matrix, and $\mathbf{y}(k+1)$ is the state at the following $k+1$ time step. Observations of the system are made according to the *measurement* model

$$\mathbf{z}(k+1) = \mathbf{H}\,\mathbf{y}(k+1) + \mathbf{w}(k+1) \tag{7.11}$$

where $\mathbf{z}(k+1)$ is the observation at time $k+1$, $\mathbf{w}(k+1)$ is the additive observation noise, and $\mathbf{H}$ is the observation matrix. The noise vectors $\mathbf{g}(k)$ and $\mathbf{w}(k)$ are assumed to be Gaussian, identically distributed, and temporally uncorrelated with zero mean. Thus, $E\{\mathbf{g}(k)\} = E\{\mathbf{w}(k)\} = \mathbf{0}$, $E\{\mathbf{g}(i)\,\mathbf{g}(j)^\top\} = \delta_{ij}\boldsymbol{\Lambda}_{\mathbf{g}}$ and $E\{\mathbf{w}(i)\,\mathbf{w}(j)^\top\} = \delta_{ij}\boldsymbol{\Lambda}_{\mathbf{w}}(i)$, where $\boldsymbol{\Lambda}_{\mathbf{g}}$ and $\boldsymbol{\Lambda}_{\mathbf{w}}$ are covariance matrices. The complete predict–observe–update cycle is:

Predict state and variance:
$$\hat{\mathbf{y}}(k+1|k) = \mathbf{F}\,\hat{\mathbf{y}}(k|k) \tag{7.12}$$
$$\mathbf{P}(k+1|k) = \mathbf{F}\,\mathbf{P}(k|k)\,\mathbf{F}^\top + \boldsymbol{\Lambda}_{\mathbf{g}} \tag{7.13}$$

Update state and variance:
$$\hat{\mathbf{y}}(k+1|k+1) = \hat{\mathbf{y}}(k+1|k) + \mathbf{W}(k+1)\,[\mathbf{z}(k+1) - \mathbf{H}\,\hat{\mathbf{y}}(k+1|k)] \tag{7.14}$$
$$\mathbf{P}(k+1|k+1) = \mathbf{P}(k+1|k) - \mathbf{W}(k+1)\,\mathbf{S}(k+1)\,\mathbf{W}^\top(k+1) \tag{7.15}$$

where $\mathbf{W}(k+1) = \mathbf{P}(k+1|k)\,\mathbf{H}^\top\,\mathbf{S}^{-1}(k+1)$ and $\mathbf{S}(k+1) - \mathbf{H}\,\mathbf{P}(k+1|k)\,\mathbf{H}^\top + \boldsymbol{\Lambda}_{\mathbf{w}}(k\mid 1)$.

We estimate s, ϕ and θ using a constant position model ($\dot{s} = \dot{\phi} = \dot{\theta} = 0$). The state vector is $\mathbf{y} = (s, \phi, \theta)^\top$ with state transition matrix $\mathbf{F} = \mathbf{I}_3$. We observe[4] s, ϕ and $\phi - \theta$,

---

[4]We could observe θ directly; however, $\phi - \theta$ is obtained naturally from $\arctan(d/c)$ in Equation (7.6).

so $\mathbf{z} = (z_1, z_2, z_3)^\top = (s + B_1, \phi + B_2, \phi - \theta + B_3)^\top$, where B_i are the relevant bias terms from Equation (7.7). The observation matrix ($\mathbf{H}$) and its noise covariance matrix ($\mathbf{\Lambda_w}(k) = E\{\mathbf{w}(k)\,\mathbf{w}(k)^\top\}$) are then

$$\mathbf{H} = \begin{bmatrix} 1 & 0 & 0 \\ 0 & 1 & 0 \\ 0 & 1 & -1 \end{bmatrix} \quad \text{and} \quad \mathbf{\Lambda_w} = \begin{bmatrix} \mathrm{Var}\{z_1\} & \mathrm{Cov}\{z_1, z_2\} & \mathrm{Cov}\{z_1, z_3\} \\ \mathrm{Cov}\{z_1, z_2\} & \mathrm{Var}\{z_2\} & \mathrm{Cov}\{z_2, z_3\} \\ \mathrm{Cov}\{z_1, z_3\} & \mathrm{Cov}\{z_2, z_3\} & \mathrm{Var}\{z_3\} \end{bmatrix}.$$

The variance and covariance terms are obtained from Equations (7.8) and (7.9). Unlike $\mathbf{\Lambda_g}$, $\mathbf{\Lambda_w}$ changes over time and must be recomputed at each iteration.

The process noise covariance matrix $\mathbf{\Lambda_g}$ is calculated by considering potential errors in the model and determining how they propagate through to the state vector. The velocities $(\dot{s}, \dot{\phi}, \dot{\theta})$ will not be exactly zero, so they are modelled as Gaussian, zero-mean, random variables (r_s, r_ϕ, r_θ) with variances (q_s, q_ϕ, q_θ) (i.e. $E\{r_s\} = 0$ and $\mathrm{Var}\{r_s\} = q_s$). This noise is assumed uncorrelated over time (e.g. $E\{r_s(i)\,r_s(j)\} = \delta_{ij}\,q_s$), giving

$$\mathbf{g} = \Delta t \begin{bmatrix} r_s \\ r_\phi \\ r_\theta \end{bmatrix}, \quad \mathbf{\Lambda_g} = \Delta t^2 \begin{bmatrix} q_s & 0 & 0 \\ 0 & q_\phi & 0 \\ 0 & 0 & q_\theta \end{bmatrix},$$

with Δt the time period between successive observations.

The filter is initialised by choosing a starting estimate for $\hat{\mathbf{y}}(0|0)$ and its variance $\mathbf{P}(0|0)$. The solution from the first frame–pair $\{I_1, I_2\}$ gives the initial state $\hat{\mathbf{y}}(0|0)$ and we set $\mathbf{P}(0|0) = 25\,\mathbf{\Lambda_g}$. The effects of these initial estimates diminish with time, though a good initial estimate improves convergence [38]. Since $\mathbf{\Lambda_w}$ changes over time, the filter doesn't settle to a steady state. The variances of the velocity perturbation variables (q_s, q_ϕ, q_θ) are determined empirically.

7.3.7   Results

Figure 7.7(b) shows the filtered results of the example from Section 7.3.5, along with the 95% confidence intervals obtained from the Kalman filter variances. The solution is clearly smoother after filtering and the variances decrease as the filter becomes more confident in its predictions. Note the increase in variances at the motion discontinuity; at that stage, the filter detects that the observation falls outside the validation region and re–initialises itself.

Figure 7.8 shows a real sequence with a car rotating on a turn–table about a (known) fixed axis. The successive two–frame estimates of the projected axis angle along with the computed errors serve as the filter input, and these are shown alongside the filter output, which gives reliable estimates of the projected axis. Figure 7.9 shows a second example with a subject shaking his head. Here the true axis is unknown, but it is approximately vertical and the results are qualitatively correct. Finally, results are shown for the images and corner data of Harris [55] (Figures 7.10 and 7.11). There is no scale change between views, and the fiducial axis is 10° off the vertical. Our unfiltered solution (using E_3) is identical to his (using E_2) since the scale here is unity (see Section 5.4). However, our error model facilitates the filtering operation, whose estimates are clearly superior.

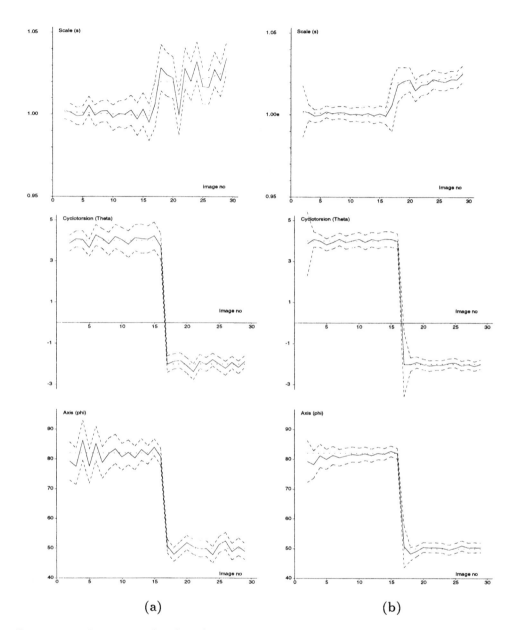

(a)   (b)

Figure 7.7: *Estimates of s, θ and φ over a 30–frame synthetic sequence with σ = 0.5 pixels and a discontinuity in constant motion. Solid lines show computed values, dotted lines show true values, and dashed lines show 95% confidence intervals: (a) Raw 2–frame estimates with associated error models (input to filter); (b) Kalman filtered estimates with 95% confidence regions (within which the true values fall).*

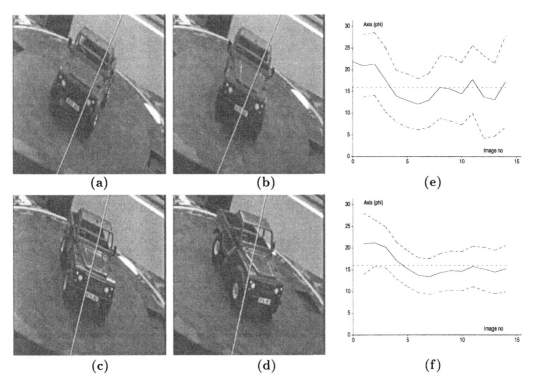

(a) (b) (e)

(c) (d) (f)

Figure 7.8: *A buggy rotates on a turntable angled at 16° off the vertical in the image (true world angle approximately 24° with aspect ratio 0.65): (a)(b)(c)(d) Frames 2, 4, 6, 8 (6° turns between successive frames), with axes drawn through the image centre; (e) Unfiltered two–frame estimates of the axis angle. Solid lines show computed values, dotted lines show true values, and dashed lines show 95% confidence intervals; (f) Filtered estimates with associated 95% confidence regions.*

7.3.8   Previous work

Harris [55] used a weak perspective camera and the Euler angle representation to solve for rotation angles over two frames. The weak perspective form of ϵ_h (Equation (3.42)), whose shortcomings were outlined in Sections 3.5.5 and 5.4.3, was minimised and shown to be *independent* of the turn angle η (see Appendix D.2), illustrating the bas–relief ambiguity. No confidence estimates in the solution were provided, and only the scale and projected axis were interpreted (not the cyclotorsion angle).

Huang and Lee [66] assumed orthographic projection and proposed a linear algorithm to solve the equation $R_{23}\Delta x' - R_{13}\Delta y' + R_{32}\Delta x - R_{31}\Delta y = 0$ (a special case of Equation (7.3)). Hu and Ahuja [64] rightly criticised their approach, noting that the equation has only *two* independent unknowns, since

$$R_{13}^2 + R_{23}^2 = R_{31}^2 + R_{32}^2 = 1 - R_{33}^2. \tag{7.16}$$

Our formulation (see Equation 7.3) has *three* independent unknowns (the scale factor s is also accounted for), making a linear solution valid.

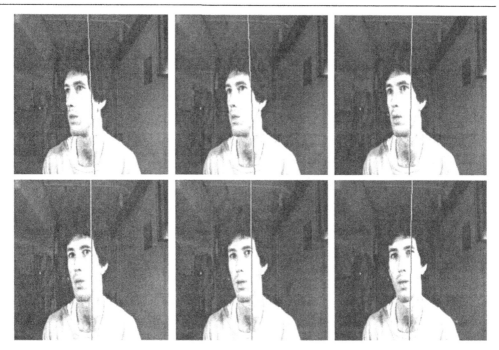

Figure 7.9: *The subject shakes his head. The true axis is roughly vertical, giving qualitatively correct results.*

Chen and Huang [29] improved on the Huang–Lee solution by incorporating Equation (7.16) as a constraint in their minimisation expression; however, this yielded a non-linear equation. None of the above authors [29, 64, 66] noted that the projections of the axis of rotation could be found directly from R_{13}, R_{23}, R_{31} and R_{32}.

Huang and Lee [66] deduced that two views yield a one–parameter family of motion (and structure) solutions, since R_{13}, R_{23}, R_{31} and R_{32} could only be recovered up to a "scale factor". It is clear from Equation (7.5) that this factor is actually $\sin \rho$. Bennet et al. [18] proved the existence of this one–parameter family of rigid interpretations using set theory.

In an algorithm involving numerous computation stages, Koenderink and van Doorn [79] determined the scale factor and the projections of the axes of rotation by means of a LCF (four non–coplanar points). Our algorithm retains their underlying principles, but uses a single set of equations and *all* available points. Lee and Huang [85] independently devised Koenderink and van Doorn's method. They termed $(R_{13}, R_{23})^\top$ and $(R_{31}, R_{32})^\top$ the "matching directions", denoting them $c\mathbf{l}_1$ and $c\mathbf{l}_2$ respectively (where $\mathbf{l}_1$ and $\mathbf{l}_2$ were unit vectors). It is clear from our notation that $c = \sin \rho$, $\mathbf{l}_1 = (\sin \phi, -\cos \phi)^\top$ and $\mathbf{l}_2 = (\sin(\phi - \theta), -\cos(\phi - \theta))^\top$, corresponding to the epipolar directions.

Aloimonos and Bandyopadhay [7] claimed that two orthographic projections of four non-coplanar points admitted only *four* interpretations of structure (up to a reflection); this is incorrect, for there are infinitely many solutions.

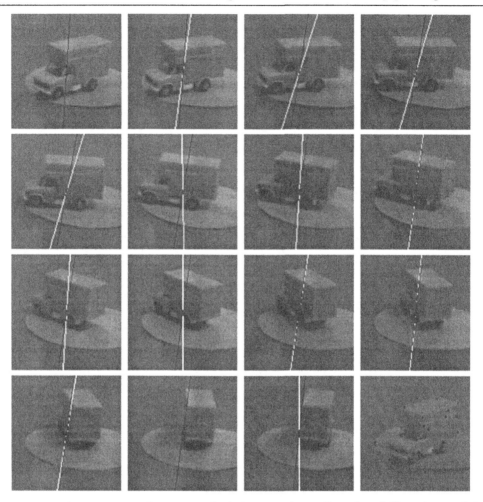

Figure 7.10: *The Harris truck sequence [55] showing the unfiltered and filtered axes (white and black respectively). A typical set of corners is also shown.*

7.4 Rigid motion: three views

Three distinct views of four rigidly connected non–coplanar points permit a unique solution for the 3D motion and structure of the object (up to a Necker reversal) [151], i.e. introducing a third view I_3 resolves the bas–relief ambiguity [55, 66, 79, 153]. This enables us to determine the scaled depths Δz_i, and the remaining rotation angle ρ for each pair of views.

This section briefly reviews previous work on the three–view problem, and outlines a new approach (further details of which can be found in Shapiro et al. [131]). Motion parameters involving images I_j and I_k are subscripted jk, e.g. θ_{23} is the cyclotorsion angle for the view–pair $\{I_2, I_3\}$.

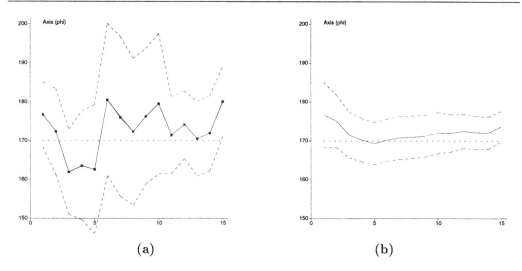

Figure 7.11: *The Harris truck sequence: solid lines give computed values, dotted lines show "true" values, and dashed lines show 95% confidence intervals: (a) Our two–frame solution (E_3, circles) is indistinguishable from that of Harris (E_2, crosses); (b) The improved filtered values (dashed lines show 95% confidence levels).*

7.4.1   Previous work

A popular method for computing rotations is the "rotation matrix constraint" [64, 66, 88]: the rotation $\mathbf{R}_{13}$ (from I_1 to I_3) must be a composite of the two rotations $\mathbf{R}_{12}$ and $\mathbf{R}_{23}$, i.e. $\mathbf{R}_{13} = \mathbf{R}_{23}\,\mathbf{R}_{12}$. These nine equations yield a solution for the angles; in particular, the "border elements" (R_{13}, R_{23}, R_{31} and R_{32}) are frequently used, and Huang and Lee [66] even devised a linear solution. However, this approach has two drawbacks. First, rotation matrices are over–determined (using nine elements to encode three independent angles), so errors in the individual elements accumulate rapidly. Second, the constraint only works in special cases. For instance, the algorithms of Huang and Lee [66] and Hu and Ahuja [64] fail if the 3D axis of rotation is fixed over the three views [131]. Fixed–axis rotation occurs frequently in practice, and a motion estimation algorithm should therefore be able to cope with it.

The first stage of Tomasi and Kanade's solution [145] (SVD of the measurement matrix $\mathbf{V}$ into $\mathbf{LS}$) was described in Section 3.5.2. Rigidity was then imposed to fix the rotation, by computing the orthogonalisation matrix (i.e. the 3D affine transformation matrix $\mathbf{A}$). This involved a set of non–linear "metric constraints", requiring each row–pair in $\mathbf{L}$ to belong to a rotation matrix. Ullman and Basri [153] used a similar method. This approach does cope with all possible rotations, but involves a non–linear system of simultaneous equations. Moreover, only the points that appeared in every view can be used in the computation.

Koenderink and van Doorn [79] used three points from I_1 and I_2 to give two constraints in the form of Equation (E.3), namely $A_i = B_i \cos \rho_{12} + \Delta z_i \sin \rho_{12}$ $(i = 1, 2)$. They then eliminated ρ_{12}, leaving a single quadratic equation in Δz_1 and Δz_2. A similar process for views I_1 and I_3 yielded the equations $G_i = H_i \cos \rho_{13} + \Delta z_i \sin \rho_{13}$ $(i = 1, 2)$, and eliminating ρ_{13} gave a second quadratic equation in Δz_1 and Δz_2. The intersection of these two quadratics yielded four possible solutions for the two depths, from which ρ_{12}, ρ_{13} and the remaining depths Δz_i ($i = 3 \ldots n - 1$) were determined. This algorithm has the drawbacks of using only three points and of processing the images in an unnatural sequence ($\{I_1, I_2\}$ and $\{I_1, I_3\}$).

7.4.2 Epipolar–based algorithm

The desiderata for a three–view algorithm are that it should: (a) process only successive view–pairs, $\{I_1, I_2\}$ and $\{I_2, I_3\}$, to facilitate filtering and extension to further frames; (b) place no constraints on the permitted motion, other than the obvious requirement that the three views be distinct (e.g. there must be rotation out of the plane [64]); and (c) allow feature points to appear and disappear at will.

Appendix E shows that our two–frame algorithm (Figure 7.6) only uses the component of image motion *orthogonal* to the epipolar line direction. The remaining information (about depth and turn) lies in the *parallel* component. We therefore obtain a partial motion solution for each frame–pair using the two–view algorithm, and then compute the remaining parameters using the parallel components.

Frame pairs $\{I_1, I_2\}$ and $\{I_2, I_3\}$ give the following equations, expressing distances along the epipolar lines in terms of Δz_i, ρ_{12} and ρ_{23} (see Appendix E and [131]):

$$A_i = B_i \cos \rho_{12} + \Delta z_i \sin \rho_{12} \tag{7.17}$$

$$C_i = D_i \cos \rho_{23} - B_i \sin \rho_{12} \sin \rho_{23} + \Delta z_i \cos \rho_{12} \sin \rho_{23}. \tag{7.18}$$

Here, A_i, B_i, C_i and D_i are known, and the task is to solve for the $n-1$ depths (Δz_i) and the two turn angles (ρ_{12}, ρ_{23}). This requires at least three points (there are $2n - 2$ equations in $n + 1$ unknowns), and there are two obvious cost functions for a least squares solution:

1. Cost function F_1

   Each pair of views provides an estimate of the scaled depth Δz_i as a function of ρ (from Equations (7.17) and (7.18)):

   $$(\Delta z_i)_{12} = \frac{A_i - B_i \cos \rho_{12}}{\sin \rho_{12}}, \quad (\Delta z_i)_{23} = \frac{C_i - D_i \cos \rho_{23} + B_i \sin \rho_{12} \sin \rho_{23}}{\cos \rho_{12} \sin \rho_{23}}.$$

   We therefore minimise the sum of squared differences between these depth estimates, i.e. $F_1(\rho_{12}, \rho_{23}) = \sum_i \left[(\Delta z_i)_{12} - (\Delta z_i)_{23} \right]^2$.

2. Cost function F_2

   Here we minimise the image distances in I_2 and I_3 along the epipolar lines:

   $$F_2(\rho_{12}, \rho_{23}, \Delta z_i) = \sum_{i=0}^{n-1} (A_i - B_i \cos \rho_{12} - \Delta z_i \sin \rho_{12})^2 +$$

   $$\sum_{i=0}^{n-1} (C_i - D_i \cos \rho_{23} + B_i \sin \rho_{12} \sin \rho_{23} - \Delta z_i \cos \rho_{12} \sin \rho_{23})^2.$$

The optimal value for Δz_i is computed from $\partial F_2/\partial \Delta z_i = 0$ and substituted back into F_2 to give a function of ρ_{12} and ρ_{23}.

F_1 uses 3D depths while F_2 uses image distances, and there are two main reasons for preferring F_2. First, the F_1 method gives two separate values for Δz_i, whereas F_2 gives a single, optimally weighted estimate. Second, F_1 has a singularity when either $\rho_{12} = 0°$ or $\rho_{23} = 0°$, whereas F_2 is smooth everywhere. This lends credence to the argument that minimisation should take place in the *image*, where the noise actually occurs. The drawback of both cost functions is that they involve non–linear minimisation, with the attendant difficulties of finding starting estimates and coping with local minima. Preliminary results can be found in [131].

7.5   Conclusions

A new framework has been proposed for computing motion from point features viewed under parallel projection. Based on the affine camera and its epipolar geometry, this framework incorporates the major theoretical results pertaining to the problem [18, 55, 66, 85, 145, 151, 153], including partial solutions, ambiguities and degeneracies. The necessary camera calibration parameters have been identified, and the facility to use all available points both ensures robustness to noise and obviates the need to choose a LCF. Error models provide confidence estimates in the computed parameters, and the processing of successive frame–pairs permits straightforward extension to long sequences in sequential mode. The rotation representation of Koenderink and van Doorn has been shown to be particularly apt since it makes explicit the ambiguities inherent in parallel projection (e.g. the bas–relief ambiguity).

Future work on computing and filtering the third angle of rotation (ρ) should focus on the *extended* (i.e. non–linear) Kalman filter (EKF), with the goal of accommodating ρ estimates in the same filter as s, θ and ϕ. Since all three rotation angles would then be known, the EKF state could express the overall rotation in *angle–axis* form (while the observations remain in KvD form), thus permitting more realistic inertia constraints (e.g. constant angular velocity about the space axis).

Chapter 8

Affine transfer

8.1 Introduction

Affine structure can be used to generate new views of an object [35, 79, 98], since the known image positions for a core point–set allow the unknown image positions of the remaining points to be deduced. This process is termed "transfer" [12]. One immediate application of transfer is the feedback link in our architecture (Figure 1.1): having tracked corners, grouped them into objects and computed their affine structure, we can use transfer to assist the low–level correspondence process in Chapter 2.

It is already known how to transfer affine views using a local coordinate frame [79], which requires four non–coplanar points in two views. This chapter presents a novel transfer technique which *doesn't* use a local coordinate frame. This improves on two alternative LCF–free methods, namely the intersection of epipolar lines and Tomasi and Kanade's "hallucination" scheme [145].

Sections 8.2 and 8.3 review existing transfer methods with and without local coordinate frames, and Section 8.4 presents the new technique. Examples on real images are given in Section 8.5.

8.2 Transfer using local coordinate frames

Suppose two images I_1 and I_2 have axes $\{e_1, e_2, e_3\}$ and $\{e'_1, e'_2, e'_3\}$ respectively, and that the affine structure $(\alpha_i, \beta_i, \gamma_i)$ of the point–set is computed as in Section 3.4. A third image I_3 can then be rendered simply by selecting a new image spanning set $\{e''_1, e''_2, e''_3\}$ and a new origin x''_0,

$$x''_i = x''_0 + \alpha_i\, e''_1 + \beta_i\, e''_2 + \gamma_i\, e''_3 = x''_0 + \begin{bmatrix} e''_1 & e''_2 & e''_3 \end{bmatrix} \begin{bmatrix} \alpha_i \\ \beta_i \\ \gamma_i \end{bmatrix}, \tag{8.1}$$

as shown in Figure 8.1. The new view is thus determined purely by *three image basis vectors,* without requiring any camera calibration – a result due to Koenderink and van Doorn [79]. It is straightforward to generalise this to m views, provided at least 4 non–coplanar points appear in all the views. Moreover, if transfer is the *sole* objective, then the affine structure itself can be bypassed to give an expression involving only image measurables. To derive

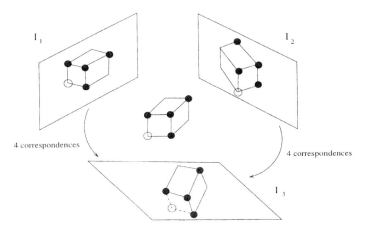

Figure 8.1: *Affine transfer using a local coordinate frame. Four non–coplanar points (sighted in all three views) are designated the basis. The affine coordinates of the point missing from I_3 are computed from its presence in I_1 and I_2, enabling its I_3 position to be reconstructed.*

this expression, recall Equations (3.27) and (3.29):

$$
\begin{bmatrix} \Delta \mathbf{x}_i(1) \\ \Delta \mathbf{x}_i(2) \\ \vdots \\ \Delta \mathbf{x}_i(m) \end{bmatrix} = \begin{bmatrix} \mathbf{e}_1(1) & \mathbf{e}_2(1) & \mathbf{e}_3(1) \\ \mathbf{e}_1(2) & \mathbf{e}_2(2) & \mathbf{e}_3(2) \\ \vdots & \vdots & \vdots \\ \mathbf{e}_1(m) & \mathbf{e}_2(m) & \mathbf{e}_3(m) \end{bmatrix} \begin{bmatrix} \alpha_i \\ \beta_i \\ \gamma_i \end{bmatrix} \quad \Longleftrightarrow \quad \mathbf{v}_i = \mathbf{L}\, \mathbf{s}_i.
$$

The structure $\mathbf{s}_i$ is eliminated using Equation (3.32), giving the location of point i in I_{m+1} as

$$
\Delta \mathbf{x}_i(m+1) = \begin{bmatrix} \mathbf{e}_1(m+1) & \mathbf{e}_2(m+1) & \mathbf{e}_3(m+1) \end{bmatrix} (\mathbf{L}^\mathsf{T} \mathbf{L})^{-1} \mathbf{L}^\mathsf{T} \mathbf{v}_i. \tag{8.2}
$$

This is a function only of the known axis vectors and the image coordinates.

8.3   Transfer without local coordinate frames

The drawbacks of local coordinate frames (LCF's) were discussed in Section 3.5, making the method in Section 8.2 unsuitable. We now review two transfer algorithms that use *all* the available features without requiring an explicit LCF (Figure 8.2). Demey, Zisserman and Beardsley [35] intersected affine epipolar lines, while Tomasi and Kanade [145] "hallucinated" the entries missing from $\mathbf{V}$ (using scaled Euclidean structure). Shortcomings in both approaches are identified.

8.3.1   Intersecting epipolar lines

Figure 8.3 illustrates the idea behind the first approach. Known correspondences in I_1 and I_3 define the epipolar geometry between these two views, yielding an epipolar line in I_3 for the missing point. Similarly, known I_2–I_3 correspondences define a second epipolar line in I_3. The transferred point lies at the intersection of these two epipolar lines. This technique

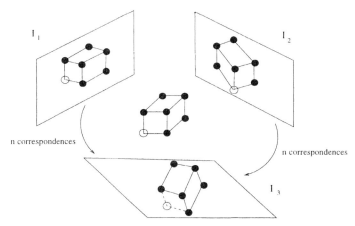

Figure 8.2: *Transfer using n correspondences: the task is to reconstruct the missing point in I_3 using all the available matches.*

fails if the direction of the epipolar lines remains *fixed* over the three views (e.g. when a rigid body rotates about a fixed space axis over the three views), in which case there is no unique intersection in I_3. To illustrate this problem, consider the two epipolar lines in I_3 (cf. Equation (3.21) and Figure 5.3):

$$\mathbf{x}_i'' = \boldsymbol{\Gamma}_{13}\,\mathbf{x}_i + Z_i\,\mathbf{d}_{13} + \boldsymbol{\varepsilon}_{13} \quad \text{and} \quad \mathbf{x}_i'' = \boldsymbol{\Gamma}_{23}\,\mathbf{x}_i' + Z_i\,\mathbf{d}_{23} + \boldsymbol{\varepsilon}_{23}.$$

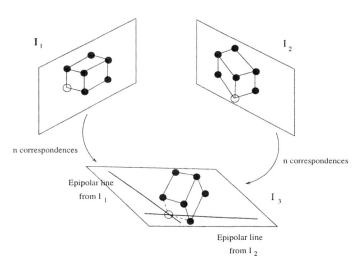

Figure 8.3: *Transfer by intersecting affine epipolar lines from $\{I_1, I_3\}$ and $\{I_2, I_3\}$.*

It is convenient to express these lines in the (p, q) epipolar–based image coordinate system of Section 7.4 and Appendix E.2, resolving $\mathbf{x}_i''$ into its components along the epipolar direction $\hat{\mathbf{d}}$ and its normal $\hat{\mathbf{d}}^\perp$, i.e.

$$\mathbf{x}_i'' = p_{i,13}\,\hat{\mathbf{d}}_{13}^\perp + q_{i,13}\,\hat{\mathbf{d}}_{13} \quad \text{and} \quad \mathbf{x}_i'' = p_{i,23}\,\hat{\mathbf{d}}_{23}^\perp + q_{i,23}\,\hat{\mathbf{d}}_{23}.$$

Figure 8.4 summarises this notation. The p values are known, while the q values are unknown (being functions of the line parameters Z_i). To construct the unknown point $\mathbf{x}_i''$, either $q_{i,13}$ or $q_{i,23}$ must be computed. Intersecting the two epipolar lines gives

$$p_{i,13}\, \hat{\mathbf{d}}_{13}^{\perp} - p_{i,23}\, \hat{\mathbf{d}}_{23}^{\perp} = q_{i,23}\, \hat{\mathbf{d}}_{23} - q_{i,13}\, \hat{\mathbf{d}}_{13}, \qquad (8.3)$$

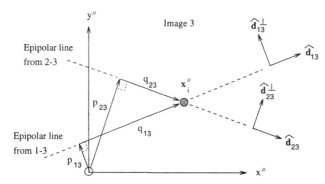

Figure 8.4: *Notation for transfer by affine epipolar lines.*

the left–hand side of which is known, so $q_{i,13}$ and $q_{i,23}$ can be determined as follows,

$$\begin{bmatrix} q_{i,13} \\ q_{i,23} \end{bmatrix} = \begin{bmatrix} \hat{\mathbf{d}}_{13} & -\hat{\mathbf{d}}_{23} \end{bmatrix}^{-1} \begin{bmatrix} -\hat{\mathbf{d}}_{13}^{\perp} & \hat{\mathbf{d}}_{23}^{\perp} \end{bmatrix} \begin{bmatrix} p_{i,13} \\ p_{i,23} \end{bmatrix}, \qquad (8.4)$$

giving the location of the transferred point. If the epipolar lines don't change direction between views (i.e. $\hat{\mathbf{d}}_{13} = \hat{\mathbf{d}}_{23}$), then $p_{i,13} = p_{i,23}$ and Equation (8.3) becomes

$$\mathbf{0} = (q_{i,23} - q_{i,13})\, \hat{\mathbf{d}}_{13} \quad \Rightarrow \quad q_{i,13} - q_{i,23} = 0.$$

Thus, $q_{i,13} = q_{i,23} = q_i$ and the actual value of q_i cannot be determined, i.e. the position of $\mathbf{x}_i''$ *along* the epipolar line in I_3 is unknown, and the method fails. This is a problem even if $\hat{\mathbf{d}}_{13}$ and $\hat{\mathbf{d}}_{23}$ do not have precisely the same direction, since Equation (8.4) becomes increasingly ill–conditioned as $\hat{\mathbf{d}}_{13}$ and $\hat{\mathbf{d}}_{23}$ tend towards alignment (the most accurate intersection arising when they are at right angles[1]).

The weakness of the epipolar line intersection method stems from its failure to measure the component of the transferred point *along* the epipolar direction (q_i); instead, reliance is placed wholly on the *perpendicular* component (p_i). However, information about the parallel component q_i *is* available from I_1 and I_2 (where point i *does* appear), and the problem disappears when this data is used. The necessary modifications were described in Shapiro et al. [131]; they are not reported here since the modified scheme still shares one other weakness with the original scheme, namely that epipolar geometry is inherently a two–view formulation and doesn't extend naturally to m frames. The epipolar method is hence inferior to the new method presented in Section 8.4.

---

[1]The conditioning of the solution may be quantified in several ways, e.g. $\hat{\mathbf{d}}_{13} \cdot \hat{\mathbf{d}}_{23}$ gives the cosine of the angle between the vectors, with the value 1 meaning poor conditioning and 0 meaning good conditioning. Alternatively, one can use the condition number of the matrix $[\hat{\mathbf{d}}_{13} - \hat{\mathbf{d}}_{23}]$ (which has to be inverted).

8.3.2 "Hallucination" via scaled Euclidean structure

Tomasi and Kanade [145] used m views ($m \geq 3$) to compute the scaled Euclidean structure of the object and the m camera rotation matrices. They then projected the computed 3D position using the computed camera into any view in which the feature wasn't seen. However, their "condition for reconstruction" is sub–optimal, stating that "an unknown image measurement pair in frame f can be reconstructed if point p is visible in at least <u>three</u> more frames" (page 147 [145], underlining added). The need for *three* frames is unnecessary since Sections 8.2 and 8.3.1 demonstrated that *two* views of a feature enable transfer to a new view. The explanation is that Tomasi and Kanade used *scaled Euclidean* structure to perform transfer, where *affine structure* suffices. A simpler, more general version of their algorithm is therefore given in Section 8.4, removing the need to solve the non–linear equations (the "metric constraints") which they employed to impose rigidity. The need for camera calibration is also removed, since we use an affine camera model.

8.4 Affine transfer using CI space

This section presents a new transfer algorithm that generalises the method of Tomasi and Kanade [145]. Suppose a set of n scene points appear in m views ($m \geq 2$), and that a subset of these (n_s points) also appear in the $(m+1)^{th}$ view, I_{m+1}. The task is to reconstruct the $n-n_s$ points missing from I_{m+1}, given their sightings in the first m views. The superscripts m and $m+1$ are used to denote quantities computed from m and $m+1$ views respectively.

First consider the problem in geometric terms. Assuming independent, isotropic, Gaussian noise, the optimal structure estimate for point i is given by orthogonally projecting $\mathbf{v}_i^m$ onto the 3D linear subspace π^m, which has been fitted to the m views in $2m$–dimensional CI space (cf. Section 3.5.3). This m–view structure estimate is $\mathbf{s}_i^m$. When view $m+1$ becomes available, the CI space expands to $2m+2$ dimensions, and the points that appear in all $m+1$ views now define a new 3D linear subspace π^{m+1}. The transfer operation then "projects" the m–view structure estimate $\mathbf{s}_i^m$ onto π^{m+1}, whence the coordinates in the new view can be determined (Figure 8.5).

The algorithm is listed in Figure 8.6, and we note two details. First, in order to use the m–view affine structure estimate for the missing points, the axis vectors $\{\boldsymbol{\ell}_1, \boldsymbol{\ell}_2, \boldsymbol{\ell}_3\}^m$ spanning π^m must be aligned with those spanning π^{m+1} (after truncating the extra two dimensions, giving $\{\tilde{\boldsymbol{\ell}}_1, \tilde{\boldsymbol{\ell}}_2, \tilde{\boldsymbol{\ell}}_3\}^{m+1}$). That is, it is necessary to determine the transformation between the two 3D linear subspaces. In general, this takes the form of a 3D affine transformation, but the translation vector can be ignored since the points are centred, leaving a 3×3 matrix $\mathbf{H}$ to be determined. Step 5 computes this by linear least squares (since noise is present).

Second, the m–view and $(m+1)$–view computations use different centroids, because the latter uses a reduced point–set (n_s versus n points). This problem was addressed by Tomasi and Kanade [145], whose solution we generalise. Recall from Equation (3.40) that in $\{\mathbf{M}, \mathbf{X}\}$

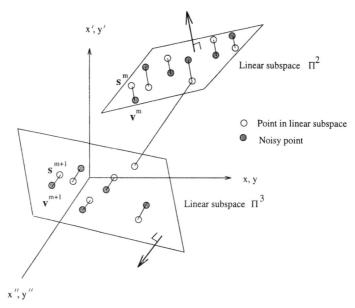

Figure 8.5: *Three–view transfer (i.e., m = 2). See text for details.*

form,

$$
\mathbf{V}^m = \mathbf{L}^m\,\mathbf{S}^m =
\begin{bmatrix}
\mathbf{M}^m(1) \\
\mathbf{M}^m(2) \\
\vdots \\
\mathbf{M}^m(m)
\end{bmatrix}
\begin{bmatrix}
\boldsymbol{\Delta}\mathbf{X}_0^m & \boldsymbol{\Delta}\mathbf{X}_1^m & \cdots & \boldsymbol{\Delta}\mathbf{X}_{n-1}^m
\end{bmatrix}.
$$

Now partition $\mathbf{L}^{m+1}$ as

$$
\mathbf{L}^{m+1} =
\begin{bmatrix}
\mathbf{M}^{m+1}(1) \\
\mathbf{M}^{m+1}(2) \\
\vdots \\
\mathbf{M}^{m+1}(m) \\
\mathbf{M}^{m+1}(m+1)
\end{bmatrix}
=
\begin{bmatrix}
\tilde{\mathbf{L}} \\
\mathbf{M}^{m+1}(m+1)
\end{bmatrix},
$$

where $\tilde{\mathbf{L}} = [\tilde{\boldsymbol{\ell}}_1\,\tilde{\boldsymbol{\ell}}_2\,\tilde{\boldsymbol{\ell}}_3]$ is the truncation of $\mathbf{L}^{m+1}$ to the m–view component. Now, the expression $\mathbf{M}^{m+1}(m+1)\,\mathbf{Hs}_i^m$ gives $\boldsymbol{\Delta}\mathbf{x}_i^m(m+1)$, the transferred point location in I_3 relative to the centroid of all n points in I_{m+1}, $\bar{\mathbf{x}}^m(m+1)$. However, this centroid isn't known; only the centroid of the n_s points in I_{m+1}, $\bar{\mathbf{x}}^{m+1}(m+1)$, is known, making $\mathbf{M}^{m+1}(m+1)\,\mathbf{Hs}_i^{m+1}$ the desired computation. Unfortunately, $\mathbf{s}_i^{m+1}$ is also unknown (for $i = n_s \ldots n$). We therefore express $\mathbf{s}_i^{m+1}$ in terms of $\mathbf{s}_i^m$, noting that $\mathbf{s}_i^m = \mathbf{X}_i - \bar{\mathbf{X}}^m$ ($i = 0 \ldots n-1$) and $\mathbf{s}_i^{m+1} = \mathbf{X}_i - \bar{\mathbf{X}}^{m+1}$ ($i = 0 \ldots n_s - 1$), whence $\mathbf{s}_i^{m+1} = \mathbf{s}_i^m + (\bar{\mathbf{X}}^m - \bar{\mathbf{X}}^{m+1})$. Also, $\sum_{i=0}^{n_s-1}\mathbf{s}_i^{m+1} = \mathbf{0}$. Thus,

$$
\bar{\mathbf{X}}^m - \bar{\mathbf{X}}^{m+1} = \sum_{i=0}^{n_s-1}(\mathbf{s}_i^{m+1} - \mathbf{s}_i^m)/n_s = -\sum_{i=0}^{n_s-1}\mathbf{s}_i^m/n_s,
$$

giving $\mathbf{s}_i^{m+1} = \mathbf{s}_i^m - \sum_{i=0}^{n_s-1} \mathbf{s}_i^m / n_s$. The final expression for the point in I_{m+1} is thus

$$\Delta \mathbf{x}_i^{m+1}(m+1) = \mathbf{M}^{m+1}(m+1)\,\mathbf{H}\,\mathbf{s}_i^{m+1} = \mathbf{M}^{m+1}(m+1)\,\mathbf{H}\left[\mathbf{s}_i^m - \sum_{j=0}^{n_s-1} \mathbf{s}_j^m / n_s\right].$$

8.5   Results

We evaluate our transfer algorithm on the images of Demey, Zisserman and Beardsley [35] (Figure 8.7). They obtained line drawings of these images using the Canny edge detector [25], obtained vertices by extrapolating and intersecting fitted lines, and did correspondence between different images by hand. Figure 8.8 shows a typical line drawing.

We assess performance by transferring to an image for which the projected structure is *known,* and measuring the difference between the transferred and actual structures. Two reference images (I_1 and I_2) are used to transfer the structure to a third view (I_3). The transfer error is then the Euclidean distance[2] $d(\mathbf{x}'', \mathbf{x}_t'')$ between the transferred point $\mathbf{x}''$ and its "correct" image position $\mathbf{x}''$ (i.e. the position extracted from the actual image). Two measures are used for the evaluation:

1. Mean error: $E_{mean} = \frac{1}{n} \sum_{i=0}^{n-1} d(\mathbf{x}_i'', \mathbf{x}_{t,i}'')$

2. Maximum error: $E_{max} = \max_i d(\mathbf{x}_i'', \mathbf{x}_{t,i}'')$ $i \in \{0 \ldots n-1\}$

In both cases n is the number of points seen in both reference images. Images A and B serve as our reference images (Figure 8.9), and we transfer to the four remaining images (C, D, E and F). The results are shown in Figures 8.10 and 8.11 using 4, 7 and 10 reference points. There is clearly a significant improvement in the estimates of the transferred points when a larger set of reference points is used. The results are summarised in Figure 8.12, which plots the error measures for each transferred image against the number of reference points[3]. Different images have different absolute errors because of perspective distortion: performance degrades for image E (where there are significant perspective effects) and is best for D (which has very minor perspective effects).

8.6   Conclusions

A new method has been proposed for generating affine views of an object. This technique subsumes the existing two–view, four–point transfer algorithms, and extends naturally to n points and m views without requiring any camera calibration.

This chapter completes the processing chain first outlined in Chapter 1, with high–level 3D affine structure information feeding back down to the low–level correspondence process.

---

[2]This measure assumes that the camera aspect ratio is known.

[3]Naturally, the result is dependent on *which* set of points is chosen as the reference set. We start from the initial set (points 2, 7, 11 and 13) and at each iteration, add in the point whose error $d(\mathbf{x}_i'', \mathbf{x}_{t,i}'')$ is greatest.

Task

Given n corresponding points $\mathbf{x}_i(k)$ in m distinct images ($i = 0 \ldots n{-}1$, $k = 1 \ldots m$), where n_s of these points $\mathbf{x}_i(m+1)$ ($i = 0 \ldots n_s{-}1$, $4 \le n_s < n$) appear in an $(m+1)^{th}$ distinct image, determine the $n - n_s$ points missing from I_{m+1}, i.e. compute $\mathbf{x}_i(m+1)$ for $i = n_s \ldots n{-}1$.

Algorithm

1. Compute the centroids of the n points that appear in the first m images, namely $\bar{\mathbf{x}}^m(k) = \sum_{i=0}^{n-1} \mathbf{x}_i(k)/n$ (for $k = 1 \ldots m$). Register the points, giving $\Delta\mathbf{x}_i^m(k) = \mathbf{x}_i(k) - \bar{\mathbf{x}}^m(k)$ (for $i = 0 \ldots n{-}1$).

2. Perform SVD on the $2m \times n$ matrix $\mathbf{V}^m$ using the three largest singular values,

$$
\mathbf{V}^m = \begin{bmatrix}
\Delta\mathbf{x}_0^m(1) & \Delta\mathbf{x}_1^m(1) & \cdots & \Delta\mathbf{x}_{n-1}^m(1) \\
\Delta\mathbf{x}_0^m(2) & \Delta\mathbf{x}_1^m(2) & \cdots & \Delta\mathbf{x}_{n-1}^m(2) \\
\vdots & \vdots & & \vdots \\
\Delta\mathbf{x}_0^m(m) & \Delta\mathbf{x}_1^m(m) & \cdots & \Delta\mathbf{x}_{n-1}^m(m)
\end{bmatrix} = \mathbf{L}^m\,\mathbf{S}^m,
$$

so $\mathbf{L}^m$ and $\mathbf{S}^m$ are respectively $2m \times 3$ and $3 \times n$ matrices. $\mathbf{S}^m$ has columns $\mathbf{s}_i^m$, and the best structure estimates for the missing points are given by its last $n{-}n_s$ columns, $[\,\mathbf{s}_{n_s}^m \mid \mathbf{s}_{n_s+1}^m \mid \cdots \mid \mathbf{s}_{n-1}^m\,]$.

3. Compute the centroids of the n_s points that appear in all $m{+}1$ views, namely $\bar{\mathbf{x}}^{m+1}(k) = \sum_{i=0}^{n_s-1} \mathbf{x}_i(k)/n_s$ (for $k = 1 \ldots m{+}1$). Write $\Delta\mathbf{x}_i^{m+1}(k) = \mathbf{x}_i(k) - \bar{\mathbf{x}}^{m+1}(k)$ ($i = 0 \ldots n_s{-}1$).

4. Perform SVD on the $(2m+2) \times n_s$ matrix $\mathbf{V}^{m+1}$ using the largest three singular values,

$$
\mathbf{V}^{m+1} = \begin{bmatrix}
\Delta\mathbf{x}_0^{m+1}(1) & \Delta\mathbf{x}_1^{m+1}(1) & \cdots & \Delta\mathbf{x}_{n_s-1}^{m+1}(1) \\
\Delta\mathbf{x}_0^{m+1}(2) & \Delta\mathbf{x}_1^{m+1}(2) & \cdots & \Delta\mathbf{x}_{n_s-1}^{m+1}(2) \\
\vdots & \vdots & & \vdots \\
\Delta\mathbf{x}_0^{m+1}(m+1) & \Delta\mathbf{x}_1^{m+1}(m+1) & \cdots & \Delta\mathbf{x}_{n_s-1}^{m+1}(m+1)
\end{bmatrix} = \mathbf{L}^{m+1}\,\mathbf{S}^{m+1},
$$

so $\mathbf{L}^{m+1}$ and $\mathbf{S}^{m+1}$ are respectively $(2m+2) \times 3$ and $3 \times n_s$ matrices. $\mathbf{L}^{m+1}$ is decomposed into $\tilde{\mathbf{L}}$ and $\mathbf{M}^{m+1}(m+1)$, where $\tilde{\mathbf{L}}$ contains the first $2m$ rows, relating to the first m views, and $\mathbf{M}^{m+1}(m+1)$ contains the last pair of rows, relating to view $m+1$.

5. Compute the 3×3 matrix $\mathbf{H}$ that accounts for the relative orientation between the spanning sets of π^m and π^{m+1}, i.e. $\tilde{\mathbf{L}}\,\mathbf{H} = \mathbf{L}^m$. The $6m$ equations in the 9 unknowns are solved by linear least–squares (pseudo–inverse).

6. The locations in I_3 of the $n - n_s$ transferred points are then

$$
\mathbf{x}_i(m+1) = \bar{\mathbf{x}}^{m+1}(m+1) + \mathbf{M}^{m+1}(m+1)\,\mathbf{H}\left[\mathbf{s}_i^m - \frac{1}{n_s}\sum_{j=0}^{n_s-1}\mathbf{s}_j^m\right], \quad i = n_s \ldots n - 1.
$$

Figure 8.6: m–view affine transfer algorithm (no local coordinate frame).

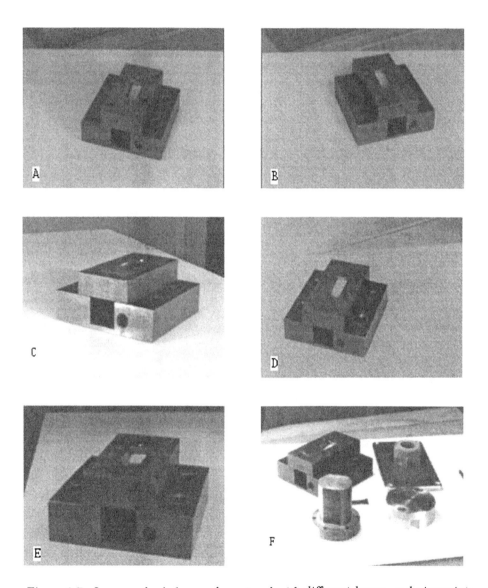

Figure 8.7: *Images of a hole punch captured with different lenses and viewpoints.*

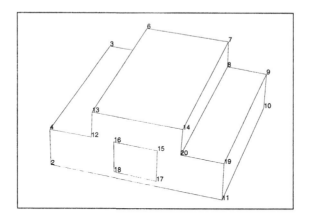

Figure 8.8: *Line drawing of the hole punch extracted from image A in Figure 8.7. Points 1 and 5 are occluded in this view.*

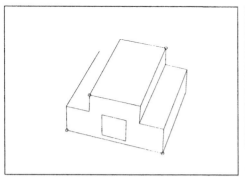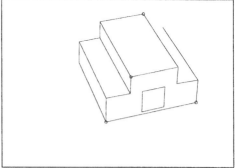

Figure 8.9: *Line drawings of the two reference images, A and B. Points 2, 7, 11 and 13 are the reference points used for 4–point transfer.*

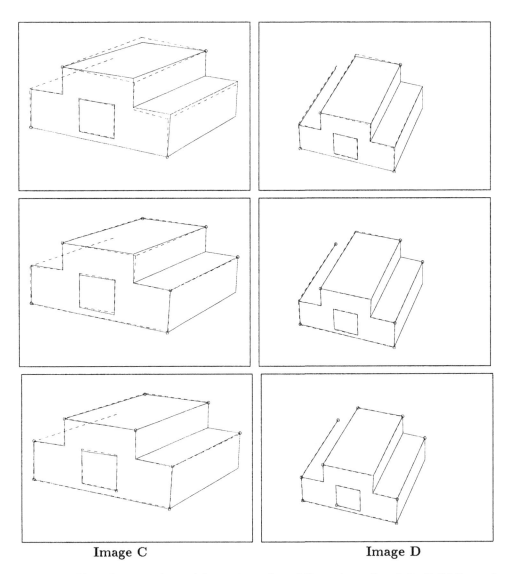

Image C   Image D

Figure 8.10: *Transfer is performed from views A and B to views C and D. Solid lines show the "correct" graph structure and dashed lines shown the transferred view ("correct" refers to the real image). The line structure is for visualisation only; it is the vertices (points) that are transferred: (a) Four reference points are used, indicated by circles; (b) Seven reference points are used, clearly improving the estimates of the transferred points; (c) Ten reference points are used, leading to a further improvement in accuracy.*

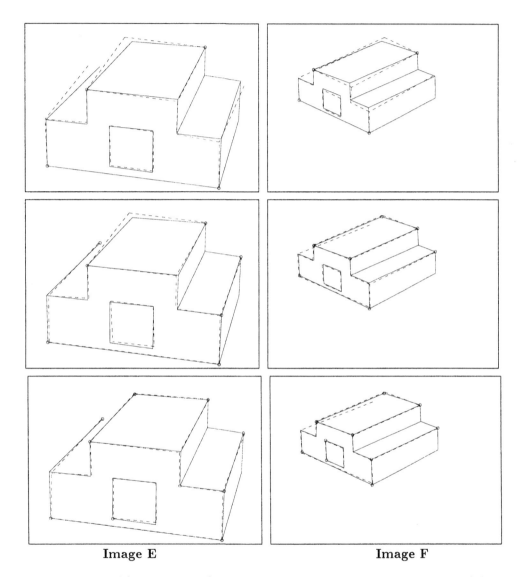

Image E   Image F

Figure 8.11: *The same procedure as in Figure 8.10, now using images E and F.*

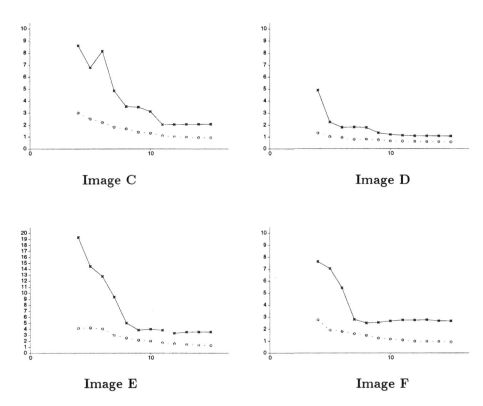

Figure 8.12: *Graphs of the mean and maximum Euclidean distance errors. Crosses show E_{max} and circles show E_{mean}. The x axis represents the number of reference points used to transfer the structure. Note that the error axis for Image E is larger than in the other graphs (due to larger perspective effects).*

Chapter 9

Conclusions

9.1 Summary

This thesis has developed a coherent framework for analysing image sequences based on the affine camera, and has demonstrated the practical feasibility of recovering 3D structure and motion in a bottom–up fashion, using "corner" features. New algorithms have been proposed to compute affine structure, and these have then been applied to the problems of clustering and view transfer. The theory of affine epipolar geometry has been derived and applied to outlier rejection and rigid motion estimation. Due consideration has been paid to error and noise models, with a χ^2 test serving as a termination criterion for cluster growth and outlier detection, and confidence limits in the motion parameters facilitating Kalman filtering.

On a practical level, all the algorithms have been implemented and tested on a wide range of sequences. The use of n points and m frames has lead to enhanced noise immunity and has also simplified the algorithms in important ways, e.g. local coordinate frames are no longer needed to compute affine structure or rigid motion parameters. Finally, the use of 3D information without explicit depth has been illustrated in a working system (e.g. for transfer).

In summary, the affine camera has been shown to provide a solid foundation both for understanding structure and motion under parallel projection, and for devising reliable algorithms.

9.2 Future work

There are many interesting problems for future work to address. First, the CI space interpretation of the motion segmentation problem is that each independently moving object contributes a different 3D linear subspace. Thus, an alternative clustering method to that of Chapter 4 would be to partition CI space directly into 3D linear subspaces. Possible approaches here are accumulator methods (e.g. a sampling technique à la Torr and Murray [147]), generalised Hough transform techniques, and perhaps a modified SVD method.

Second, the proposed affine structure and motion algorithms use batch methods. However, one would ideally like to update affine structure and motion ($\mathbf{L}$ and $\mathbf{S}$) recursively over time (much as the Kalman filter performs this function for the LCF–based solution in [159]). Recent progress in this direction has been reported by [93].

Third, since corners are a sparse shape representation, it would be desirable to use them in conjunction with other features; edge information in particular would be useful for eliciting motion boundaries (as in [50, 134]). Combined corner and edge detectors have been reported [54, 134], and affine distortion of closed contours has been analysed in [21, 30]. A sound theoretical framework for integrating the constraints offered by edges and corners would thus be the next logical step.

Finally, the affine camera is only valid under restricted viewing conditions, the more general model being the projective camera (cf. Section 3.2). It would thus be useful to establish which theoretical contributions of this thesis generalise to the projective case (e.g. "transfer by epipolar lines" is known to fail identically under projective viewing). Especially interesting would be the nature of CI space in the projective case: what is the projective analogue of the 3D linear subspace, and how exactly are these two "surfaces" related? It would also be worthwhile to try boot–strap perspective/projective structure and motion estimates from the weak–perspective/affine solutions, in the spirit of [88, 139].

Appendix A

Clustering proofs

A.1 MAST generation

Theorem 1 establishes that trusting the acquisition decisions of neighbouring processors gives the same evolving MAST's as the parallel Prim algorithm (see Section 4.2.3).

Theorem 1 *In a graph $\mathcal{G}$, let an evolving MAST $\mathcal{M}_a$ (grown from root point p_a and spanning $\mathcal{P}_a$) acquire the point p_b (having MAST $\mathcal{M}_b$ and span $\mathcal{P}_b$). Then $\mathcal{M}_a$ is justified in immediately incorporating the whole of $\mathcal{P}_b$, since its affinity score remains optimal.*

Proof: Let p_k be the point in $\mathcal{M}_a$ with the best affinity link to p_b (possibly $p_k = p_a$); this link is ℓ_{bk} with affinity $a(\ell_{bk})$. Assume initially that all affinity values are unique (this restriction is removed shortly). Clearly, $a(\ell_{bk})$ exceeds any affinities between $\mathcal{M}_a$ and its other neighbours, since ℓ_{bk} was selected as the best available link. Also, since ℓ_{bk} wasn't chosen sooner, the affinities of the links *already* within $\mathcal{M}_a$ must exceed $a(\ell_{bk})$. Thus, $a(\ell_{bk})$ is the smallest affinity value in $\mathcal{M}_a$.

Now consider the points already acquired by $\mathcal{M}_b$. There are two possibilities:

- $\mathcal{M}_b$ has not yet incorporated ℓ_{bk}

  In this case, $\mathcal{M}_b$'s internal links must possess higher affinities than $a(\ell_{bk})$, since ℓ_{bk} was available for selection and was passed over. Thus $\mathcal{M}_a$ is justified in acquiring the remaining points in $\mathcal{M}_b$.

- $\mathcal{M}_b$ has incorporated ℓ_{bk}

  After acquiring p_k, $\mathcal{M}_b$ will immediately begin acquiring the remainder of $\mathcal{P}_a$, because all the affinities in $\mathcal{M}_a$ exceed $a(\ell_{bk})$. If $\mathcal{M}_b$ has not yet finished acquiring $\mathcal{P}_a$, then the theorem holds (since any points that $\mathcal{M}_b$ acquired *before* selecting ℓ_{bk} are optimal choices with regard to $\mathcal{M}_a$, and overlapping points are irrelevant). If $\mathcal{M}_b$ has already acquired all of $\mathcal{P}_a$, then it has access to all $\mathcal{M}_a$'s neighbours, and so its decisions will be optimal with respect to $\mathcal{M}_a$. The theorem therefore holds in this case too.

Now suppose that $\mathcal{G}$ contains tie affinities. In this case, the choice of links is arbitrary, and $\mathcal{M}_a$ is no worse off (in an affinity score sense) by accepting $\mathcal{M}_b$'s choices than by selecting alternative points; $\mathcal{M}_a$'s freedom to choose between equally valid alternatives has simply been curtailed. The theorem is therefore still valid when ties are present. □

A.2 Cluster Formation

Some notation and definitions are necessary before proving the remaining theorems. Denote by $\mathcal{L}(p_a)$ (or simply $\mathcal{L}_a$) the set of links incident on point a, i.e. the links joining p_a to its neighbours Γ_a (Figure A.1(a)),

$$\mathcal{L}_a = \{\ell_{ai} \mid p_i \in \Gamma_a\}. \tag{A.1}$$

Also, denote by $\mathcal{L}^\star(\mathcal{P})$ the set of links connecting a point from the point–set $\mathcal{P}$ to a point not in $\mathcal{P}$, i.e. the links joining $\mathcal{P}$ to its neighbours $\Gamma(\mathcal{P})$ (Figure A.1(b)),

$$\mathcal{L}^\star(\mathcal{P}) = \{\ell_{ij} \mid p_i \in \mathcal{P}, p_j \notin \mathcal{P}, \ell_{ij} \in \mathcal{G}\} = \{\ell_{ij} \mid p_i \in \mathcal{P}, p_j \in \Gamma(\mathcal{P})\}. \tag{A.2}$$

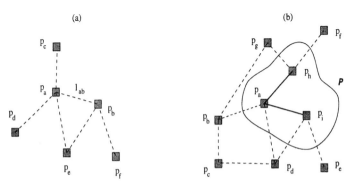

Figure A.1: *Notation: (a) The links incident on p_a and p_b are $\mathcal{L}_a = \{\ell_{ab}, \ell_{ac}, \ell_{ad}, \ell_{ae}\}$ and $\mathcal{L}_b = \{\ell_{ba}, \ell_{be}, \ell_{bf}\}$; (b) The links connecting $\mathcal{P} = \{p_a, p_h, p_i\}$ to its neighbours are $\mathcal{L}^\star(\mathcal{P}) = \{\ell_{ab}, \ell_{ad}, \ell_{di}, \ell_{ei}, \ell_{fh}, \ell_{gh}\}$.*

Corollary 1 *A MAST grown from any point in a k–point cluster $\mathcal{C}$ will select the remaining $k-1$ points in $\mathcal{C}$ before selecting any other points.*

Proof: This follows directly from the cluster definition (Definition 2 in Section 4.3.2). Thus, no MAST grown from a point within $\mathcal{C}$ can acquire a point *outside* $\mathcal{C}$ before first acquiring the rest of the points inside $\mathcal{C}$. □

Corollary 2 *The affinities in a MAST $\mathcal{M}_\mathcal{C}$ spanning the cluster $\mathcal{C}$ exceed or equal the affinities of the links joining points in $\mathcal{C}$ to their neighbours outside $\mathcal{C}$, that is*

$$a(\ell) \geq \max_{\ell^\star \in \mathcal{L}^\star(\mathcal{C})} a(\ell^\star), \quad \ell \in \mathcal{M}_\mathcal{C}.$$

Proof: This follows from Corollary 1, for if any link $\ell^\star$ in $\mathcal{L}^\star(\mathcal{C})$ had a greater affinity value than the links inside $\mathcal{C}$, then $\ell^\star$ would be acquired before some other point in $\mathcal{C}$, contradicting the cluster definition. The equality only arises if there are tie affinities. □

Lemma 1 *Let p_a belong to the cluster C_a with k_a points and MAST M_a, and let p_b belong to the cluster C_b with k_b points and MAST M_b. If M_a acquires p_b (via link ℓ_{ab}), then it will acquire all the other points in C_b before acquiring any other points.*

Proof: First assume there are no tie affinities. Then, by Corollary 2, the affinities in M_b exceed $a(\ell_{ab})$:

$$a(\ell) > a(\ell_{ab}), \quad \ell \in M_b.$$

Furthermore, since ℓ_{ab} was selected in preference to other neighbouring links, $a(\ell_{ab})$ exceeds the affinities to all other neighbours of C_a:

$$a(\ell_{ab}) > a(\ell^\star), \quad \ell^\star \in \mathcal{L}^\star(C_a).$$

Thus, all the links in M_b have higher affinities than C_a's other neighbours,

$$a(\ell) > a(\ell^\star), \quad \ell \in M_b, \ \ell^\star \in \mathcal{L}^\star(C_a),$$

and M_a will therefore acquire C_b's points first. Note that M_a cannot first acquire any neighbours of C_b since $a(\ell_{ab})$ also exceeds the affinities to C_b's neighbours ($a(\ell_{ab}) > a(\ell^\star)$ for $\ell^\star \in \mathcal{L}^\star(C_b)$).

When tie affinities are present, the inequalities are relaxed, giving

$$a(\ell) \geq a(\ell^\star), \quad \ell \in M_b, \ \ell^\star \in \mathcal{L}^\star(C_a).$$

However, since no link in M_b has *lower* affinity than C_a's remaining neighbours, M_a is again no worse off (in an affinity score sense) by accepting M_b's choices than by choosing alternative points. The theorem is thus proved. $\qquad\square$

Theorem 2 now proves that the cardinality dendogram of the parallel evolving MAST algorithm in Section 4.3.3 (hereafter termed the "parallel algorithm") coincides with that of the "sequential algorithm" (Section 4.3.1), i.e. the identical clusters emerge.

Theorem 2 *If an N–point graph $\mathcal{G}$ with point set $\mathcal{P}$ has a unique MAST M, then the nested cluster hierarchy generated by the parallel evolving MAST algorithm is equivalent to that generated by a sequential hierarchical agglomerative single–link algorithm.*

Proof: The proof is by induction on the cluster cardinality k. First assume $k = 1$ (i.e. N singleton clusters), and let the sequential algorithm accept link ℓ_{ab}, forming the two–point cluster $(p_a; p_b)$. Clearly, ℓ_{ab} must have a larger affinity value than any other link incident on p_a or p_b (Figure A.2(a)), else p_a and/or p_b would belong to some other cluster by the time ℓ_{ab} was selected from the sorted link list. Thus, the mutual attraction between the points exceeds the attraction that either has for any other point:

$$a(\ell_{ab}) = \max_{\ell \in (\mathcal{L}_a \cup \mathcal{L}_b)} a(\ell). \tag{A.3}$$

It follows that under these conditions, the parallel algorithm will have the MAST M_a (grown from p_a) select p_b as its first acquisition, and similarly the MAST M_b (grown from p_b) select

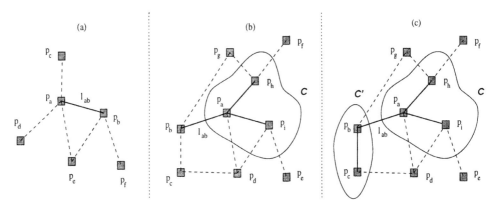

Figure A.2: *Cluster formation. Dotted links indicate affinities and solid links indicate clustered points: (a) The affinity of link ℓ_{ab} exceeds the affinities of the other links incident on p_a and p_b; (b) The cluster $\mathcal{C} = (p_a; p_h; p_i)$ acquires p_b (singleton cluster); (c) Clusters $\mathcal{C} = (p_a; p_h; p_i)$ and $\mathcal{C}' = (p_b; p_c)$ are merged by ℓ_{ab}.*

p_a. Thus, $\mathcal{S}(\mathcal{M}_a) = \mathcal{S}(\mathcal{M}_b) = \{p_a, p_b\}$ and the parallel algorithm will correctly identify the cluster $(p_a; p_b)$.

Now assume there is a k–point cluster $\mathcal{C}$ (with MAST $\mathcal{M}_\mathcal{C}$) to which the sequential method adds link ℓ_{ab}, with $p_a \in \mathcal{C}$ and $p_b \notin \mathcal{C}$ (see Figures A.2(b) and (c)). To have been chosen, ℓ_{ab} must have the largest affinity of the links $\mathcal{L}^*(\mathcal{C})$:

$$a(\ell_{ab}) = \max_{\ell \in \mathcal{L}^*(\mathcal{C})} a(\ell). \tag{A.4}$$

Let p_b belong to the cluster $\mathcal{C}'$ with k' points and MAST $\mathcal{M}_{\mathcal{C}'}$. It must be shown that $\mathcal{M}_\mathcal{C}$ acquires all of $\mathcal{C}'$ while $\mathcal{M}_{\mathcal{C}'}$ simultaneously acquires all of $\mathcal{C}$. Of course, p_b could either be a singleton cluster (Figure A.2(b)) or belong to a compound cluster (Figure A.2(c)). Equation (A.4) ensures that the next acquisition of $\mathcal{M}_\mathcal{C}$ will be p_b. Thereafter, by Lemma 1, it acquires all the points in $\mathcal{C}'$. Similarly, by reversing the argument, $\mathcal{M}_{\mathcal{C}'}$ acquires all the points in $\mathcal{C}$ and the theorem is proved. Note that the new cluster contains $k + k'$ points, so will only be identified by the parallel algorithm at step $k + k'$.

The cluster hierarchies of the sequential and parallel algorithms are thus identical. $\square$

Theorem 2 ignored tie affinities, because the MAST is not unique when they are present. However, provided the termination criterion is suitable (i.e. based on affinities rather than, say, the number of points in the cluster), ties will not affect the final clusters: either all points with the same affinity will be accepted into a cluster, or all will be rejected. Tie affinities *do* nonetheless affect the links chosen by the evolving MAST's; this in turn affects the subclusters formed en route to the final cluster, and can cause discontinuities in cluster cardinality. For instance, consider the "equi–affinity triangle" in Figure A.3. Different link choices in triangle abc generate different two–point subclusters before the correct three–point cluster emerges. Certain choices can even suppress the sub–clusters entirely, with the complete three point cluster emerging suddenly (Figure A.3(d)). In all cases, however, the three–point cluster is identified correctly.

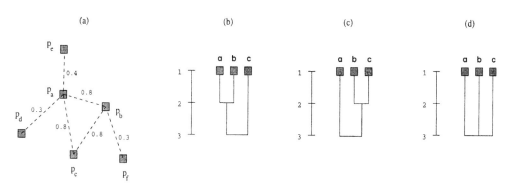

Figure A.3: *Clustering with tie affinities: (a) Triangle (p_a, p_b, p_c) has equal affinity links and the subclusters formed after the first acquisition depend on arbitrary choices of links; Cardinality dendograms arising from (b) $\mathcal{M}_a \rightarrow p_b, \mathcal{M}_b \rightarrow p_a, \mathcal{M}_c \rightarrow p_b$; (c) $\mathcal{M}_a \rightarrow p_b, \mathcal{M}_b \rightarrow p_c, \mathcal{M}_c \rightarrow p_b$; and (d) $\mathcal{M}_a \rightarrow p_b, \mathcal{M}_b \rightarrow p_c, \mathcal{M}_c \rightarrow p_a$. The last dendogram contains a cardinality discontinuity.*

Finally, Theorem 3 shows that all the MAST's grown from root points within a k–point cluster will contain exactly k points at some time when the grapevine clustering algorithm is used, and that no point outside the cluster $\mathcal{C}$ will have been incorporated when this occurs. This ensures that clusters are identical to those of the one–step parallel algorithm.

Theorem 3 *Let k points $\mathcal{C} = \{p_1, p_2, \ldots, p_k\}$ be a cluster in the universal point set $\mathcal{P}$, i.e. $\mathcal{C} \subset \mathcal{P}$. Then every MAST grown from a point within $\mathcal{C}$ using the grapevine algorithm will span exactly k points at some stage of its evolution (and these k points will be $\mathcal{C}$).*

Proof: Consider the k evolving MAST's being grown from the points $p_i \in \mathcal{C}$, $i = 1 \ldots k$. There are only two ways in which one of these k evolving MAST's $\mathcal{M}_i$ can acquire a point p_o outside $\mathcal{C}$: either by selecting it directly, or by acquiring a neighbour that has itself selected it. Direct selection is impossible if $\mathcal{M}_i$ has fewer than k points (Corollary 1). Thus, no outside point can be incorporated into any MAST $\mathcal{M}_i$ until $|\mathcal{P}_i| = k$.

Now consider indirect selection. For every MAST $\mathcal{M}_i$ spanning less than k points, all its valid potential neighbours are subject to the Corollary 1 restrictions above, since they too are members of $\mathcal{C}$; their MAST's also cannot contain an outside point while their spans are smaller than $k + 1$, since they can't acquire it directly and none of their selected neighbours can either. A crucial factor here is hibernation, which prevents any single MAST $\mathcal{M}_i$ growing beyond k points (thereby introducing outsiders) before the other MAST's span k points.

Thus, no MAST $\mathcal{M}_i$ spanning less than k points will span more than k points after incorporating a neighbour's MAST. Consequently, no MAST can grow beyond $\mathcal{C}$ before all the trees $\mathcal{M}_i$ span $\mathcal{C}$, in which case the cluster is correctly identified. $\qquad\square$

Appendix B

Proofs for epipolar geometry minimisation

Sections B.1, B.2 and B.3 derive the solutions to the three minimisation problems of Section 5.2, and Section B.4 then relates the line–to–point cost functions to their point–to–point counterparts.

B.1 Cost function E_1

Consider minimising the expression

$$E_1(\mathbf{n}_1, \mathbf{n}_2, e) = \left(\frac{1}{|\mathbf{n}_1|^2} + \frac{1}{|\mathbf{n}_2|^2} \right) \sum_{i=0}^{n-1} (\mathbf{n}_1 \cdot \mathbf{x}_i + \mathbf{n}_2 \cdot \mathbf{x}'_i + e)^2.$$

Write $\mathbf{n}_1 = s\mathbf{n}_3$, where $|\mathbf{n}_3| = |\mathbf{n}_2| = 1$, and express the constraints in terms of Lagrange multipliers, λ and μ:

$$E' = \left(1 + \frac{1}{s^2} \right) \sum_{i=0}^{n-1} (s\mathbf{n}_3 \cdot \mathbf{x}_i + \mathbf{n}_2 \cdot \mathbf{x}'_i + e)^2 - \lambda(\mathbf{n}_2^\mathsf{T} \mathbf{n}_2 - 1) - \mu(\mathbf{n}_3^\mathsf{T} \mathbf{n}_3 - 1) \to \min.$$

To solve, set the partial derivatives of the Lagrangian to zero. Differentiating with respect to e gives

$$\frac{\partial E'}{\partial e} = 0 = 2 \left(1 + \frac{1}{s^2} \right) \sum_{i=0}^{n-1} (\mathbf{n} \cdot \mathbf{r}_i + e) \quad \Rightarrow \quad e = -\frac{1}{n} \sum_{i=0}^{n-1} (\mathbf{n} \cdot \mathbf{r}_i) = -\mathbf{n} \cdot \bar{\mathbf{r}},$$

so the solution $\mathbf{n}$ passes through the data centroid $\bar{\mathbf{r}}$. Now substitute for e in E',

$$E' = \left(1 + \frac{1}{s^2} \right) \sum_{i=0}^{n-1} (s\mathbf{n}_3 \cdot \Delta\mathbf{x}_i + \mathbf{n}_2 \cdot \Delta\mathbf{x}'_i)^2 - \lambda(\mathbf{n}_2^\mathsf{T} \mathbf{n}_2 - 1) - \mu(\mathbf{n}_3^\mathsf{T} \mathbf{n}_3 - 1),$$

and differentiate with respect to $\mathbf{n}_2$ and $\mathbf{n}_3$, giving

$$\left(1 + \frac{1}{s^2} \right) (\mathbf{K}_1 \mathbf{n}_2 + s\mathbf{K}_2 \mathbf{n}_3) = \lambda \mathbf{n}_2 \quad \text{and} \quad s \left(1 + \frac{1}{s^2} \right) (\mathbf{K}_2^\mathsf{T} \mathbf{n}_2 + s\mathbf{K}_3 \mathbf{n}_3) = \mu \mathbf{n}_3,$$

where $\mathbf{K}_j$ are defined in Section 5.4.1. Finally, differentiate with respect to s, giving

$$\left(1 + \frac{1}{s^2} \right) \mathbf{n}_3^\mathsf{T} (\mathbf{K}_2^\mathsf{T} \mathbf{n}_2 + s\mathbf{K}_3 \mathbf{n}_3) = \frac{1}{s^3} \left[\mathbf{n}_2^\mathsf{T} (\mathbf{K}_1 \mathbf{n}_2 + s\mathbf{K}_2 \mathbf{n}_3) + s\mathbf{n}_3^\mathsf{T} (\mathbf{K}_2^\mathsf{T} \mathbf{n}_2 + s\mathbf{K}_3 \mathbf{n}_3) \right],$$

whence

$$s^2 \mu = \lambda \quad \Rightarrow \quad \mu = \frac{\lambda}{s^2}.$$

The final system of equations is therefore

$$\left(1 + \frac{1}{s^2}\right) \begin{bmatrix} \mathbf{K}_1 & \mathbf{K}_2 \\ s^4 \, \mathbf{K}_2^\mathsf{T} & s^4 \, \mathbf{K}_3 \end{bmatrix} \mathbf{n} = \lambda \mathbf{n} \tag{B.1}$$

This is not a conventional eigenvector problem since $\mathbf{n}$ is also a function of s and requires $|\mathbf{n}_2| = |\mathbf{n}_3|$ $(\mathbf{n}^\mathsf{T} = (\mathbf{n}_2^\mathsf{T}, \mathbf{n}_1^\mathsf{T}) = (\mathbf{n}_2^\mathsf{T}, s\mathbf{n}_3^\mathsf{T}))$; solving this system of equations thus requires non–linear methods. The minimum cost is given by substituting the solution into E_1,

$$E_{1,min} = \lambda \left(1 + \frac{1}{s^2}\right).$$

B.2 Cost function E_2

Consider minimising the expression

$$E_2(\mathbf{n}_1, \mathbf{n}_2.e) = \frac{1}{|\mathbf{n}_2|^2} \sum_{i=0}^{n-1} (\mathbf{x}_i \cdot \mathbf{n}_1 + \mathbf{x}_i' \cdot \mathbf{n}_2 + e)^2.$$

Use a Lagrange multiplier λ and remove e (see Section B.1) to obtain

$$E' = \sum_{i=0}^{n-1} (\Delta \mathbf{x}_i \cdot \mathbf{n}_1 + \Delta \mathbf{x}_i' \cdot \mathbf{n}_2)^2 - \lambda(\mathbf{n}_2^\mathsf{T} \mathbf{n}_2 - 1).$$

Now differentiate with respect to $\mathbf{n}_1$ and $\mathbf{n}_2$,

$$\frac{\partial E'}{\partial \mathbf{n}_1} = 0 = 2 \sum_{i=0}^{n-1} (\Delta \mathbf{x}_i \cdot \mathbf{n}_1 + \Delta \mathbf{x}_i' \cdot \mathbf{n}_2) \, \Delta \mathbf{x}_i \quad \Rightarrow \quad \mathbf{K}_3 \, \mathbf{n}_1 + \mathbf{K}_2^\mathsf{T} \, \mathbf{n}_2 = 0 \tag{B.2}$$

$$\frac{\partial E'}{\partial \mathbf{n}_2} = 0 = 2 \sum_i (\Delta \mathbf{x}_i \cdot \mathbf{n}_1 + \Delta \mathbf{x}_i' \cdot \mathbf{n}_2) \Delta \mathbf{x}_i' - 2\lambda \mathbf{n}_2 \quad \Rightarrow \quad \mathbf{K}_2 \, \mathbf{n}_1 + \mathbf{K}_1 \, \mathbf{n}_2 = \lambda \, \mathbf{n}_2$$

whence

$$(\mathbf{K}_1 - \mathbf{K}_2 \, \mathbf{K}_3^{-1} \, \mathbf{K}_2^\mathsf{T}) \, \mathbf{n}_2 = \lambda \, \mathbf{n}_2$$

Thus, $\mathbf{n}_2$ is a unit eigenvector of a real, symmetric 2×2 matrix. To decide which eigenvalue λ to select, substitute in E_2:

$$E_{2,min} = \mathbf{n}_1^\mathsf{T}(\mathbf{K}_3 \, \mathbf{n}_1 + \mathbf{K}_2^\mathsf{T} \, \mathbf{n}_2) + \mathbf{n}_2^\mathsf{T}(\mathbf{K}_2 \, \mathbf{n}_1 + \mathbf{K}_1 \, \mathbf{n}_2) = \mathbf{n}_2^\mathsf{T} \lambda \, \mathbf{n}_2 = \lambda \, |\mathbf{n}_2|^2 = \lambda.$$

Thus, λ is the minimum eigenvalue of $(\mathbf{K}_1 - \mathbf{K}_2 \mathbf{K}_3^{-1} \mathbf{K}_2^\mathsf{T})$ and $\mathbf{n}_2$ is its associated eigenvector. Finally, $\mathbf{n}_1$ is obtained from the equation $\mathbf{n}_1 = -\mathbf{K}_3^{-1} \, \mathbf{K}_2^\mathsf{T} \mathbf{n}_2$.

B.3   Cost function E_3

Consider minimising the expression

$$E_3(\mathbf{n}, e) = \frac{1}{|\mathbf{n}|^2} \sum_{i=0}^{n-1} (\mathbf{r}_i \cdot \mathbf{n} + e)^2.$$

Use a Lagrange multiplier λ,

$$E' = \sum_{i=0}^{n-1} (\mathbf{n} \cdot \mathbf{r}_i + e)^2 - \lambda(\mathbf{n}^\mathsf{T}\mathbf{n} - 1),$$

and as before, the optimum hyperplane will pass through the data centroid $\bar{\mathbf{r}}$. Substitute $e = -\mathbf{n} \cdot \bar{\mathbf{r}}$ and write $\mathbf{W} = \sum_i \mathbf{v}_i \mathbf{v}_i^\mathsf{T}$, giving

$$E' = \mathbf{n}^\mathsf{T}\,\mathbf{W}\,\mathbf{n} - \lambda(\mathbf{n}^\mathsf{T}\mathbf{n} - 1).$$

Now differentiate with respect to $\mathbf{n}$:

$$\frac{\partial E'}{\partial \mathbf{n}} = 0 = 2\mathbf{W}\mathbf{n} - 2\lambda\,\mathbf{n} \quad \Rightarrow \quad \mathbf{W}\,\mathbf{n} = \lambda\,\mathbf{n}. \tag{B.3}$$

Thus, $\mathbf{n}$ is a unit eigenvector of $\mathbf{W}$ corresponding to the eigenvalue λ. To decide *which* eigenvalue, substitute into E_3:

$$E_{3,min} = \mathbf{n}^\mathsf{T}\mathbf{W}\,\mathbf{n} = \mathbf{n}^\mathsf{T}\lambda\,\mathbf{n} = \lambda\,|\mathbf{n}|^2 = \lambda.$$

Thus, λ must be the minimum eigenvalue of $\mathbf{W}$, with $\mathbf{n}$ its associated eigenvector.

B.4   Line–to–point and point–to–point cost functions

This section establishes that the point–to–point cost functions from Sections 3.5,

$$\epsilon_h(\boldsymbol{\Gamma}, \mathbf{d}, Z_i) = \sum_{i=0}^{n-1} |\Delta\mathbf{x}'_i - \boldsymbol{\Gamma}\,\Delta\mathbf{x}_i - \Delta Z_i\,\mathbf{d}|^2 \quad \text{and} \quad \epsilon_{tk}(\mathbf{L}, \mathbf{s}_i) = \sum_{i=0}^{n-1} |\mathbf{v}_i - \mathbf{L}\mathbf{s}_i|^2$$

reduce respectively to the cost functions in Section 5.4,

$$E_2(\boldsymbol{\Gamma}, \mathbf{d}) = \sum_{i=0}^{n-1} [\,(\Delta\mathbf{x}'_i - \boldsymbol{\Gamma}\,\Delta\mathbf{x}_i) \cdot \hat{\mathbf{d}}^\perp\,]^2 \quad \text{and} \quad E_3(\boldsymbol{\ell}_4) = \sum_{i=0}^{n-1} (\mathbf{v}_i \cdot \boldsymbol{\ell}_4)^2$$

after minimisation with respect to structure (ΔZ_i and $\mathbf{s}_i$ respectively). The proofs use simple geometry, resolving the error vectors into mutually orthogonal components by Pythagoras's theorem.

B.4.1 Cost function ϵ_h

Resolve ϵ_h into components perpendicular to the epipolar line (direction $\hat{\mathbf{d}}^\perp$) and parallel to it (direction $\hat{\mathbf{d}}$), noting that $\hat{\mathbf{d}} \cdot \hat{\mathbf{d}}^\perp = 0$:

$$
\begin{aligned}
\epsilon_h &= \sum_{i=0}^{n-1} [\,(\boldsymbol{\Delta}\mathbf{x}_i' - \boldsymbol{\Gamma}\,\boldsymbol{\Delta}\mathbf{x}_i - \Delta Z_i\,\mathbf{d}) \cdot \hat{\mathbf{d}}^\perp\,]^2 + [\,(\boldsymbol{\Delta}\mathbf{x}_i' - \boldsymbol{\Gamma}\,\boldsymbol{\Delta}\mathbf{x}_i - \Delta Z_i\,\mathbf{d}) \cdot \hat{\mathbf{d}}\,]^2 \\
&= \sum_{i=0}^{n-1} [\,(\boldsymbol{\Delta}\mathbf{x}_i' - \boldsymbol{\Gamma}\,\boldsymbol{\Delta}\mathbf{x}_i) \cdot \hat{\mathbf{d}}^\perp\,]^2 + [\,(\boldsymbol{\Delta}\mathbf{x}_i' - \boldsymbol{\Gamma}\,\boldsymbol{\Delta}\mathbf{x}_i) \cdot \hat{\mathbf{d}} - \Delta Z_i\,|\mathbf{d}|\,]^2,
\end{aligned}
\tag{B.4}
$$

Differentiating ϵ_h with respect to ΔZ_i yields the optimal depth estimate,

$$
\Delta Z_i = \frac{(\boldsymbol{\Delta}\mathbf{x}_i' - \boldsymbol{\Gamma}\,\boldsymbol{\Delta}\mathbf{x}_i) \cdot \hat{\mathbf{d}}}{|\mathbf{d}|},
\tag{B.5}
$$

and after resubstitution (noting that $|\hat{\mathbf{d}}| = |\hat{\mathbf{d}}^\perp| = 1$),

$$
\epsilon_h = \sum_{i=0}^{n-1} [\,(\boldsymbol{\Delta}\mathbf{x}_i' - \boldsymbol{\Gamma}\,\boldsymbol{\Delta}\mathbf{x}_i) \cdot \hat{\mathbf{d}}^\perp\,]^2,
\tag{B.6}
$$

which is E_2. An alternative explanation is that the second term in Equation (B.4) (distance *along* the epipolar line) is the sole source of information about depth, so ΔZ_i must satisfy the equality and make the error in that term zero. This leaves only *motion* degrees of freedom to explain the remaining error (in the first term).

B.4.2 Cost function ϵ_{tk}

A similar proof is used for ϵ_{tk}, with the error vectors resolved along the four mutually orthogonal unit–length axes $\boldsymbol{\ell}_1 \ldots \boldsymbol{\ell}_4$ (recall that $\mathbf{L} = [\,\boldsymbol{\ell}_1\ \boldsymbol{\ell}_2\ \boldsymbol{\ell}_3\,]$ and $\mathbf{L}^\top \boldsymbol{\ell}_4 = 0$):

$$
\begin{aligned}
\epsilon_{tk}\,(\mathbf{L}, \mathbf{S}) &= \sum_{i=0}^{n-1} [(\mathbf{v}_i - \mathbf{L}\mathbf{s}_i) \cdot \boldsymbol{\ell}_1]^2 + [(\mathbf{v}_i - \mathbf{L}\mathbf{s}_i) \cdot \boldsymbol{\ell}_2]^2 + [(\mathbf{v}_i - \mathbf{L}\mathbf{s}_i) \cdot \boldsymbol{\ell}_3]^2 + [(\mathbf{v}_i - \mathbf{L}\mathbf{s}_i) \cdot \boldsymbol{\ell}_4]^2 \\
&= \sum_{i=0}^{n-1} |(\mathbf{v}_i - \mathbf{L}\mathbf{s}_i)^\top \mathbf{L}|^2 + (\mathbf{v}_i \cdot \boldsymbol{\ell}_4)^2
\end{aligned}
$$

Differentiating ϵ_{tk} with respect to $\mathbf{s}_i$ yields

$$
\mathbf{s}_i = (\mathbf{L}^\top \mathbf{L})^{-1}\,\mathbf{L}^\top\,\mathbf{v}_i
\tag{B.7}
$$

and after resubstitution,

$$
\epsilon_{tk}\,(\boldsymbol{\ell}_4) = \sum_{i=0}^{n-1} (\mathbf{v}_i \cdot \boldsymbol{\ell}_4)^2,
\tag{B.8}
$$

which equals[1] E_3. Clearly, the first term (resolved distance *in* the hyperplane) provides the only available information about structure, so $\mathbf{s}_i$ satisfies the equality in that term. The structure has therefore been factored out in an optimal way.

---

[1] A comparison with the E_3 form in Equation (5.13) shows that $\boldsymbol{\ell}_4 = \mathbf{n}/|\mathbf{n}|$.

Appendix C

Proofs for outlier rejection

C.1 Matrix perturbation theory

C.1.1 Definitions and notation

Let $\mathbf{A}$ be an $m \times m$ matrix with eigenvalues $\lambda(\mathbf{A}) = \{\lambda_1, \ldots, \lambda_m\}$. The non–zero m–vectors satisfying $\mathbf{A}\mathbf{u}_j = \lambda_j \mathbf{u}_j$ $(j = 1 \ldots m)$ are the *right* eigenvectors (or simply the eigenvectors) of $\mathbf{A}$, while those satisfying $\mathbf{q}_j^\mathsf{T} \mathbf{A} = \lambda_j \mathbf{q}_j^\mathsf{T}$ are the *left* eigenvectors. The p–norm of the vector $\mathbf{x}$ is

$$\|\mathbf{x}\|_p = (|x_1|^p + |x_2|^p + \cdots + |x_n|^p)^{\frac{1}{p}}, \quad p = 1, 2, \ldots, \infty ,$$

so the 2–norm is simply the Euclidean length $|\mathbf{x}|$. The p–norm of $\mathbf{A}$ is

$$\|\mathbf{A}\|_p = \sup_{\mathbf{x} \neq 0} \frac{\|\mathbf{A}\mathbf{x}\|_p}{\|\mathbf{x}\|_p} = \max_{\|\mathbf{x}\|_p = 1} \|\mathbf{A}\mathbf{x}\|_p ,$$

the p–norm of the longest vector obtained by applying $\mathbf{A}$ to a unit p–norm vector. Importantly, $\|\mathbf{A}\|_2$ is the square–root of the largest eigenvalue of $\mathbf{A}^\mathsf{T}\mathbf{A}$ [165].

C.1.2 Eigensolution perturbation

Consider the effect on the eigensolution when $\mathbf{A}$ is perturbed to $\mathbf{A} + \Delta\mathbf{A}$. A well–established body of theory describes the sensitivity of eigenvalues and eigenvectors to perturbations in matrix elements (e.g. [48, 165]). The relations for the general asymmetric case simplify considerably when $\mathbf{A}$ is symmetric, since the left and right eigenvectors are then equal ($\mathbf{u}_j = \mathbf{q}_j$). A further simplification applies in our case (see Section 6.4), where $\mathbf{A} = \mathbf{W}$ and $\Delta\mathbf{A} = \Delta\mathbf{W}_i = -\frac{n}{n-1}\mathbf{v}_i\mathbf{v}_i^\mathsf{T}$, since $\Delta\mathbf{A}$ then has unit rank and its 2–norm equals $\frac{n}{n-1}|\mathbf{v}_i|^2$.

Eigenvalue perturbation

Suppose that λ_j is a simple (i.e. non–repeated) eigenvalue of $\mathbf{A}$, and that the left and right eigenvectors of $\mathbf{A}$ have unit 2–norm. If the perturbation $\Delta\mathbf{A}$ equals $\epsilon\mathbf{B}$, where ϵ is small and $\|\mathbf{B}\|_2 = 1$, then it can be shown (see [48]) that in the neighbourhood of the origin there exist differentiable $\mathbf{u}_j(\epsilon)$ and $\lambda_j(\epsilon)$ such that

$$(\mathbf{A} + \epsilon\mathbf{B})\mathbf{u}_j(\epsilon) = \lambda_j(\epsilon)\mathbf{u}_j(\epsilon), \quad j = 1 \ldots m.$$

Differentiating with respect to ϵ (and setting $\epsilon = 0$ in the result) yields

$$\mathbf{A}\dot{\mathbf{u}}_j(0) + \mathbf{B}\mathbf{u}_j = \dot{\lambda}_j(0)\mathbf{u}_j + \lambda_j(0)\dot{\mathbf{u}}_j(0),$$

where $\lambda_j(0) = \lambda_j$ and $\lambda_j(\epsilon) = \lambda_j(0) + \dot{\lambda}_j(0)\epsilon + \frac{1}{2}\ddot{\lambda}_j(0)\epsilon^2 + O(\epsilon^3)$. Premultiplying by $\mathbf{q}_j^{\mathsf{T}}$ and simplifying gives [48, 165]:

$$\dot{\lambda}_j(0) = \frac{\mathbf{q}_j^{\mathsf{T}}\mathbf{B}\mathbf{u}_j}{\mathbf{q}_j^{\mathsf{T}}\mathbf{u}_j}.$$

If $\mathbf{A}$ is symmetric ($\mathbf{q}_j = \mathbf{u}_j$),

$$\dot{\lambda}_j(0) = \mathbf{u}_j^{\mathsf{T}}\mathbf{B}\mathbf{u}_j,$$

and since in our case $\epsilon\mathbf{B} = \Delta\mathbf{W}_i = -\frac{n}{n-1}\mathbf{v}_i\mathbf{v}_i^{\mathsf{T}}$, the first order change in λ_j is

$$\dot{\lambda}_j(0)\epsilon = -\frac{n}{n-1}(\mathbf{u}_j \cdot \mathbf{v}_i)^2, \quad j \in \{1\ldots m\}, \ i \in \{1\ldots n\}, \tag{C.1}$$

for the ith data vector and the jth eigenvector (corresponding to eigenvalue λ_j). This varies between 0 (no perturbation) and $-\frac{n}{n-1}|\mathbf{v}_i|^2$ (maximum perturbation). Evidently, the first order change is always non–positive. The second order perturbation can be obtained in a similar fashion [165, 60]:

$$\frac{1}{2}\ddot{\lambda}_j(0) = \frac{1}{\mathbf{q}_j^{\mathsf{T}}\mathbf{u}_j}\sum_{\substack{k=1\\k\neq j}}^{m}\frac{(\mathbf{q}_k^{\mathsf{T}}\mathbf{B}\mathbf{u}_j)(\mathbf{q}_j^{\mathsf{T}}\mathbf{B}\mathbf{u}_k)}{(\lambda_j - \lambda_k)\,\mathbf{q}_k^{\mathsf{T}}\mathbf{u}_k}.$$

With $\mathbf{A}$ symmetric,

$$\frac{1}{2}\ddot{\lambda}_j(0) = \sum_{\substack{k=1\\k\neq j}}^{m}\frac{(\mathbf{u}_k^{\mathsf{T}}\mathbf{B}\mathbf{u}_j)(\mathbf{u}_j^{\mathsf{T}}\mathbf{B}\mathbf{u}_k)}{\lambda_j - \lambda_k},$$

and with $\epsilon\mathbf{B} = -\frac{n}{n-1}\mathbf{v}_i\mathbf{v}_i^{\mathsf{T}}$, the second order change in λ_j is

$$\frac{1}{2}\ddot{\lambda}_j(0)\epsilon^2 = \frac{n^2}{(n-1)^2}(\mathbf{u}_j \cdot \mathbf{v}_i)^2\sum_{\substack{k=1\\k\neq j}}^{m}\frac{(\mathbf{u}_k \cdot \mathbf{v}_i)^2}{\lambda_j - \lambda_k}. \tag{C.2}$$

This second order variation is small when λ_j is well–separated from the other eigenvalues.

Eigenvector perturbation

The Taylor series expansion for the jth eigenvector is

$$\mathbf{u}_j(\epsilon) = \mathbf{u}_j + \epsilon\dot{\mathbf{u}}_j(0) + O(\epsilon^2),$$

and Golub and van Loan [48] give

$$\dot{\mathbf{u}}_j(0) = \sum_{\substack{k=1\\k\neq j}}^{m}\frac{\mathbf{q}_k^{\mathsf{T}}\mathbf{B}\mathbf{u}_j}{(\lambda_j - \lambda_k)\,\mathbf{q}_k^{\mathsf{T}}\mathbf{u}_k}\mathbf{u}_k,$$

showing that the sensitivity of the jth eigenvector depends both on eigenvalue sensitivity and on the separation of λ_j from the other eigenvalues. Substituting the expressions for $\mathbf{A} = \mathbf{W}$ and $\epsilon\mathbf{B} = \Delta\mathbf{W}_i$ gives:

$$\dot{\mathbf{u}}_j(0)\epsilon = -\frac{n}{n-1}(\mathbf{u}_j \cdot \mathbf{v}_i) \sum_{\substack{k=1 \\ k \neq j}}^{m} \frac{\mathbf{u}_k \cdot \mathbf{v}_i}{\lambda_j - \lambda_k}\mathbf{u}_k. \tag{C.3}$$

C.2 Variance proofs

C.2.1 Eigenvector covariance matrix

We have from Equation (6.21) in Section 6.5.1:

$$
\begin{aligned}
\mathbf{\Lambda}_{\mathbf{u}_1} &= E\{\delta\mathbf{u}_1 \, \delta\mathbf{u}_1^{\mathsf{T}}\} = E\{\hat{\mathbf{J}}\,\hat{\mathbf{V}}\,\delta\mathbf{V}^{\mathsf{T}}\,\hat{\mathbf{u}}_1\,\hat{\mathbf{u}}_1^{\mathsf{T}}\,\delta\mathbf{V}\,\hat{\mathbf{V}}^{\mathsf{T}}\,\hat{\mathbf{J}}^{\mathsf{T}}\} \\
&= \hat{\mathbf{J}}\,E\left\{\left(\sum_{i=0}^{n-1}\hat{\mathbf{v}}_i\,(\delta\mathbf{v}_i \cdot \hat{\mathbf{u}}_1)\right)\left(\sum_{j=0}^{n-1}\hat{\mathbf{v}}_j^{\mathsf{T}}\,(\delta\mathbf{v}_j \cdot \hat{\mathbf{u}}_1)\right)\right\}\hat{\mathbf{J}}^{\mathsf{T}} \\
&= \hat{\mathbf{J}}\left[\sum_{i=0}^{n-1}\hat{\mathbf{v}}_i\left(\sum_{j=0}^{n-1}\hat{\mathbf{v}}_j^{\mathsf{T}}\,\hat{\mathbf{u}}_1^{\mathsf{T}}\,E\{\delta\mathbf{v}_i\,\delta\mathbf{v}_j^{\mathsf{T}}\}\,\hat{\mathbf{u}}_1\right)\right]\hat{\mathbf{J}}^{\mathsf{T}}.
\end{aligned}
$$

Now

$$E\{\delta\mathbf{v}_i \, \delta\mathbf{v}_j^{\mathsf{T}}\} = \begin{cases} \sigma^2(1-\frac{1}{n})\,\mathbf{I}_m & i = j \\ -\sigma^2\,\frac{1}{n}\,\mathbf{I}_m & i \neq j \end{cases},$$

and since $\hat{\mathbf{u}}_1^{\mathsf{T}}\hat{\mathbf{u}}_1 = 1$,

$$\hat{\mathbf{u}}_1^{\mathsf{T}}E\{\delta\mathbf{v}_i \, \delta\mathbf{v}_j^{\mathsf{T}}\}\,\hat{\mathbf{u}}_1 = \begin{cases} \sigma^2\left(1-\frac{1}{n}\right) & i = j \\ -\sigma^2\,\frac{1}{n} & i \neq j \end{cases}.$$

Noting that $\sum_{j=0}^{n-1}\hat{\mathbf{v}}_j = \mathbf{0}$, we get

$$\sum_{j=0}^{n-1}\hat{\mathbf{v}}_j^{\mathsf{T}}\,\hat{\mathbf{u}}_1^{\mathsf{T}}E\{\delta\mathbf{v}_i\,\delta\mathbf{v}_j^{\mathsf{T}}\}\,\hat{\mathbf{u}}_1 = \sigma^2\hat{\mathbf{v}}_i^{\mathsf{T}} - \frac{\sigma^2}{n}\sum_{j=0}^{n-1}\hat{\mathbf{v}}_j^{\mathsf{T}} = \sigma^2\hat{\mathbf{v}}_i^{\mathsf{T}},$$

whence

$$\sum_{i=0}^{n-1}\hat{\mathbf{v}}_i\left(\sum_{j=0}^{n-1}\hat{\mathbf{v}}_j^{\mathsf{T}}\,\hat{\mathbf{u}}_1^{\mathsf{T}}E\{\delta\mathbf{v}_i\,\delta\mathbf{v}_j^{\mathsf{T}}\}\,\hat{\mathbf{u}}_1\right) = \sigma^2\sum_{i=0}^{n-1}\hat{\mathbf{v}}_i\,\hat{\mathbf{v}}_i^{\mathsf{T}} = \sigma^2\,\hat{\mathbf{W}}.$$

Since $\hat{\mathbf{W}}\hat{\mathbf{u}}_j = \hat{\lambda}_j\hat{\mathbf{u}}_j$ and $\hat{\mathbf{u}}_i \cdot \hat{\mathbf{u}}_j = \delta_{ij}$,

$$
\begin{aligned}
\mathbf{\Lambda}_{\mathbf{u}_1} = \sigma^2\,\hat{\mathbf{J}}\,\hat{\mathbf{W}}\,\hat{\mathbf{J}}^{\mathsf{T}} &= \sigma^2\left(\sum_{k=2}^{m}\frac{\hat{\mathbf{u}}_k\,\hat{\mathbf{u}}_k^{\mathsf{T}}}{\hat{\lambda}_k}\right)\left(\sum_{l=2}^{m}\frac{\hat{\mathbf{W}}\,\hat{\mathbf{u}}_l\,\hat{\mathbf{u}}_l^{\mathsf{T}}}{\hat{\lambda}_l}\right) = \sigma^2\left(\sum_{k=2}^{m}\frac{\hat{\mathbf{u}}_k\,\hat{\mathbf{u}}_k^{\mathsf{T}}}{\hat{\lambda}_k}\right)\left(\sum_{l=2}^{m}\frac{\hat{\lambda}_l\,\hat{\mathbf{u}}_l\,\hat{\mathbf{u}}_l^{\mathsf{T}}}{\hat{\lambda}_l}\right) \\
&= \sigma^2\sum_{k=2}^{m}\frac{\hat{\mathbf{u}}_k\,\hat{\mathbf{u}}_k^{\mathsf{T}}}{\hat{\lambda}_k}.
\end{aligned}
$$

Thus

$$\mathbf{\Lambda}_{\mathbf{u}_1} = -\sigma^2\,\hat{\mathbf{J}}.$$

Note that in Section 6.4, we could not assume $\lambda_1 \approx 0$ in the denominator terms $(\lambda_k - \lambda_1)$ because outliers were present. The approximation does hold once the contaminants are eliminated, since then $\lambda_1 \ll \lambda_k$.

C.2.2 Residual variance

From Equation (6.23) in Section 6.5.2, the variance of the residual for point i is

$$
\begin{aligned}
\text{Var}\,\{\delta h_i\} &= \hat{\mathbf{u}}_1^{\mathsf{T}} \mathbf{\Lambda_v} \hat{\mathbf{u}}_1 + \hat{\mathbf{v}}_i^{\mathsf{T}} \mathbf{\Lambda_{u_1}} \hat{\mathbf{v}}_i + 2\,\hat{\mathbf{v}}_i^{\mathsf{T}}\, E\,\{\delta\mathbf{u}_1\,\delta\mathbf{v}_i^{\mathsf{T}}\}\hat{\mathbf{u}}_1 \\
&= \frac{n-1}{n}\sigma^2\,\hat{\mathbf{u}}_1^{\mathsf{T}}\,\mathbf{I}_m\,\hat{\mathbf{u}}_1 - \sigma^2\,\hat{\mathbf{v}}_i^{\mathsf{T}}\,\hat{\mathbf{J}}\,\hat{\mathbf{v}}_i + 2\,\hat{\mathbf{v}}_i^{\mathsf{T}}\,E\,\left\{\hat{\mathbf{J}}\left(\sum_{j=0}^{n-1}\hat{\mathbf{v}}_j\,(\delta\mathbf{v}_j\cdot\hat{\mathbf{u}}_1)\right)\delta\mathbf{v}_i^{\mathsf{T}}\right\}\hat{\mathbf{u}}_1 \\
&= \frac{n-1}{n}\sigma^2\,\hat{\mathbf{u}}_1^{\mathsf{T}}\,\hat{\mathbf{u}}_1 + \sigma^2\,\hat{\mathbf{v}}_i^{\mathsf{T}}\left(\sum_{k=2}^{m}\frac{\hat{\mathbf{u}}_k\,\hat{\mathbf{u}}_k^{\mathsf{T}}}{\hat{\lambda}_k}\right)\hat{\mathbf{v}}_i + 2\,\hat{\mathbf{v}}_i^{\mathsf{T}}\,\hat{\mathbf{J}}\left(\sum_{j=0}^{n-1}\hat{\mathbf{v}}_j\,\hat{\mathbf{u}}_1^{\mathsf{T}}E\{\delta\mathbf{v}_j\,\delta\mathbf{v}_i^{\mathsf{T}}\}\hat{\mathbf{u}}_1\right).
\end{aligned}
$$

Now $\hat{\mathbf{u}}_1^{\mathsf{T}}\hat{\mathbf{u}}_1 = 1$ and from Section C.2.1

$$
\sum_{j=0}^{n-1}\hat{\mathbf{v}}_j\,\hat{\mathbf{u}}_1^{\mathsf{T}}E\{\delta\mathbf{v}_i\,\delta\mathbf{v}_j^{\mathsf{T}}\}\,\hat{\mathbf{u}}_1 = \sigma^2\,\hat{\mathbf{v}}_i,
$$

thus

$$
\begin{aligned}
\text{Var}\,\{\delta h_i\} &= \frac{n-1}{n}\sigma^2 + \sigma^2\sum_{k=2}^{m}\frac{(\hat{\mathbf{v}}_i\cdot\hat{\mathbf{u}}_k)^2}{\hat{\lambda}_k} + 2\,\sigma^2\,\hat{\mathbf{v}}_i^{\mathsf{T}}\,\hat{\mathbf{J}}\,\hat{\mathbf{v}}_i \\
&= \sigma^2\left[\frac{n-1}{n} + \sum_{k=2}^{m}\frac{(\hat{\mathbf{v}}_i\cdot\hat{\mathbf{u}}_k)^2}{\hat{\lambda}_k} - 2\sum_{k=2}^{m}\frac{(\hat{\mathbf{v}}_i\cdot\hat{\mathbf{u}}_k)^2}{\hat{\lambda}_k}\right] = \sigma^2\left[\frac{n-1}{n} - \sum_{k=2}^{m}\frac{(\hat{\mathbf{v}}_i\cdot\hat{\mathbf{u}}_k)^2}{\hat{\lambda}_k - \hat{\lambda}_1}\right].
\end{aligned}
$$

For any point i, $\sum_{k=2}^{m}(\hat{\mathbf{v}}_i\cdot\hat{\mathbf{u}}_k)^2/\hat{\lambda}_k$ has a maximum value of $(n-1)/n$ and a minimum value of 0. The variance thus has respective lower and upper bounds of 0 and $(n-1)\sigma^2/n$.

C.2.3 Residual covariance

We derive Equation (6.26) in Section 6.5.2. The covariance between two residuals h_i and h_j $(i\neq j)$ is

$$
\begin{aligned}
\text{Cov}\,\{\delta h_i, \delta h_j\} &= E\,\{(\hat{\mathbf{u}}_1\cdot\delta\mathbf{v}_i + \hat{\mathbf{v}}_i\cdot\delta\mathbf{u}_1)\,(\hat{\mathbf{u}}_1\cdot\delta\mathbf{v}_j + \hat{\mathbf{v}}_j\cdot\delta\mathbf{u}_1)^{\mathsf{T}}\} \\
&= \hat{\mathbf{u}}_1^{\mathsf{T}}E\{\delta\mathbf{v}_i\,\delta\mathbf{v}_j^{\mathsf{T}}\}\hat{\mathbf{u}}_1 + \hat{\mathbf{v}}_j^{\mathsf{T}}E\{\delta\mathbf{u}_1\,\delta\mathbf{v}_i^{\mathsf{T}}\}\hat{\mathbf{u}}_1 + \hat{\mathbf{v}}_i^{\mathsf{T}}E\{\delta\mathbf{u}_1\,\delta\mathbf{v}_j^{\mathsf{T}}\}\hat{\mathbf{u}}_1 + \hat{\mathbf{v}}_i^{\mathsf{T}}\mathbf{\Lambda_{u_1}}\hat{\mathbf{v}}_j,
\end{aligned}
$$

and knowing $E\{\delta\mathbf{u}_1\,\delta\mathbf{v}_i^{\mathsf{T}}\}\hat{\mathbf{u}}_1 = \hat{\mathbf{J}}\sigma^2\hat{\mathbf{v}}_i$ from Section C.2.1,

$$
\begin{aligned}
\text{Cov}\,\{\delta h_i, \delta h_j\} &= -\frac{1}{n}\sigma^2 + \sigma^2\,\hat{\mathbf{v}}_j^{\mathsf{T}}\hat{\mathbf{J}}\,\hat{\mathbf{v}}_i + \sigma^2\,\hat{\mathbf{v}}_i^{\mathsf{T}}\hat{\mathbf{J}}\,\hat{\mathbf{v}}_j - \sigma^2\,\hat{\mathbf{v}}_i^{\mathsf{T}}\hat{\mathbf{J}}\,\hat{\mathbf{v}}_j \\
&= -\frac{1}{n}\sigma^2 - \sigma^2\,\hat{\mathbf{v}}_j^{\mathsf{T}}\sum_{k=2}^{m}\frac{\hat{\mathbf{u}}_k\,\hat{\mathbf{u}}_k^{\mathsf{T}}}{\hat{\lambda}_k}\,\hat{\mathbf{v}}_i.
\end{aligned}
$$

The final form is therefore

$$
\text{Cov}\,\{\delta h_i, \delta h_j\} = -\sigma^2\left[\frac{1}{n} + \sum_{k=2}^{m}\frac{(\hat{\mathbf{v}}_i\cdot\hat{\mathbf{u}}_k)\,(\hat{\mathbf{v}}_j\cdot\hat{\mathbf{u}}_k)}{\hat{\lambda}_k}\right]. \tag{C.4}
$$

Appendix D

Rotation matrices

Three rotation representations are described and the relationships between them are demonstrated. A general rotation matrix $\mathbf{R}$, with rows $\mathbf{R}_i^\mathsf{T}$, is denoted

$$\mathbf{R} = \begin{bmatrix} R_{11} & R_{12} & R_{13} \\ R_{21} & R_{22} & R_{23} \\ R_{31} & R_{32} & R_{33} \end{bmatrix} = \begin{bmatrix} \mathbf{R}_1^\mathsf{T} \\ \mathbf{R}_2^\mathsf{T} \\ \mathbf{R}_3^\mathsf{T} \end{bmatrix}.$$

There are only *three* independent parameters in $\mathbf{R}$ since it is orthogonal ($\mathbf{R}\mathbf{R}^\mathsf{T} = \mathbf{I}_3$).

D.1   Angle–axis form

Consider a rotation about the unit axis $\mathbf{a} = (a_x, a_y, a_z)^\mathsf{T}$ through angle χ. The Rodrigues equation gives the rotation matrix as [74]

$$\begin{bmatrix} a_x^2(1 - \cos\chi) + \cos\chi & a_x a_y(1 - \cos\chi) - a_z \sin\chi & a_x a_z(1 - \cos\chi) + a_y \sin\chi \\ a_y a_x(1 - \cos\chi) + a_z \sin\chi & a_y^2(1 - \cos\chi) + \cos\chi & a_y a_z(1 - \cos\chi) - a_x \sin\chi \\ a_z a_x(1 - \cos\chi) - a_y \sin\chi & a_z a_y(1 - \cos\chi) + a_x \sin\chi & a_z^2(1 - \cos\chi) + \cos\chi \end{bmatrix}$$

$$(\text{D.1})$$

The rotation parameters are obtained from the matrix elements as follows:

$$2\cos\chi = \mathrm{trace}\,(\mathbf{R}) - 1 \quad \text{and} \quad 2\sin\chi\,\mathbf{a} = \begin{bmatrix} R_{32} - R_{23} \\ R_{13} - R_{31} \\ R_{21} - R_{12} \end{bmatrix} \qquad (\text{D.2})$$

The angle–axis formulation is identical to the *quaternion* representation, where the unit quaternion $\mathbf{u} = (s_u, \mathbf{v}_u)$ comprises a scalar component $s_u = \cos(\chi/2)$ and a vector component $\mathbf{v}_u = (x_u, y_u, z_u) = \sin(\chi/2)\mathbf{a}$. The corresponding rotation matrix [74],

$$\mathbf{R} = \begin{bmatrix} s_u^2 + x_u^2 - y_u^2 - z_u^2 & 2(x_u y_u - s_u z_u) & 2(x_u z_u + s_u y_u) \\ 2(y_u x_u + s_u z_u) & s_u^2 - x_u^2 + y_u^2 - z_u^2 & 2(y_u z_u - s_u z_u) \\ 2(z_u x_u - s_u y_u) & 2(z_u y_u + s_u x_u) & s_u^2 - x_u^2 - y_u^2 + z_u^2 \end{bmatrix},$$

reduces to Equation (D.2)) after substituting the half–angle formulae $1 + \cos\chi = 2\cos^2(\chi/2)$ and $1 - \cos\chi = 2\sin^2(\chi/2)$.

D.2 Euler–angle form

The rotation is decomposed into three simpler rotations, first about the Z axis (by φ), then about the X axis (by η), and finally about the Z axis again (by μ):

$$\mathbf{R} = \begin{bmatrix} \cos\mu & -\sin\mu & 0 \\ \sin\mu & \cos\mu & 0 \\ 0 & 0 & 1 \end{bmatrix} \begin{bmatrix} 1 & 0 & 0 \\ 0 & \cos\eta & -\sin\eta \\ 0 & \sin\eta & \cos\eta \end{bmatrix} \begin{bmatrix} \cos\varphi & -\sin\varphi & 0 \\ \sin\varphi & \cos\varphi & 0 \\ 0 & 0 & 1 \end{bmatrix}. \tag{D.3}$$

D.3 KvD form

Koenderink and van Doorn [79] decomposed $\mathbf{R}$ into a rotation *in* the image plane followed by a rotation *out of* the image plane (see Section 3.4.4). Thus $\mathbf{R} = \mathbf{R}_\rho \mathbf{R}_\theta$, where $\mathbf{R}_\rho$ and $\mathbf{R}_\theta$ are obtained from Equation (D.1) with $\mathbf{a}_\rho = (\cos\phi, \sin\phi, 0)^\mathsf{T}$ and $\mathbf{a}_\theta = \mathbf{k} = (0,0,1)^\mathsf{T}$:

$$\mathbf{R} = \begin{bmatrix} (1-\cos\rho)\cos^2\phi + \cos\rho & (1-\cos\rho)\sin\phi\cos\phi & \sin\phi\sin\rho \\ (1-\cos\rho)\sin\phi\cos\phi & (1-\cos\rho)\sin^2\phi + \cos\rho & -\cos\phi\sin\rho \\ -\sin\phi\sin\rho & \cos\phi\sin\rho & \cos\rho \end{bmatrix} \begin{bmatrix} \cos\theta & -\sin\theta & 0 \\ \sin\theta & \cos\theta & 0 \\ 0 & 0 & 1 \end{bmatrix}$$

giving the final elements

$$\begin{bmatrix} (1-\cos\rho)\cos\phi\cos(\phi-\theta) + \cos\rho\cos\theta & (1-\cos\rho)\cos\phi\sin(\phi-\theta) - \cos\rho\sin\theta & \sin\phi\sin\rho \\ (1-\cos\rho)\sin\phi\cos(\phi-\theta) + \cos\rho\sin\theta & (1-\cos\rho)\sin\phi\sin(\phi-\theta) + \cos\rho\cos\theta & -\cos\phi\sin\rho \\ -\sin\rho\sin(\phi-\theta) & \sin\rho\cos(\phi-\theta) & \cos\rho \end{bmatrix}$$

The rotation parameters can then be obtained from the matrix elements as follows:

$$\cos\rho = R_{33}, \quad \tan\phi = -\frac{R_{13}}{R_{23}} \quad \text{and} \quad \tan(\phi-\theta) = -\frac{R_{31}}{R_{32}} \tag{D.4}$$

To relate ρ, ϕ and θ to the Euler angles φ, η and μ, write Equation (D.3) as

$$\mathbf{R} = \mathbf{R}^Z(\mu)\,\mathbf{R}^X(\eta)\,\mathbf{R}^Z(\varphi),$$

where $\mathbf{R}^Z(\mu)$ denotes rotation about the Z axis by angle μ, and so on. Noting that $\mathbf{R}(\mu)^{-1} = \mathbf{R}(\mu)^\mathsf{T} = \mathbf{R}(-\mu)$, we obtain

$$\mathbf{R} = \mathbf{R}^Z(\mu)\,\mathbf{R}^X(\eta)\,\left[\mathbf{R}^Z(-\mu)\,\mathbf{R}^Z(\mu)\right]\mathbf{R}^Z(\varphi) = \left[\mathbf{R}^Z(\mu)\,\mathbf{R}^X(\eta)\,\mathbf{R}^Z(-\mu)\right]\mathbf{R}^Z(\mu+\varphi).$$

Now, $\mathbf{R}^Z(\mu)\,\mathbf{R}^X(\eta)\,\mathbf{R}^Z(-\mu)$ represents a rotation out of the plane by η about a line lying in the plane at angle μ: this is equivalent to $\mathbf{R}_\rho$, with $\rho = \eta$ and $\phi = \mu$. The matrix $\mathbf{R}^Z(\mu+\varphi)$ gives a rotation in the image plane through $\mu + \varphi$, equivalent to $\mathbf{R}_\theta$ with $\theta = \mu + \varphi$. Hence

$$\rho = \eta, \quad \phi = \mu \quad \text{and} \quad \theta - \phi = \varphi.$$

Appendix E
KvD motion equations

E.1 KvD image motion equations

In KvD form, Equation (7.2) becomes

$$\Delta \mathbf{x}_i' = s \, \cos \rho \, \mathbf{R}(\theta) \, \Delta \mathbf{x}_i + s \, (1 - \cos \rho) \, (\mathbf{R}(-\theta) \, \mathbf{\Phi} \cdot \Delta \mathbf{x}_i) \, \mathbf{\Phi} + s \, \sin \rho \, \Delta z_i \, \mathbf{\Phi}^{\perp}$$

with $\mathbf{R}(\theta)$ the upper left 2×2 submatrix of $\mathbf{R}_\theta$ (see Appendix D.3). Using the relation $\mathbf{\Phi}\mathbf{\Phi}^{\mathsf{T}} = \mathbf{I}_2 - \mathbf{\Phi}^{\perp}(\mathbf{\Phi}^{\perp})^{\mathsf{T}}$, where $\mathbf{I}_2$ is the 2×2 identity matrix, we get

$$\boxed{\Delta \mathbf{x}_i' = s\mathbf{R}(\theta) \, \Delta \mathbf{x}_i - s \left\{ (1 - \cos \rho) \, (\mathbf{R}(\theta) \, \Delta \mathbf{x}_i \cdot \mathbf{\Phi}^{\perp}) - \sin \rho \, \Delta z_i \right\} \, \mathbf{\Phi}^{\perp}} \qquad \text{(E.1)}$$

This describes the image motion of point i between I_1 and I_2. The first term in Equation (E.1) rotates the vector about the line of sight by θ (positions A and B in Figure E.1(a)); this is the effect of $\mathbf{R}_\theta$. The second term *compresses* the vector in a direction orthogonal to $\mathbf{\Phi}$ (i.e. along $\mathbf{\Phi}^{\perp}$). This is the *foreshortening* effect of $\mathbf{R}_\rho$, which rotates $\Delta \mathbf{X}_i$ out of the plane about $\mathbf{\Phi}$ (positions B and C in Figure E.1(b)). Finally, the vector is scaled by s to account for the change in depth. To interpret the foreshortening coefficient,

$$(1 - \cos \rho) \, (\mathbf{R}(\theta) \, \Delta \mathbf{x}_i \cdot \mathbf{\Phi}^{\perp}) - \sin \rho \, \Delta z_i, \qquad \text{(E.2)}$$

consider the axis $\mathbf{oq}$ in Figure E.2(a). This axis is perpendicular to $\mathbf{\Phi}$ and passes through $\mathbf{R}(\theta) \, \Delta \mathbf{x}_i$, intersecting $\mathbf{\Phi}$ in o. Now consider a depth slice through $\mathbf{oq}$, with the $\mathbf{oz}$ axis directed out of the page through o, i.e. treat $\mathbf{oq}$ as the edge of a plane seen side–on. The 3D vector rotates in this plane, as shown in Figure E.2(b). The point initially has depth Δz_i and ordinate $q_i = \mathbf{R}(\theta) \, \Delta \mathbf{x}_i \cdot \mathbf{\Phi}^{\perp}$ (position B), and rotates in the q–z plane through ρ, giving

$$\begin{bmatrix} q_i'/s \\ \Delta z_i'/s \end{bmatrix} = \begin{bmatrix} \cos \rho & \sin \rho \\ -\sin \rho & \cos \rho \end{bmatrix} \begin{bmatrix} q_i \\ \Delta z_i \end{bmatrix}.$$

The scale factor s is present since all I_2 quantities have been referred back to I_1. Then

$$\frac{q_i'}{s} = q_i \cos \rho + \Delta z_i \sin \rho, \qquad \text{(E.3)}$$

and the *change* in q (seen from I_1) is the compression term in Equation (E.2),

$$q_i - \frac{q_i'}{s} = (1 - \cos \rho) \, q_i - \sin \rho \, \Delta z_i.$$

The new scaled depth is

$$\Delta z_i' = -sq_i \sin \rho + s\Delta z_i \cos \rho. \qquad \text{(E.4)}$$

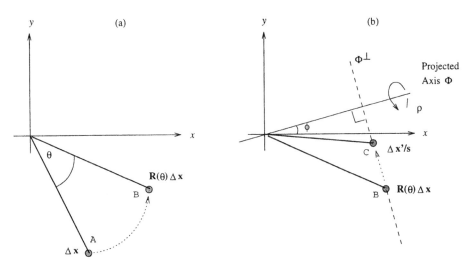

Figure E.1: *The image motion equation: (a) The vector $\Delta\mathbf{x}$ rotates in the image plane through θ°; (b) The vector is foreshortened orthogonal to $\mathbf{\Phi}$.*

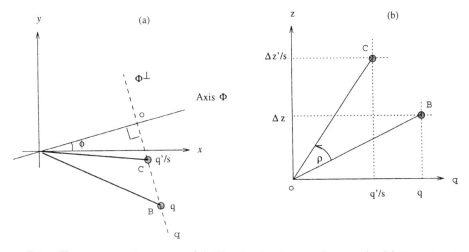

Figure E.2: *The compression term: (a) The depth slice $\mathbf{oq}$ (see text); (b) Rotation in depth through ρ°.*

E.2   Epipolar–based image coordinates

The default image coordinate system is $\{\mathbf{i}, \mathbf{j}\}$, the x and y axes. However, Section E.1 suggests an alternative coordinate system $\{\boldsymbol{\Phi}, \boldsymbol{\Phi}^{\perp}\}$, namely the projected axis and epipolar line directions (Figure E.3). This is a *motion–based*, orthogonal coordinate system anchored at the object centroid (or some other object–based reference point), and the coordinates along the $\{\boldsymbol{\Phi}, \boldsymbol{\Phi}^{\perp}\}$ axes are denoted $(p, q)^{\mathsf{T}}$. Since the projected axis in I_1 is $\mathbf{R}(-\theta)\,\boldsymbol{\Phi}$ (the I_2 axis $\boldsymbol{\Phi}$ counter–rotated by θ), the components of an image point projected along these axes are

$$p_i = \Delta\mathbf{x}_i \cdot \mathbf{R}(-\theta)\,\boldsymbol{\Phi}, \quad q_i = \Delta\mathbf{x}_i \cdot \mathbf{R}(-\theta)\,\boldsymbol{\Phi}^{\perp}, \quad p_i' = \Delta\mathbf{x}_i' \cdot \boldsymbol{\Phi} \quad \text{and} \quad q_i' = \Delta\mathbf{x}_i' \cdot \boldsymbol{\Phi}^{\perp}.$$

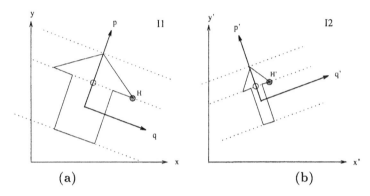

Figure E.3: *An epipolar–based coordinate frame, with components p measured along the axis direction $\boldsymbol{\Phi}$ and q along the epipolar direction $\boldsymbol{\Phi}^{\perp}$.*

We now relate the I_2 components to the I_1 components. First, consider the components *orthogonal* to the epipolar direction. From Equation (E.1),

$$p_i' = \Delta\mathbf{x}_i' \cdot \boldsymbol{\Phi} = s\,\mathbf{R}(\theta)\,\Delta\mathbf{x}_i \cdot \boldsymbol{\Phi} = s\,\Delta\mathbf{x}_i \cdot \mathbf{R}(-\theta)\,\boldsymbol{\Phi} = s\,p_i. \tag{E.5}$$

This is an alternative statement of Equation (7.5), and states that after accounting for scale, the projections of corresponding image points onto their corresponding axes are equal. Depth (Δz_i) and turn (ρ) are factored out, since they determine how far *along* the epipolar line a point lies.

Similarly, the component along the epipolar line is

$$q_i' = \Delta\mathbf{x}_i' \cdot \boldsymbol{\Phi}^{\perp} = s\,\mathbf{R}(\theta)\,\Delta\mathbf{x}_i \cdot \boldsymbol{\Phi}^{\perp}\,\cos\rho + s\,\Delta z_i\,\sin\rho = sq_i\cos\rho + s\Delta z_i\sin\rho, \tag{E.6}$$

giving an alternative derivation of Equation (E.3). This equation neatly exposes the bas–relief ambiguity: excluding the reference point, each pair (q_i, q_i') provides one constraint, i.e. n points provide $n{-}1$ equations. There are, however, n unknowns, namely the turn angle ρ and the $n{-}1$ depths Δz_i. Hence, two views will never provide a complete solution; at best, they give a *one–parameter family* of solutions.

Bibliography

[1] R.J. Adcock, "Note on the method of least squares", *The Analyst*, London, Vol. 4, No. 6, 1877, pp. 183–184.

[2] R.J. Adcock, "A problem in least squares", *The Analyst*, London, Vol. 5, No. 2, 1878, pp. 53–54.

[3] G. Adiv, "Determining 3D motion and structure from optical flow generated by several moving objects", *IEEE Trans. Pattern Anal. Machine Intell.*, Vol. PAMI–7, July 1985, pp. 384–401.

[4] J.K. Aggarwal and N. Nandhakumar, "On the computation of motion from sequences of images – a review", *Proceedings of the IEEE*, Vol. 76, No. 8, Aug. 1988, pp. 917–935.

[5] K. Aizawa, H. Harashima and T. Saito, "Model–based analysis synthesis image coding (MBASIC) system for a person's face", *Signal Processing: Image Communication*, Vol. 1, No. 2, Oct. 1989, pp. 139–152.

[6] T. Akimoto, R. Wallace and Y. Suenaga, "Feature extraction from front and side views of faces for 3D facial model creation", *IAPR Workshop on Machine Vision Applications (MVA '90)*, Tokyo, Nov. 1990, pp. 291–294.

[7] J. Aloimonos and A. Bandyopadhyay, "Perception of structure from motion: lower bound results", Tech. Report 158, Dept. Computer Science, University of Rochester, March 1985.

[8] J.Y. Aloimonos, "Perspective approximations", *Image and Vision Computing*, Vol. 8, No. 3, Aug. 1990, pp. 179–192.

[9] R.D. Arnold and T.O. Binford, "Geometrical constraints in stereo vision", *Proceedings S.P.I.E.*, Vol. 238, pp. 281–292, 1980.

[10] H. Asada and M. Brady, "The curvature primal sketch", *IEEE Trans. Pattern Anal. Machine Intell.*, Vol. PAMI–8, No. 1, Jan. 1986, pp. 2–14.

[11] Y. Bar–Shalom and T.E. Fortmann, *Tracking and data association*, Academic Press Inc., USA, 1988.

[12] E.B. Barrett, M.H. Brill, N.N. Haag and P.M. Hayton, "Invariant linear methods in photogrammetry and model–matching" in J.L. Mundy and A. Zisserman (eds), *Geometric Invariance in Computer Vision,* MIT Press, USA, 1992, pp. 277–292.

[13] S.T. Barnard and W.B. Thomson, "Disparity analysis of images", *IEEE Trans. Pattern Anal. Machine Intell.,* Vol. 2, No. 4, July 1980, pp. 333–340.

[14] V. Barnett and T. Lewis, *Outliers in Statistical Data,* 2nd ed., John Wiley & Sons, UK, 1984.

[15] P.A. Beardsley, A. Zisserman and D. Murray, "Projective structure from image sequences", Tech. Report OUEL 1985/93, Dept. Engineering Science, University of Oxford, June 1993.

[16] P.A. Beardsley, A. Zisserman and D.W. Murray, "Navigation using affine structure from motion", submitted to ECCV'94.

[17] D.A. Belsley, E. Kuh and R.E. Welsch, *Regression Diagnostics,* John Wiley & Sons, USA, 1980.

[18] B.M. Bennett, D.D. Hoffman, J.E. Nicola and C. Prakash, "Structure from two orthographic views of rigid motion", *Journal of Optical Society of America,* Vol. 6, No. 7, July 1989, pp. 1052–1069.

[19] J.R. Bergen, P. Anandan, K.J. Hanna and R. Hingorani, "Hierarchical model–based motion estimation" in G. Sandini (ed.), *Proceedings European Conference on Computer Vision* (ECCV–92), 1992, pp. 237–249.

[20] M. Berger, *Geometry I,* Springer Verlag, 1980.

[21] A. Blake, R. Curwen and A. Zisserman, "A framework for spatio–temporal control in the tracking of visual contours", *Proceedings International Conference on Computer Vision (ICCV–4),* Berlin, May 1993, pp. 66–75.

[22] A.T. Brint and M. Brady, "Stereo matching of curves", *Image and Vision Computing,* Vol. 8, No. 1, Feb. 1990, pp. 50–56.

[23] J.M. Brady, "Seeds of perception", *Proceedings of the 3rd Alvey Vision Conference,* Cambridge University, Sept. 1987, pp. 259–265.

[24] J.M. Brady and H. Wang, "Vision for mobile robots", *Proceedings of the Royal Society of London,* Vol. B, 1992.

[25] J.F. Canny, "A computational approach to edge detection," *IEEE Trans. Pattern Anal. Machine Intell.,* Vol. 6, No. 6. 1986, pp. 679–698.

[26] D. Charnley, C. Harris, M. Pike, E. Sparks and M. Stephens, "The DROID 3D vision system: algorithms for geometric integration", Plessey Research, Roke Manor, Technical Note 72/88/N488U, Dec. 1988.

[27] D. Charnley and R.J. Blissett, "Surface reconstruction from outdoor image sequences", *Proceedings of the 4th Alvey Vision Conference,* 1988, pp. 153–158.

[28] C. Chatfield and A.J. Collins, *Introduction to Multivariate Analysis,* Chapman and Hall, UK, 1980.

[29] H.C. Chen and T.S. Huang, "Using motion from orthographic views to verify 3D point matches", *IEEE Trans. Pattern Anal. Machine Intell.,* Vol. PAMI–13, No. 9, Sept. 1991, pp. 872–878.

[30] R. Cipolla, "Active visual inference of surface shape", D. Phil thesis, Dept. Engineering Science, Oxford University, 1991.

[31] R. Cipolla, Y. Okamoto and Y. Kuno, "Robust structure from motion using motion parallax", *Proceedings International Conference on Computer Vision (ICCV–4),* Berlin, May 1993, pp. 374–382.

[32] R.D. Cook and S. Weisberg, *Residuals and Influence in Regression,* Chapman Hall, UK, 1982.

[33] J. Cooper, S. Venkatesh and L. Kitchen, "Early jump–out corner detectors", *IEEE Trans. Pattern Anal. Machine Intell.,* Vol. PAMI–15, No. 8, Aug. 1993, pp. 823–828.

[34] I. Craw, D. Tock and A. Bennett, "Finding face features" in G. Sandini (ed.), *Proceedings European Conference on Computer Vision* (ECCV–92), 1992, pp. 92–96.

[35] S. Demey, A. Zisserman and P. Beardsley, "Affine and projective structure from motion", *Proceedings British Machine Vision Conference* (BMVC'92), 1992, pp. 49–58.

[36] R. Deriche and G. Giraudon, "A computational approach for corner and vertex detection", *International Journal of Computer Vision,* Vol. 10, No. 2, Nov. 1993, pp. 101–124.

[37] R.O. Duda and P.E. Hart, *Pattern Classification and Scene Analysis,* John Wiley & Sons, USA, 1973.

[38] H.F. Durrant–Whyte, "Multi–sensor fusion methods and applications", in press, 1993.

[39] L. Dreschler and H. Nagel, "Volumetric model and 3D trajectory of a moving car derived from monocular TV–frame sequence of a street scene", *Computer Vision, Graphics and Image Processing,* Vol. 20, No. 3, Nov. 1982, pp. 199–228.

[40] M. Etoh and Y. Shirai, "Segmentation and 2D motion estimation by region fragments", *Proceedings International Conference on Computer Vision (ICCV–4),* Berlin, May 1993, pp. 192–199.

[41] O.D. Faugeras, F. Lustman and G. Toscani, "Motion and structure from motion from point and line matches", *Proceedings International Conference on Computer Vision (ICCV–1),* London, UK, May 1987, pp. 25–34.

[42] O.D. Faugeras, Q–T. Luong and S.J. Maybank, "Camera self–calibration: theory and experiments" in G. Sandini (ed.), *Proceedings European Conference on Computer Vision* (ECCV–92), 1992, pp. 321–334.

[43] O.D. Faugeras, "What can be seen in three dimensions with an uncalibrated stereo rig?" in G. Sandini (ed.), *Proceedings European Conference on Computer Vision* (ECCV–92), 1992, pp. 563–578.

[44] R. Forchheimer and T. Kronander, "Image coding – from waveforms to animation", *IEEE Transactions on Acoustics, Speech and Signal Processing*, Vol. 37, No. 12, Dec. 1989, pp. 2008–2023.

[45] A. Gibbons, *Algorithmic graph theory*, Cambridge University Press, UK, 1985.

[46] R. Gnanadesikan and J.R. Kettenring, "Robust estimates, residuals and outlier detection with multi–response data", *Biometrics*, Vol. 28, 1972, pp. 81–124.

[47] G.H. Golub, "Some modified matrix eigenvalue problems", *SIAM Review*, Vol. 15, No. 2, 1973, pp. 318–334.

[48] G.H. Golub and C.F. van Loan, *Matrix Computations*, 2nd ed., Johns Hopkins University Press, USA, 1989.

[49] M. Gondran and M. Minoux, *Graphs and algorithms*, John Wiley & Sons, UK, 1984.

[50] S. Gong and M. Brady, "Parallel computation of optic flow" in *Proceedings European Conference on Computer Vision* (ECCV–90), 1990, pp. 124–133.

[51] J.C. Gower and G.J.S. Ross, "Minimum spanning trees and single linkage cluster analysis", *Applied Statistics*, Vol. 18, No. 1, 1969, pp. 54–64.

[52] W.E.L. Grimson, *From Images to Surfaces*, MIT Press, USA, 1981.

[53] F.R. Hampel, E.M. Ronchetti, P.J. Rousseeuw and W.A. Stahel, *Robust Statistics: The Approach Based on Influence Functions*, John Wiley & Sons, USA, 1986.

[54] C.G. Harris and M. Stephens, "A combined corner and edge detector", *Proceedings 4th Alvey Vision Conference*, 1988, pp. 147–151.

[55] C. Harris, "Structure–from–motion under orthographic projection", *First European Conference on Computer Vision* (ECCV–90), 1990, pp. 118–123.

[56] H.L. Harter, "The method of least squares and some alternatives: I", *International Statistical Review*, Vol. 42, No. 2, 1974, pp. 147–174.

[57] R.I. Hartley, R. Gupta and T. Chang, "Stereo from uncalibrated cameras," *Proceedings CVPR'92*, 1992, pp. 761–764.

[58] D.M. Hawkins, *Identification of Outliers*, Chapman and Hall, USA, 1980.

[59] E.C. Hildreth, *The Measurement of Visual Motion*, MIT Press, USA, 1984.

[60] E.J. Hinch, *Perturbation Methods*, Cambridge University Press, Mexico, 1991.

[61] B.K.P. Horn and B.G. Schunk, "Determining optical flow", *Artificial Intelligence*, Vol. 17, 1981, pp. 185–203.

[62] B.K.P. Horn, *Robot Vision*, MIT Press, USA, 1986.

[63] A.S. Householder and G. Young, "Matrix approximations and latent roots", *American Mathematical Monthly*, Vol. 45, pp. 165–171.

[64] X. Hu and N. Ahuja, "Motion estimation under orthographic projection", *IEEE Transactions on Robotics and Automation*, Vol. 7, No. 6, 1991, pp. 848–853.

[65] T.S. Huang (ed.), *Image Sequence Analysis*, Springer–Verlag, USA, 1981.

[66] T.S. Huang and C.H. Lee, "Motion and structure from orthographic projections", *IEEE Trans. Pattern Anal. Machine Intell.*, Vol. PAMI–11, No. 5, 1989, pp. 536–40.

[67] P.J. Huber, *Robust Statistics*, John Wiley & Sons, USA, 1981.

[68] M. Irani, B. Rousso and S. Peleg, "Detecting and tracking multiple moving objects using temporal integration" in G. Sandini (ed.), *Proceedings European Conference on Computer Vision* (ECCV–92), 1992, pp. 282–287.

[69] A.K. Jain and R.C. Dubes, *Algorithms for Clustering Data*, Prentice Hall, USA, 1988.

[70] C.P. Jerian and R. Jain, "Structure from motion – a critical analysis of methods", *IEEE Trans. Systems, Man and Cybernetics*, Vol. 21, No. 3, May/June, 1991, pp. 572–588.

[71] G. Johansson, "Visual perception of biological motion and a model for its analysis", *Perception and Psychophysics*, Vol. 14, No. 2, 1973, pp. 201–211.

[72] S.C. Johnson, "Hierarchical clustering schemes", *Psychometrika*, Vol. 32, No. 3, Sept. 1967, pp. 241–254.

[73] K. Kanatani, "Unbiased estimation and statistical analysis of three–dimensional rigid motion from two views", *IEEE Trans. Pattern Anal. Machine Intell.*, Vol. PAMI–15, No. 1, Jan. 1993, pp. 37–50.

[74] K. Kanatani, *Geometric Computation for Computer Vision*, Oxford University Press, 1993.

[75] M. Kass, A. Witkin and D. Terzopoulos, "Snakes: active contour models", *International Journal of Computer Vision*, Vol. 1, 1988, pp. 321–331.

[76] N.D. Kenyon, "Videoconferencing", *British Telecom Technical Journal*, Vol. 2, No. 2, April 1984, pp. 5–18.

[77] L. Kitchen and A. Rosenfeld, "Gray level corner detection", *Pattern Recognition Letters,* Vol. 1, Dec. 1982, pp. 95–102.

[78] J.J. Koenderink and A.J. van Doorn, "Optic flow", *Vision Research,* Vol. 26, No. 1, 1986, pp. 161–179.

[79] J.J. Koenderink and A.J. van Doorn, "Affine structure from motion", *Journal of Optical Society of America,* Vol. 8, No. 2, Feb. 1991, pp. 377-385.

[80] D. Koller, N. Heinze and H.H. Nagel, "Algorithmic characterisation of vehicle trajectories from image sequences by motion verbs" in *Proceeding CVPR'91,* Hawaii, June 1991, pp. 90–95.

[81] W.J. Krazanowski, *Principles of Multivariate Analysis,* Clarendon Press, UK, 1988.

[82] J.B. Kruskal, "On the shortest spanning subtree of a graph and the traveling salesman problem", *Proceedings American Mathematical Society,* Vol. 7, No. 1, 1956, pp. 48–50.

[83] C.H. Kummel, "Reduction of observation equations which contain more than one observed quantity", *The Analyst,* London, Vol. 6, No. 4, 1879, pp. 97–105.

[84] D.T. Lawton, "Processing translational motion sequences", *Computer Vision, Graphics and Image Processing,* Vol. 22, 1983, pp. 116–144.

[85] C. Lee and T. Huang, "Finding point correspondences and determining motion of a rigid object from two weak perspective views", *Computer Vision, Graphics and Image Processing,* Vol. 52, 1990, pp. 309–327.

[86] H. Li, P. Roivainen and R. Forchheimer, "3D motion estimation in model–based facial image coding", Internal Report LITH–ISY–I–1278, Dept. Electrical Engineering, Linköping University, Sweden, 1991.

[87] H.C. Longuet-Higgins, "A computer algorithm for reconstructing a scene from two projections", *Nature,* Vol. 293, 1981, pp. 133–135.

[88] H.C. Longuet-Higgins, "A method of determining the relation positions of 4 points from 3 perspective projections" in P. Mowforth (ed.), *Proceedings BMVC'91,* pp. 86–94.

[89] Q-T. Luong, R. Deriche, O. Faugeras and T. Papadopoulo, "On determining the fundamental matrix: analysis of different methods and experimental results", Tech. Report 1894, INRIA (Sophia Antipolis), April 1993.

[90] D. Marr, *Vision,* W.H. Freeman & Company, USA, 1982.

[91] A.M. McIvor, "A test of camera noise models", *Proceedings BMVC'90,* Oxford, Sept. 1990, pp. 355–359.

[92] P.F. McLauchlan, I.D. Reid and D.W. Murray, "Coarse motion for saccade control", in D. Hogg and R. Boyle (eds), *Proceedings BMVC'92*, Leeds, Springer–Verlag, UK, 1992.

[93] P.F. McLauchlan, I.D. Reid and D.W. Murray, "Recursive affine structure and motion from image sequences", submitted to 3rd ECCV, Stockholm, 1994.

[94] G. Medioni and Y. Yasumoto, "Corner detection and curve representation using cubic B–splines", *Proceedings of the IEEE International Conference on Robotics and Automation*, San Francisco, CA, April 1986, pp. 764–769.

[95] F. Meyer and P. Bouthemy, "Region–based tracking in an image sequence" in G. Sandini (ed.), *Proceedings European Conference on Computer Vision* (ECCV–92), 1992, pp. 476–484.

[96] H.P. Moravec, "The Stanford cart and the CMU rover", *Proceedings of the IEEE*, Vol. 71, No. 7, 1983, pp. 872–884.

[97] H. Mulholland and C.R. Jones, "Fundamentals of statistics", Butterworth & Co., Great Britain, 1982.

[98] J.L. Mundy and A. Zisserman (eds), *Geometric Invariance in Computer Vision*, MIT Press, USA, 1992.

[99] F. Murtagh and A. Heck, *Multivariate Data Analysis*, D. Reidel Publishing Co., Holland, 1987.

[100] D.W. Murray and B.F. Buxton, *Experiments in the Machine Interpretation of Visual Motion*, MIT Press, USA, 1990.

[101] D.W. Murray and L.S. Shapiro, "Dynamic updating of planar structure and motion: the case of constant motion", Oct. 1992. Submitted for journal publication.

[102] H.G. Mussman, P. Pirsch and H–J. Grallert, "Advances in picture coding", *Proceedings IEEE*, Vol. 73, No. 4, April 1985, pp. 523–548.

[103] H.G. Mussman, M. Hötter and J. Ostermann, "Object–oriented analysis–synthesis coding of moving images", *Signal Processing: Image Communication*, Vol. 1, No. 2, Oct. 1989, pp. 117–138.

[104] R.H. Myers, *Classical and Modern Regression with Applications*, 2nd ed., PWS–Kent, USA, 1990.

[105] H–H. Nagel, "Displacement vectors derived from second–order intensity variations in image sequences", *Computer Vision, Graphics and Image Processing*, Vol. 21, 1983, pp. 85–117.

[106] H.H. Nagel, "Image sequences – ten (octal) years: from phenomenology towards a theoretical foundation" in *Proc. 8th International Conference on Pattern Recognition*, Paris, Oct. 1986, pp. 1174–1185.

[107] J.A. Noble, *Description of Image Surface*, D.Phil Thesis, Department of Engineering Science, Oxford University, 1989.

[108] O. Ore, *Graphs and Their Uses*, Mathematical Association of America, revised R.J. Wilson, USA, 1990.

[109] K. Pearson, "On lines and planes of closest fit to systems of points in space", *Philosophical Magazine and Journal of Science*, Series 6, Vol. 2, Nov. 1901, pp. 559–572.

[110] D. Pearson, "Model–based image coding", *Proceedings IEEE Global Telecommunications Conference (GLOBECOM–89)*, Dallas, Texas, Nov. 1989, Vol. 1, Paper 16.1, pp. 554–558.

[111] T. Poggio, "3D object recognition: on a result of Basri and Ullman", IRST–Technical Report, May 1990.

[112] S.B. Pollard, J.E.W. Mayhew and J.P. Frisby, "PMF: a stereo correspondence algorithm using a disparity gradient limit", *Perception*, Vol. 14, 1985, pp. 449–470.

[113] S.B. Pollard, T.P. Pridmore, J. Porrill, J.E.W. Mayhew and J.P. Frisby, "Geometrical modelling from multiple stereo views", *International Journal of Robotics Research*, Vol. 8, No. 4, 1989, pp. 132–138.

[114] S.B. Pollard, J.E.W. Mayhew and J.P. Frisby, "Implementation details of the PMF stereo algorithm" in J.E.W. Mayhew and J.P. Frisby (eds.), *3D Model Recognition from Stereoscopic Cues*, MIT Press, 1991, pp. 33-39.

[115] J. Porrill, T.P. Pridmore, J.E.W. Mayhew and J.P. Frisby, "Fitting planes, lines and circles to stereo disparity data", AIVRU Tech. Report 17, University of Sheffield, Sept. 1986.

[116] F.P. Preparata and M.I. Shamos, *Computational geometry.: an introduction*, Springer-Verlag, New York, 1985.

[117] R.C. Prim, "Shortest connection networks and some generalisations", *Bell System Technical Journal*, Vol. 36, Nov. 1957, pp. 1389–1401.

[118] L. Quan and R. Mohr, "Towards structure from motion for linear features through reference points", *IEEE Workshop on Visual Motion*, New Jersey, 1991.

[119] R.F. Rashid, "Towards a system for the interpretation of moving light displays", *IEEE Trans. Computers*, Vol. PAMI-2, No. 6, Nov. 1980, pp. 574–581.

[120] J.O. Rawlings, *Applied Regression Analysis: A Research Tool*, Wadsworth and Brooks, USA, 1988.

[121] I.D. Reid and D.W. Murray, "Tracking foveated corner clusters using affine structure", *Proceedings International Conference on Computer Vision (ICCV-4)*, Berlin, May 1993, pp. 76–83.

[122] I.D. Reid, "The SVD minimizes image distance", Oxford University Robotics Research Group Internal Memo, Sept. 1993.

[123] J. M. Roberts and D. Charnley, "Parallel visual tracking", *First IFAC International Workshop on Intelligent Autonomous Vehicles*, Southampton, April 1993, pp. 127-132.

[124] P.J. Rousseeuw and A.M. Leroy, *Robust Regression and Outlier Detection*, John Wiley & Sons, USA, 1987.

[125] G.L. Scott and H.C. Longuet–Higgins, "An algorithm for associating the features of two patterns", Proceedings of the Royal Society of London, Vol. B244, 1991, pp. 21–26.

[126] L.S. Shapiro, "Towards a motion based vision framework", First Year Report, Dept. Engineering Science, University of Oxford, May 1991.

[127] L.S. Shapiro and J.M. Brady, "Feature–based correspondence: an eigenvector approach" in P. Mowforth (ed.), *Proc. British Machine Vision Conference (BMVC'91)*, Glasgow, Springer–Verlag, Sept. 1991, pp. 79–86. Also in *Image and Vision Computing*, Vol. 10, No. 5, June 1992, pp. 283–288.

[128] L.S. Shapiro, H. Wang and J.M. Brady, "A matching and tracking strategy applied to videophony", Tech. Report OUEL 1933/92, Dept. Engineering Science, University of Oxford, 1992. Also as "A matching and tracking strategy for independently moving objects" in D. Hogg and R. Boyle (eds), *Proceedings BMVC'92*, Springer–Verlag, UK, 1992, pp. 139–148.

[129] L.S. Shapiro and J.M. Brady, "Rejecting outliers and estimating errors in an orthogonal regression framework", Tech. Report OUEL 1974/93, Dept. Engineering Science, University of Oxford, Feb. 1993. To appear in *Philosophical Transactions of the Royal Society.*

[130] L.S. Shapiro, A. Zisserman and J.M. Brady, "What can one see with an affine camera?", Tech. Report 1993/93, Dept. Engineering Science, University of Oxford, June 1993.

[131] L.S. Shapiro, A. Zisserman and J.M. Brady, "Motion from point matches using affine epipolar geometry", Tech. Report 1994/93, Dept. Engineering Science, University of Oxford, June 1993. To appear in *European Conference of Computer Vision (ECCV'94)*, Stockholm, May 1994 and in *International Journal of Computer Vision.*

[132] A. Shashua and S. Ullman, "Structural saliency: the detection of globally salient structures using a locally connected network", *Proceedings International Conference on Computer Vision (ICCV-2)*, Florida, 1988, pp. 321–327.

[133] A. Shashua, "Projective structure from two uncalibrated images: structure from motion and recognition", MIT A.I. Lab, Memo No. 1363, Sept. 1992.

[134] S. Smith, "Feature based image sequence understanding", D. Phil thesis, Dept. Engineering Science, Oxford University, 1992.

[135] I. So, O. Nakamura and T. Minami, "A study on a model–based coding system based on isodensity maps of facial images", *Abstracts of the Picture Coding Symposium (PCS-91)*, Article 10.1, 1991, pp. 299–302.

[136] H. Spath, *Cluster Analysis Algorithms for Data Reduction and Classification of Objects*, Ellis Horwood Ltd., UK, 1980.

[137] G.W. Stewart and J. Sun, *Matrix Perturbation Theory*, Academic Press Inc., USA, 1990.

[138] G. Strang, *Linear Algebra and its Applications*, 3rd ed., Harcourt Brace Jovanovich Inc., USA, 1988.

[139] R. Szeliski and S.B. Kang, "Recovering 3D shape and motion from image streams using non–linear least squares", DEC Technical Report 93/3, 1993.

[140] D. Terzopolous and K. Waters, "Analysis of facial images using physical and anatomical models", *Proceedings International Conference on Computer Vision (ICCV–3)*, Osaka, Japan, 4–7 Dec. 1990, pp. 727–732.

[141] N.A. Thacker, Y. Zheng and R. Blackbourn, "Using a combined stereo/temporal matcher to determine ego–motion", *Proceedings BMVC'90*, Oxford, Sept. 1990, pp. 121–126.

[142] N.A. Thacker and J.E.W. Mayhew, "Optimal combination of stereo camera calibration from arbitrary stereo images", *Image and Vision Computing*, Vol. 9, No. 1, Feb. 1991, pp. 27–32.

[143] N.A. Thacker and P. Courtney, "Statistical analysis of a stereo matching algorithm" in D. Hogg and R. Boyle (eds), *Proceedings BMVC'92*, Springer–Verlag, UK, 1992, pp. 528–537.

[144] D.W. Thompson and J.L. Mundy, "Three dimensional model matching from an unconstrained viewpoint" in *IEEE Conference on Robotics and Automation*, Raleigh, NC, 1987, pp. 208–220.

[145] C. Tomasi and T. Kanade, "Shape and motion from image streams under orthography: a factorization method", *International Journal of Computer Vision*, Vol. 9, No. 2, Nov. 1992, pp. 137–154.

[146] P.H.S. Torr and D. W. Murray, "Statistical detection of independent movement from a moving camera", *Image and Vision Computing*, Vol. 11, No. 4, May 1993, pp. 180–187.

[147] P.H.S. Torr and D. W. Murray, "Outlier detection and motion segmentation", Technical Report 1987/93, University of Oxford, 1993. Also in Schenker (ed.), *Sensor Fusion VI*, SPIE Vol. 2059, Boston, 1993, pp. 432–443.

[148] R.Y. Tsai and T.S. Huang, "Uniqueness and estimation of 3D motion parameters of rigid objects with curved surfaces", *IEEE Trans. Pattern Anal. Machine Intell.*, Vol. PAMI–6, No. 1, Jan. 1984, pp. 13–27.

[149] S. Tsuji, M. Osada and M. Yachida, "Tracking and segmentation of moving objects in dynamic line images", *IEEE Trans. Pattern Anal. Machine Intell.*, Vol. PAMI–2, No. 6, Nov. 1980, pp. 516–522.

[150] S. Ullman, "Filling in the gaps: the shape of subjective contours and a model for their generation", *Biological Cybernetics*, Vol. 25, 1976, pp. 1–6.

[151] S. Ullman, *The Interpretation of Visual Motion*, MIT Press, USA, 1979.

[152] S. Ullman, "Visual routines". *Cognition*, Vol. 18, 1984, pp. 97–159.

[153] S. Ullman and R. Basri, "Recognition by linear combinations of model", *IEEE Trans. Pattern Anal. Machine Intell.*, Vol. 13, No. 10, Oct. 1991, pp. 992–1006.

[154] A. Verri and T. Poggio, "Against quantitative optic flow", *Proceedings International Conference on Computer Vision (ICCV-1)*, London, UK, May 1987, pp. 171–180.

[155] H. Wang, J.M. Brady and I. Page, "A fast algorithm for computing optic flow and its implementation on a transputer array", *Proceedings of the British Machine Vision Conference (BMVC90)*, Oxford, UK, Sept. 1990, pp. 175–180.

[156] H. Wang and J.M. Brady, "A structure–from–motion vision algorithm for robot guidance" in I. Masaki (ed.), *Proceedings IEEE Symposium on Intelligent Vehicles*, Detroit, June 1992.

[157] H. Wang and J.M. Brady, "Corner detection: some new results", *IEE Colloquium Digest of Systems Aspects of Machine Perception and Vision*, London, 1992, pp. 1.1–1.4.

[158] H. Wang, J.M. Brady and L.S. Shapiro, "Video–rate detection and tracking of coplanar objects for visual navigation" in *ICARCV'92: 2nd International Conference on Automation, Robotics, and Computer Vision*, Singapore, Sept. 1992.

[159] D. Weinshall and C. Tomasi, "Linear and incremental acquisition of invariant shape models from image sequences", *Proceedings International Conference on Computer Vision (ICCV-4)*, Berlin, May 1993, pp. 675–682.

[160] S. Weisberg, *Applied Linear Regression*, 2nd ed., John wiley & Sons, USA, 1985.

[161] J. Walsh, "Videoconferencing comes of age", *Communications International*, Oct. 1991, pp. 157–159.

[162] W.J. Welsh, S. Searby and J.B. Waite, "Model–based image coding", *British Telecom Technology Journal,* Vol. 8, No. 3, July 1990, pp. 94–105.

[163] J. Weng, T.S. Huang and N. Ahuja, "Motion and structure from two perspective views: algorithms, error analysis and error estimation", *IEEE Trans. Pattern Anal. Machine Intell.,* Vol. PAMI–11, No. 5, May 1989, pp. 451–476.

[164] C.S. Wiles, "Image sequence understanding", First Year Report, Dept. Engineering Science, Oxford University, 1993.

[165] J.H. Wilkinson, *The Algebraic Eigenvalue Problem,* Clarendon Press, Oxford, 1965.

[166] R.J. Wilson and J.J. Watkins, *Graphs: An Introductory Approach,* John Wiley & Sons, USA, 1990.

[167] A.P. Witkin, "Scale–space filtering", *Proceedings of the 8th International Joint Conference on Artificial Intelligence,* West Germany, Aug. 1983, pp. 1019–1022.

[168] G. Xu, E. Nishimura and S. Tsuji, "Image correspondence and segmentation by epipolar lines: theory, algorithm and applications", Technical Report, Dept. Systems Engineering, Osaka University, July 1993.

[169] A.C. Yao, "An $O(|E| \log\log |V|)$ algorithm for finding minimum spanning trees", *Information Processing Letters,* Vol. 4, No. 1, Sept. 1975, pp. 21–23.

[170] C.T. Zahn, "Graph–theoretical methods for detecting and describing Gestalt clusters", *IEEE Trans. Computers,* Vol. C–20, No. 1, Jan. 1971, pp. 68–86.

[171] Z. Zhang and O. Faugeras, *3D Dynamic Scene Analysis,* Springer–Verlag, 1992.

[172] Z. Zhang and O.D. Faugeras, "Finding clusters and planes from 3D line segments with application to 3D motion determination" in G. Sandini (ed.), *Proceedings European Conference on Computer Vision* (ECCV–92), 1992, pp. 227–236.

[173] A. Zisserman, *Notes on geometric invariance in vision: BMVC'92 tutorial,* Leeds, Sept. 1992.

Index

χ^2, 86, 123, 127

affine
    camera, 2, 35, 41, 101
    coordinates, 45
    epipolar geometry, 100, 115, 138, 144,
        146
    epipolar line, 100, 101, 147, 148, 162
    fundamental matrix, 103
    stereo, 43
    structure, 6, 36, 55, 162, 166
        using local coordinate frame, 44
        without local coordinate frame, 52
    transfer, 162
    transformation
        2D, 37
        3D, 43
affinity
    definition, 62
    matrix, 65
    measures, 63, 81
    score, 63
ambiguities, *See* rigid motion
angle–axis form, 146, 190
aperture problem, 11
aspect ratio, 36, 37, 144, 147
axis of rotation, *See* rotation (axis)

background removal, 29
bandwidth compression, 2, 4
bas–relief ambiguity, 145, 158

calibration, 2
    extrinsic parameters, 37
    intrinsic parameters, 36, 37
        aspect ratio, 36, 37, 144, 147
        focal length, 36, 37, 14

    principal point, 36, 37
camera
    affine, 2, 35, 41, 101
    calibration, 36, 37
    para–perspective, 35, 40
    perspective, 2, 35, 37
    projective, 36
    scaled orthographic, 35, 38
    weak perspective, 38
cardinality dendogram, 76, 80, 179
central projection, *See* perspective (projec-
        tion)
CI space, *See* concatenated image space
clustering, 2, 61, 71
    criterion, 72
    definition, 75
    proofs, 177
complete–link clustering, 74
computer vision, 1
concatenated image space, 36, 53, 55, 112,
        166
coordinates
    affine, 45
    epipolar–based, 194
    homogeneous, 36
    relative, 43
corner, 1, 9
    definition, 11
    detection, 13
    false, 15, 29
    matcher, 9, 16
    tracker, 9, 24
correlation, *See* normalised cross–correlation
correlation–based correspondence, 10
correspondence problem, *See* corner (matcher)
cost functions

ϵ, 46, 53
ϵ_h, 59, 107, 156, 184
ϵ_{tk}, 53, 54, 58, 59, 106, 107, 112, 184
E_1, 105, 140, 182
E_2, 105, 183, 184
E_3, 105, 138, 184
F_1, 160
F_2, 160
ε, 118
covariance, 18, 151
    in CI space, 56
    of eigenvector, 110, 188
    of hyperplane, 134
    of residual, 136, 189
cyclotorsion angle, 144, 148

Delaunay triangulation, 88
dendogram, 75
depth–scale ambiguity, 146
depth variation, 2, 35, 38, 40
DROID, 23, 33

edge detection, 11
eigensolution, 118, 121, 123, 186
eigenvalue identity, 124
epipolar geometry
    affine, 100, 115, 138, 144, 146
    perspective, 100
epipolar line, See affine (epipolar line)
epipolar plane, 100, 148
epipole, 100
error analysis, 134, 151
Euclidean structure, 4, 46, 55, 16
Euler angles, 146, 156, 19
extrinsic camera parameters, 37

Faugeras, 107
feature–based correspondence, 9
field of view, 2, 35, 38, 40
focal length, 36, 37, 14
fundamental matrix
    affine, 103
    projective, 103, 107

gradient–based correspondence, 9

grapevine clustering algorithm, 80, 181
graph theory, 61-62

Harris algorithm, 59, 154, 156
hibernation, 71
hierarchical clustering, 73
homogeneous coordinates, 36
Huang–Lee algorithm, 156, 159
hyperplane, 106, 112, 116, 132
    definition, 56
    fitting, 56, 115

image coding, 4
image motion, 9
image trajectories, 2, 9, 27, 87
influence measures, 116, 121
intrinsic camera parameters, 36, 37

Kalman filter, 24, 33, 144, 152
Koenderink–van Doorn, 44, 102, 159, 192
    algorithm, 51, 145, 157
    representation, 144, 147, 191
Kruskal algorithm, 65, 75
KvD, See Koenderink–van Doorn

LCF, See local coordinate frame
least squares regression, See regression
linear regression, See regression
linear subspace, 56, 58, 166
local coordinate frame, 4, 36, 44, 52, 145,
    162

MAST, See maximum affinity spanning tree
matcher, See corner (matcher)
matrix perturbation, See perturbation
maximum affinity spanning tree, 61, 62
    algorithms, 65
    definition, 64
    proofs, 177
minimisation, See regression
minimum eigenvalue method, 122
model–based image coding, 4
motion, See rigid motion

Necker reversal, 145, 158

noise models, 4, 56, 86, 104, 127, 132, 134, 140

normalised cross–correlation, 17

OLS, *See* ordinary least squares

optic centre, 38, 101

optic flow, 2, 10, 11

optimisation, *See* regression

OR, *See* orthogonal regression

ordinary least squares, *See* regression (least-squares:linear)

orthogonal regression, *See* regression (least-squares:orthogonal)

orthographic projection, 35, 147

outlier, 2, 115
    masking, 128
    rejection, 122

parallel projection, 42, 145

para–perspective projection, 35, 40

partitional clustering, 73

perspective
    projection, 2, 35, 37
    stereo geometry, 100

perturbation theory, 123, 125, 186

planar object, 45, 48, 84, 152

predictor, 25-26

Prim algorithm, 65-66

principal component regression, *See* regression (orthogonal)

principal point, 36, 37

projection
    orthographic, 35, 147
    parallel, 42, 145
    para–perspective, 35, 40
    perspective, 2, 35, 37
    projective, 36
    scaled orthographic, 35, 38
    weak perspective, 38

projective
    fundamental matrix, 103, 107
    projection, 36

pseudo–inverse, 47

quaternion representation, 190

rank relations, 47, 55, 107, 110, 152

region detection, 10

regression, 116
    coefficients, 116
    diagnostics, 116, 120
    least–squares, 106, 115, 116
      linear, 116
      orthogonal, 57, 106, 116-118

relative coordinates, 43

residuals, 57, 113, 116, 119, 126

rigid motion
    ambiguities, 145
    estimation, 144
      from 2 views, 146
      from 3 views, 158
    transformation, 37, 146

robust statistics, 120, 122

Rodrigues equation, 190

rotation
    axis, 144, 148
    matrix, 37, 146, 190
    representations
      angle–axis form, 146, 190
      Euler angle form, 146, 156, 19
      KvD form, 144, 147, 191
      quaternion form, 190

scale factor, 144, 148, 192

scaled orthographic projection, 35, 38

segmentation, 2

single–link clustering, 74

singular value decomposition, 54

snakes, 11

span (of graph), 63

spanning tree, 64

standard deviation, 18

stereo
    correspondence, 21
    geometry
      affine, 43, 100
      perspective, 100

structure and motion problem, 116, 144

SVD, *See* singular value decomposition

termination criteria, 61, 76, 86
tie affinities, 177, 180
token–based correspondence, *See* feature–
      based correspondence
Tomasi–Kanade algorithm, 4, 51, 53, 55,
      58, 159, 162, 166
total least squares, *See* regression (orthog-
      onal)
tracker, *See* corner (tracker)
trajectories, *See* image trajectories
transfer, 6
    using local coordinate frame, 162
    without local coordinate frame, 163

Ullman, 2, 10, 21, 23, 61, 159

variance, 151
    of residual, 136, 189
video–conferencing, 4
video–phones, 4, 29

Wang–Brady corner detector, 9, 13
weak perspective projection, 38
wire–frame model, 47, 104, 108